Microsoft® Word 2000 MOUS Cheat Sheet

Mary Millhollon

A Division of Macmillan USA
201 W. 103rd Street, Indianapolis, Indiana 46290 USA

Microsoft® Word 2000 MOUS Cheat Sheet
Copyright © *1999* by *Que*

All rights reserved. No part of this book shall be reproduced, stored in a retrieval system, or transmitted by any means, electronic, mechanical, photocopying, recording, or otherwise, without written permission from the publisher. No patent liability is assumed with respect to the use of the information contained herein. Although every precaution has been taken in the preparation of this book, the publisher and author assume no responsibility for errors or omissions. Neither is any liability assumed for damages resulting from the use of the information contained herein.

International Standard Book Number: 0-7897-2114-7

Library of Congress Catalog Card Number: 99-63288

Printed in the United States of America

First Printing: *September 1999*

00 99 98   4 3 2 1

All terms mentioned in this book that are known to be trademarks or service marks have been appropriately capitalized. *Que* cannot attest to the accuracy of this information. Use of a term in this book should not be regarded as affecting the validity of any trademark or service mark.

Every effort has been made to make this book as complete and as accurate as possible, but no warranty or fitness is implied. The information provided is on an "as is" basis. The author and the publisher shall have neither liability nor responsibility to any person or entity with respect to any loss or damages arising from the information contained in this book or from the use of the CD or programs accompanying it.

"Microsoft and the Microsoft Office User Specialist Logo are registered trademarks of Microsoft Corporation in the United States and other countries. Que is an independent entity from Microsoft Corporation, and not affiliated with Microsoft Corporation in any manner. This book and CD may be used in assisting students to prepare for a Microsoft Office User Specialist Exam. Neither Microsoft Corporation, its designated review company, nor Que warrants that use of this book and CD will ensure passing the relevant Exam.

"Use of the Microsoft Office User Specialist Approved Courseware Logo on this product signifies that it has been independently reviewed and approved in complying with the following standards:

'Acceptable coverage of all content related to the Microsoft Office Exams entitled, "Word 2000 Core and Word 2000 Expert;" and sufficient performance-based exercises that relate closely to all required content, based on sampling of text.'"

> Executive Editor *Angela Wethington*
> Acquisitions Editor *Tracy Williams*
> Development Editors *Howard Jones, Jill Hayden*
> Managing Editor *Lisa Wilson*
> Project Editor *Sara Bosin*
> Copy Editor *Christy Parrish*
> Indexer *Mary Gammons*
> Proofreader *Andy Beaster*
> Technical Editor *Connie Myers*
> Software Development Specialist *Andrea Duvall*
> Interior Design *Anne Jones*
> Cover Design *Karen Ruggles*
> Copy Writer *Eric Borgert*
> Layout Technicians *Stacey DeRome, Ayanna Lacey, Heather Hiatt Miller, Mark Walchle*
> Series Editor *Jill Hayden*

Contents at a Glance

Introduction

Part 1 Core Level

   1   Managing Files
   2   Saving a Document
   3   Working with Text
   4   Formatting Text
   5   Formatting Paragraphs
   6   Working with Documents
   7   Formatting a Document
   8   Adding Columns, Tables, and Objects
   9   Working with Art
  10   Printing

Part 2 Expert Level

  11   Applying Advanced Paragraph Formatting
  12   Applying Advanced Page Formatting
  13   Using Document Reference Features
  14   Collaborating with Workgroups
  15   Adding Spreadsheet Capabilities to Tables
  16   Working with Advanced Graphics and Charts Features
  17   Designing Forms
  18   Using Mail Merge
  19   Activating Macros and Customizing Toolbars

Appendices

   A   Student Preparation Guide
   B   Objectives Index

Index

Contents

PART I CORE LEVEL

Chapter 1 Managing Files   3

1	**Display Existing Documents in Word**	4
	Displaying the Open Dialog Box	4
	Find a Document	5
	Open a Document	6
	Open a Document with Windows Explorer	6
2	**Create New Documents**	7
	New Blank Document	7
	Use Templates	8
	Use the New Document Wizard	9
3	**Send Documents via E-mail**	10

Take the Test   11
    Task 1   11
    Task 2   12

Cheat Sheet   13
    Open a Document   *13*
    Open a Document with Windows Explorer   *13*
    Open a New Blank Document   *13*
    Create a New Document Based on a Template   *13*
    Create a New Document with a Wizard   *13*
    Send Documents via E-mail   *14*

Chapter 2 Saving a Document   15

4	**Use Save**	16
5	**Use Save As**	17
	Save a Document with a Different Name	18
	Save a Document in a Different Location	18
	Save a Document in a Different Format	19
	Save a Document as a Web Page	19

6	**Manage Folders**	**22**
	Create a New Folder	22
	Rename a Folder	22
Take the Test		**24**
	Task 1	24
Cheat Sheet		**25**
	Save a Document	*25*
	Save a Document with a Different Name	*25*
	Save a Document in a Different Location	*25*
	Save a Document in a Different Format	*25*
	Save a Document as a Web Page	*25*
	Create a New Folder	*26*
	Rename a Folder	*26*

Chapter 3 Working with Text   27

7	**Add Text**	**28**
	Insert Text	28
	Overtype Text	29
	Use Click and Type	30
8	**Select, Delete, and Move Text**	**31**
	Select Text	32
	Delete Text	33
	Move Text	34
	Cut Text	34
	Paste Text	35
	Copy Text	35
	Use Paste Special	36
9	**Find and Replace Text**	**37**
	Find	37
	Replace	38
10	**Undo, Redo, and Repeat Options**	**40**
	Undo	40
	Redo	40
	Repeat	41

v

Microsoft Word 2000 MOUS Cheat Sheet

11 Insert the Date and Time	42
12 Insert Symbols	43
13 Use AutoCorrect	44
Take the Test	**46**
Task 1	46
Task 2	47
Cheat Sheet	**48**
Insert vs. Overtype	*48*
Use Click and Type	*48*
Select Text	*48*
Delete Text	*48*
Move Text	*48*
Cut Text	*48*
Paste Text	*49*
Copy Text	*49*
Use Paste Special	*49*
Find Text	*49*
Replace Text	*49*
Undo Actions	*50*
Redo Actions	*50*
Repeat Actions	*50*
Insert the Date and Time	*50*
Insert Symbols	*50*
Use AutoCorrect	*50*

Chapter 4   Formatting Text   51

14 Apply Character Effects	52
Apply Bold	53
Italicize Text	54
Add Underlines	54
15 Apply Advanced Character Effects	56
Create Subscripts and Superscripts	57
Format Strike-through Text	57
Create Small Caps	57
Apply Outlined Formatting	57
16 Change Font Color	58

17 Select and Change Font and Font Size	59
Change Font Sizes	59
18 Add a Hyperlink	61
19 Highlight Text	64
20 Use Format Painter	65
Take the Test	**66**
Task 1	66
Task 2	66
Cheat Sheet	**68**
Apply Bold	*68*
Italicize Text	*68*
Add Underlines	*68*
Create Subscripts and Superscripts	*68*
Format Strikethrough Text	*68*
Create Small Caps	*68*
Apply Outline Formatting	*69*
Change Font Color	*69*
Change Font Families	*69*
Change Font Sizes	*69*
Add a Hyperlink	*69*
Highlight Text	*69*
Use Format Painter	*70*

Chapter 5 Formatting Paragraphs 71

21 Create Bulleted Lists	72
22 Create Numbered Steps	75
23 Work in Outline View	77
Display a Document in Outline View	78
Hide and Display Outline Information	79
Move Sections	79
24 Align Text in Paragraphs	80
25 Adjust Paragraph Spacing	83
Set Character Spacing	83
Adjust Line Spacing	84
Modify Spacing Above and Below Paragraphs	85

Microsoft Word 2000 MOUS Cheat Sheet

✓ 26	Add Borders to Paragraphs	86
✓ 27	Apply Shading to Paragraphs	89
✓ 28	Indent Paragraphs	91
	Increase and Decrease Indents	91
	Indent the First Line	92
	Create Hanging Indents	93
✓ 29	Place Tabs	94
✓ 30	Use Tab Leaders	97

Take the Test   **98**

   Task 1   98
   Task 2   98
   Task 3   99

Cheat Sheet   **100**

Create Bulleted Lists   *100*
Create Numbered Steps   *100*
Display a Document in Outline View   *100*
Hide and Display Outline Information   *100*
Move Sections   *100*
Align Text in Paragraphs   *101*
Set Character Spacing   *101*
Adjust Line Spacing   *101*
Modify Spacing Above and Below Paragraphs   *101*
Add Borders to Paragraphs   *102*
Apply Shading to Paragraphs   *102*
Increase and Decrease Indents   *102*
Indent the First Line   *103*
Create Hanging Indents   *103*
Place Tabs   *103*
Use Tab Leaders   *104*

Chapter 6   Working with Documents   105

✓ 31	Navigate through Documents	106
✓ 32	Run the Spelling Feature	110
✓ 33	Access the Thesaurus Feature	113

Contents

34 Run the Grammar Feature	115
35 Work with the Office Assistant	117
36 Run the Go To Feature	119
37 Configure Page Numbers	120
Add Page Numbers	120
Modify Page Numbers	121
38 Use Headers and Footers	122
Create Headers and Footers	122
Modify Headers and Footers	124
Take the Test	**125**
Task 1	125
Task 2	125
Cheat Sheet	**127**
Navigate through Documents	*127*
Run the Spelling Feature	*127*
Access the Thesaurus Feature	*127*
Use the Grammar Feature	*127*
Use the Office Assistant	*127*
Use the Go To Option	*128*
Add Page Numbers	*128*
Modify Page Numbers	*128*
Create Headers and Footers	*128*
Modify Headers and Footers	*128*

Chapter 7 Formatting a Document 129

39 Set Page Orientation	130
40 Set Margins	131
41 Align Text Vertically	133
42 Insert a Page Break	135
43 Create Sections	136
Create a Section	137
Format a section	137
44 Apply a Style	138

Take the Test	**140**
Task 1	140
Task 2	140
Cheat Sheet	**141**
Set Page Orientation	*141*
Set Margins	*141*
Align Text Vertically	*141*
Insert a Page Break	*141*
Create Sections	*141*
Format Sections	*142*
Apply a Style	*142*

Chapter 8 Adding Columns, Tables, and Objects   143

45 Format Text into Columns	**144**
Create Columns	145
Revise Columns	146
46 Create a Table	**147**
Insert A Table	147
Draw A Table	149
Add Table Borders	152
Add Table Shading	153
47 Revise a Table	**154**
Insert Rows and Columns	154
Delete Rows and Columns	155
48 Modify Table Cells	**157**
Merge Cells	157
Change Cell Height and Width	157
49 Rotate Table Text	**159**
Take the Test	**160**
Task 1	160
Task 2	160

Cheat Sheet	**162**
Create Columns	*162*
Revise Columns	*162*
Insert a Table	*162*
Draw a Table	*162*
Add Table Borders	*162*
Add Table Shading	*163*
Insert Columns	*163*
Insert Rows	*163*
Delete Rows and Columns	*163*
Merge Cells	*164*
Change Cell Height and Width	*164*
Rotate Table Text	*164*

Chapter 9 Working with Art   165

50 Use the Drawing Toolbar	**166**
Draw Lines	167
Create Shapes and 3D Shapes	168
AutoShapes	169
51 Insert Objects	**171**
Insert WordArt	171
Insert Clip Art	172
Insert Images	173
Take the Test	**175**
Task 1	175
Cheat Sheet	**176**
Draw Lines	*176*
Create Shapes and 3D Shapes	*176*
AutoShapes	*176*
Insert WordArt	*176*
Insert ClipArt	*176*
Insert Images	*177*

xi

Microsoft Word 2000 MOUS Cheat Sheet

Chapter 10   Printing   179

52 Use Print Preview	180
53 Use Web Page Preview	183
54 Print a Document	184
55 Print Envelopes	185
Prepare and Print Envelopes	185
Work with Attached Envelopes	187
56 Prepare and Print labels	189
Take the Test	191
Task 1	191
Task 2	191
Cheat Sheet	192
Use Print Preview	*192*
Use Web Page Preview	*192*
Print a Document	*192*
Prepare and Print Envelopes	*192*
Work with Attached Envelopes	*193*
Prepare and Print Labels	*193*

PART II   EXPERT LEVEL

Chapter 11   Applying Advanced Paragraph Formatting   197

57 Implement Text Flow Options	198
Use the Widows/Orphans Feature	198
Keep Text Lines Together	199
58 Insert Nonbreaking Spaces	201
59 Insert Fields	202
60 Sort Information	205
Sort Paragraphs	205
Sort Tables	207
61 Perform Advanced Find and Replace Tasks	209
Take the Test	212
Task 1	212
Task 2	212

Contents

Cheat Sheet — 213
   Use The Widows/Orphans Feature — *213*
   Keep Text Lines Together — *213*
   Insert Nonbreaking Spaces — *213*
   Insert Fields — *213*
   Sort Paragraphs — *213*
   Sort Tables — *214*
   Find and Replace Formats, Special Characters, and Nonprinting Elements — *214*

Chapter 12   Applying Advanced Page Formatting   215

62 Format the First Page Differently   216
63 Create Watermarks   217
64 Add Page Borders   219
65 Using Footnotes   221
   Create Footnotes — 221
   Modify Footnotes — 223
66 Insert Endnotes   224
67 Create and Edit Styles   225
   Create a Style — 226
   Edit a Style — 227
68 Balance Column Lengths   229

Take the Test — 231
   Task 1 — 231
   Task 2 — 231

Cheat Sheet — 232
   Format the First Page Differently — *232*
   Create Watermarks — *232*
   Add Page Borders — *232*
   Create Footnotes — *232*
   Modify Footnotes and Endnotes — *233*
   Insert Endnotes — *233*
   Create a Style — *233*
   Edit a Style — *233*
   Balance Columns Lengths — *234*

> **Microsoft Word 2000 MOUS Cheat Sheet**

Chapter 13 Using Document Reference Features — 235

69 Add a Bookmark	236
70 Insert a Cross-Reference	238
71 Generate a Table of Contents	240
Generate a Table of Contents	240
Modify a Table of Contents	242
72 Create an Index	243
Mark Index Entries	243
Generate an Index	245
Take the Test	246
Task 1	246
Cheat Sheet	247
Add a Bookmark	*247*
Insert a Cross-Reference	*247*
Generate a Table of Contents	*247*
Modify a Table of Contents	*247*
Mark Index Entries	*248*
Generate an Index	*248*

Chapter 14 Collaborating with Workgroups — 249

73 Track Changes to a Document	250
Turn On the Revisions Feature	251
View Revisions	252
Accept and Reject Revisions	253
74 Insert Comments	255
75 Work with Master Documents	257
Create a Master Document	258
Add an Existing Document to a Master Document	259
76 Apply Document Protection	261
77 Create Multiple Versions of a Document	263
78 Set the Default Location for Workgroup Templates	265
79 Use Round Trip Documents	267

Contents

Take the Test 270
    Task 1 270
    Task 2 270
Cheat Sheet 272
    Turn On The Revisions Feature 272
    View Revisions 272
    Accept and Reject Revisions 272
    Insert Comments 272
    Create a Master Document 272
    Add an Existing Document to a Master Document 273
    Apply Document Protection 273
    Create Multiple Versions of a Document 273
    Set the Default Location for Workgroup Templates 274
    Use Round Trip Documents 274

Chapter 15 Adding Spreadsheet Capabilities to Tables 275

80 Perform Calculations 276
81 Embed Worksheets 278
    Embed a New Blank Worksheet 278
    Embed Existing Worksheets 279
    Embed Selected Worksheet Data 281
82 Link Excel Data 283
    Link Excel Worksheets 283
    Link Selected Worksheet Data 284
83 Modify Worksheets 285
Take the Test 287
    Task 1 287
    Task 2 287
Cheat Sheet 288
    Perform Calculations 288
    Embed a New Blank Worksheet 288
    Embed Existing Worksheets 288
    Embed Selected Worksheet Data 288
    Link Excel Worksheets 289
    Link Selected Worksheet Data 289
    Modify Worksheets 289

> **Microsoft Word 2000 MOUS Cheat Sheet**

Chapter 16 Working with Advanced Graphics and Charts Features   291

84 Add Bitmapped Graphics	292
85 Delete Graphics	294
86 Reposition Graphics	295
87 Align Text with Graphics	296
88 Create a Chart	298
89 Modify a Chart	300
90 Import Data into Charts	304
Create a Chart from a Word Table	304
Import Data from Other Programs	305
Take the Test	**306**
Task 1	306
Task 2	306
Cheat Sheet	**307**
Add Bitmapped Graphics	*307*
Delete Graphics	*307*
Reposition Graphics	*307*
Align Text with Graphics	*307*
Create a Chart	*307*
Modify a Chart	*308*
Create a Chart from a Word Table	*308*
Import Data from Other Programs	*308*

Chapter 17 Designing Forms   309

91 Create and Modify Form	310
Create Printed Forms	311
Create Online Forms	312
Modify Forms	313
92 Work with Form Controls	315
Take the Test	**319**
Task 1	319
Task 2	319

Cheat Sheet   **321**
    Create Printed Forms   *321*
    Create Online Forms   *321*
    Modify Forms   *321*
    Work with Form Controls   *322*

Chapter 18   Using Mail Merge   323

93   Merge a Main Document with a Data Source   324

94   Create a Data Source   327

95   Create a Main Document   330

96   Sort Merge Records   332

97   Generate Labels   333

98   Merge a Document Using Alternate Data Sources   335

Take the Test   **337**
    Task 1   337
    Task 2   337

Cheat Sheet   **338**
    Merge a Main Document with a Data Source   *338*
    Create a Data Source   *338*
    Create a Main Document   *338*
    Sort Merge Records   *339*
    Generate Labels   *339*
    Merge a Document Using Alternate Data Sources   *339*

Chapter 19   Activating Macros and Customizing Toolbars   341

99   Create, Apply, and Edit Macros   342
    Record a Macro   342
    Run a Macro   345
    Edit a Macro   346

100   Copy, Rename and Delete Macros   348
    Copy a Macro   348
    Rename a Macro   349
    Delete a Macro   349

101 Customize Toolbars	**350**
Add and Remove Toolbar Buttons	350
Reset Toolbars	351
Create Custom Toolbars	352
Take the Test	**354**
Task 1	354
Task 2	354
Cheat Sheet	**355**
Record a Macro	*355*
Run a Macro	*355*
Edit a Macro	*355*
Copy a Macro	*356*
Rename a Macro	*356*
Delete a Macro	*356*
Add and Remove Toolbar Buttons	*356*
Reset Toolbars	*357*
Create Custom Toolbars	*357*

PART III APPENDICES

Appendix A Student Preparation Guide	**361**
Test Specs	361
During the Test	362
Be Prepared	362
For More Information	363
Take a Break	*363*

Appendix B Objectives Index	**365**

Index	**369**

About the Author

Mary Millhollon is a Microsoft Certified Professional and Internet Expert. Among other accomplishments, she has passed both the core-level and expert-level Word MOUS exams. Throughout the 1990s, Mary has focused her career on writing, developing, and editing computer-related books for a number of publishers. In addition to writing *Microsoft Word 2000 MOUS Cheat Sheet* (Macmillan), Mary's recent publications include *Microsoft Internet Explorer Step-by-Step* (Microsoft Press), *Outlook 2000 I and II* courseware books (ComputerPREP), and *Online Auctions: The Internet Guide for Bargain Hunters and Collectors* (McGraw-Hill).

When Mary's not writing or developing computer books, she enjoys music, literature, art, traveling, Web surfing, and spending time with her family and friends. Finally, because Mary never strays far from her computer, she can be easily reached at `mcmail@primenet.com`.

Dedication

With love for Cale, Robert, and Matthew Taylor

Acknowledgments

I would like to thank Debbie McKenna at the Moore Literary Agency for being a great go-between and friendly cohort.

In addition, I'd like to thank the team at Que—they've been exceptional to work with. Howard Jones, Jill Hayden, Tracy Williams, and Vicki Harding are intelligent, fast, efficient, and extremely helpful at getting questions answered, providing useful information, and coordinating the entire process. Also, a special thanks to Connie Myers, the Technical Editor; the editing team of Sara Bosin, Christy Parrish, Mary Gammons, and Andy Beaster; and the production team of Stacey DeRome, Ayanna Lacey, Heather Hiatt Miller, and Mark Walchle for their hard work and attention to detail.

I would also like to thank my sister, Julie Pickering (Thanks Julie!), as well as the rest of my family; Tim, AJ, Archie, Shiela, Jill, and Jean just for being a part of my life.

And finally, a heartfelt thanks to the Bughouse (Ir)regulars for being so eclectic, creative, intriguing, and entertaining—Miss Christy Lynn Annos, Matt and Paul Corroo, Jeff Castrina, Patrick Kaminsky, Jake Engelking, Dave Ramsey, and (too far away) Joyce Chaney.

Tell Us What You Think!

As the reader of this book, *you* are our most important critic and commentator. We value your opinion and want to know what we're doing right, what we could do better, what areas you'd like to see us publish in, and any other words of wisdom you're willing to pass our way.

As an *Associate Publisher* for *Que*, I welcome your comments. You can fax, email, or write me directly to let me know what you did or didn't like about this book—as well as what we can do to make our books stronger.

Please note that I cannot help you with technical problems related to the topic of this book, and that due to the high volume of mail I receive, I might not be able to reply to every message.

When you write, please be sure to include this book's title and author as well as your name and phone or fax number. I will carefully review your comments and share them with the author and editors who worked on the book.

Fax: 317.581.4666

Email: `office@mcp.com`

Mail: *Associate Publisher*
Que
201 West 103rd Street
Indianapolis, IN 46290 USA

Introduction

The Microsoft Office User Specialist (MOUS) exams give trainers, consultants, and company experts a chance to prove themselves. Intermediate to advanced users can use the tests to review Office features, gain recognition, request a promotion or raise, validate their experience, or beef up their résumés.

The goal of this book is to help you pass the MOUS exams for Word 2000, including both the Core exam and the Expert exam. Appendix A, "Student Preparation Guide," outlines some strategies you can use for taking the tests.

The 19 chapters in this book combine to cover the 100 objectives on the tests. In the book, each objective is clearly identified and accompanied by steps and procedures necessary to successfully master the objective. Appendix B lists the tests' objectives and page numbers. In the week before you take the exam, look through the objectives list. If you don't understand one of the objectives, quickly review the objective in the book again.

Furthermore, this book is set up so that each chapter incorporates a set of practice tasks that help you prepare for the exam. The practice tasks are designed to closely simulate Microsoft's certification exams' exercises. As mentioned, the exams are "hands-on," which means that you will be completing procedures instead of answering questions when you take the exam. Therefore, the enclosed CD-ROM contains task-oriented practice files focusing on each chapter's key objectives. To effectively use the practice files, review the chapter, then open the chapter's exercise file(s), perform the specified tasks, and check your work against the designated answer file(s). When you can confidently complete all the tasks presented on the CD-ROM, you're ready to pass the Word 2000 certification exams!

Following the practice elements, each chapter concludes with a Cheat Sheet short list, which details, in abbreviated form, any steps or terms used in the chapter and on the exam. This element is designed to be a quick reference for you to review before walking into the testing center.

As you work through the book's objectives, notice the different ways to perform a procedure. Remember, the test is timed, so you should focus on what is quickest for you. The cheat sheet short list at the end of each chapter is a last-minute reference and review tool for you to use before you take the test.

This book is specifically aimed at providing quick, expert advice and instruction that is clear and easy to understand and pertains directly to the MOUS Word 2000 certification exams.

PART I

Core Level

- Managing Files
- Saving a Document
- Working with Text
- Formatting Text
- Formatting Paragraphs
- Working with Documents
- Formatting a Document
- Adding Columns, Tables, and Objects
- Working with Art
- Printing

CHAPTER 1

Managing Files

At first glance, you might wonder why a Microsoft Word book would start with file management topics. The answer is simple—this isn't your typical Word 2000 book; it's a complete guide to passing the Word 2000 Microsoft Office Users Specialist (MOUS) exams. Mastering file management from within Word 2000 is fundamental to passing the MOUS exams. Not only will you be directly tested on file management, but you'll also have to use file management techniques to complete tasks that focus on other skills. Further, you'll need to use your file management skills as you work through this book. Therefore, this chapter shows you how to

- Display Existing Documents in Word
- Create New Documents
- Send Documents via E-mail

OBJECTIVE 1

Display Existing Documents in Word

This first objective tests your ability to display Word documents. Displaying an existing document in Word involves three steps. Namely, you must display the Open dialog box, find the document, and then open it.

Displaying the Open Dialog Box

After starting Word, you can access documents that are stored on your hard drive, floppy disk, CD-ROM, and network through the Open dialog box. You can display the Open dialog box in three ways:

- Click the File menu and select Open.
- Click 📂 Open on the Standard toolbar.
- Press Ctrl+O.

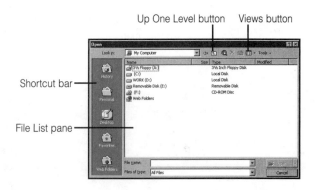

4

After you display the Open dialog box, you can use the dialog box to display drives, directories, and filenames in the File List pane. You can either click the dialog box options or open the Find dialog box to find documents. To access the Find dialog box, click <u>T</u>ools to open a drop-down list. On the drop-down list, click [🏛] <u>F</u>ind to display the Find dialog box.

Find a Document

To find a file in the Open dialog box, click the Look <u>i</u>n drop-down arrow to open an Explorer-type dialog box. Then, select the drive or the directory (folder) that stores the file you are looking for and click subdirectories (folders within folders) until the desired filename appears in the File List pane. You can change directories and display files in the File List pane by clicking any of the following:

- Look <u>i</u>n drop-down list box
- Shortcut bar icons
- Up One Level button

The Files of type field in the Open dialog box displays All Files by default.

On the MOUS Word 2000 exams, you will be told where files are stored, and then you'll be required to find and open those files. You should be able to use standard processes to find existing files without resorting to opening the Find dialog box. However, it's good to know that the Find dialog box is available in case you get "lost" during navigation. In the Open dialog box, click Too<u>l</u>s to open a drop-down list. On the drop-down list, click [🏛] <u>F</u>ind to display the Find dialog box.

5

Open a Document

After you locate a document's filename in the Open dialog box, double-click the document's [W] Word icon in the File List to open it. Alternatively, select the document's name in the File List pane, and click <u>O</u>pen.

Open a Document with Windows Explorer

You can open a Word document without first opening Word by double-clicking the document's name in Windows Explorer. When you double-click a Word file, the Word application opens automatically.

2 OBJECTIVE

Create New Documents

You can create new documents in a number of ways. You can create a new blank document, or you can use templates and wizards. This objective tests your ability to create new blank documents, as well as your ability to use templates and wizards to create new documents based on pre-existing settings.

Regardless of how you create it, every Word document is based on a template that provides the basic format settings for the document. Word comes with a number of predefined templates. By default, new blank documents are based on Word's Normal template.

When you want to create a new blank document, several methods are available to you:

- Click ☐ New Blank Document on the Standard toolbar.
- Press Ctrl+N.
- Click the File menu, select New, and double-click the Blank Document icon in the New dialog box.

Word document files have the .DOC file extension.

New Blank Document

Word template files have the .DOT file extension.

7

Part 1 • Core Level

Use Templates

Each tab in the New dialog box contains a collection of templates and wizards. Templates in the New dialog box are identified by the Template icon.

Aside from the Normal template, most templates contain placeholder text. Simply type over the placeholder text to insert your own text, or delete placeholder text where you do not want to include information.

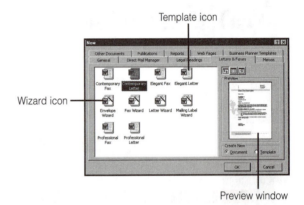

When you select a template in the New dialog box, a preview appears in the Preview window.

After you open a new document based on a template (other than the Normal template), a Word document containing placeholder text opens. You replace the placeholder text with your own text. In this way, your information appears within the boundaries of the template's settings.

1. On the File menu, click New. The New dialog box opens.
2. Click the tab that contains the template you want to use.
3. Select the template you want to use, view the template in the Preview pane, verify that the Document option is selected in the Create New area, and then click OK. Alternatively, verify Document is selected in the Create New area, and double-click the template that you want to use.

Objective 2 • Create New Documents

4. Replace sample text in the template, insert any additional information you want to include, and delete any template information you do not want to use.

A wizard presents a series of dialog boxes that enable you to customize a template as you build your document. After you answer a series of questions, the wizard displays a new document with preexisting text and formatting based on how you answered the wizard's queries. Common wizards include Word's Fax Wizard, Letter Wizard, Memo Wizard, Web Page Wizard, and Résumé Wizard.	**Use the New Document Wizard**
Some templates are accompanied by wizards. In the New dialog box, wizards are identified by the Wizard icon. Notice that the Wizard icon contains a magic wand for easy identification. When you select a wizard in the New dialog box, you see a preview of the template in the Preview pane. After you choose a wizard, you are presented with a series of steps in custom dialog boxes (sometimes accompanied by Word's Office Assistant).	*Wizard template files have the .WIZ file extension.*

Outline of wizard's steps

Notice that the left side of the wizard's dialog box outlines the wizard's steps. In each step, you are required to provide specific information, and then you click Next to move on to the next step. As you work through the wizard's steps, the outline in the wizard's dialog box marks which step you are currently viewing. After you complete all the steps, click Finish, and Word presents you with a document containing template components based on your responses to the wizard's queries. At this point, you can add, delete, and change the document's information to complete the document.	*While working through the wizard steps, you can click Back to return to a wizard screen you've already viewed.*

9

OBJECTIVE 3

Send Documents via E-mail

Using Word 2000, you can send both existing and new Word documents as e-mail messages. Simply open or create a document and then click 📧 E-mail in the Standard toolbar to open Word's e-mail header pane.

E-mail button

E-mail header pane

By default, the current document's name appears in the Subject field on the E-mail Header pane. You can delete, replace, and edit the subject text to suit your needs. If the document is not yet named, the subject line will be empty. Adding or changing the subject text will not affect a document's name. After you complete your document, you should connect to a network (if necessary), enter the recipient's e-mail address in the To: text box in the e-mail header pane, and then click Send a Copy to send the Word document. If you decide not to send the document, you can click 📧 E-mail in the Standard toolbar to close the e-mail header pane without sending the document.

1. Open a Word document.

2. Click 📧 E-mail in the Standard toolbar. The e-mail header pane displays.

3. To send the e-mail, verify that you are connected to a network, insert an e-mail address in the To: text box, and click Send a Copy in the e-mail header pane.

TAKE THE TEST

Objectives covered: 1, Display existing documents in Word; and 3, Send documents via e-mail. To complete this task, open the Word document named Life in The 1500s, which is stored in the Practice folder on the CD-ROM included with this book.

Task 1

Display the e-mail header pane as if you are going to send an electronic copy of the document to an associate.

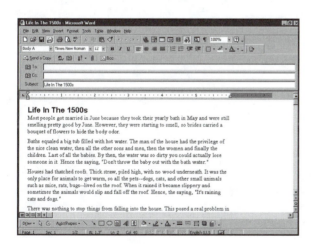

Compare your screen to the preceding figure to check your work.

Part 1 • Core Level

Task 2

Objective covered: 2, Create new documents.

1. Open a new blank document, and then close the document without saving changes.

2. Create a memo with the Memo Wizard in the Elegant style.

3. Indicate that the title of the memo is "This Month's Birthday Luncheon," that the topic line is "Next Friday," and that the memo is from you. Address the memo to the Research Department, and ensure that the memo is not marked as confidential.

Open solution file 1147A on the CD to check your work.

Cheat Sheet

Open a Document

1. 📂 File, Open (Ctrl+O).
2. Drill down to the desired file by clicking:
   - Up One Level
   - Look in drop-down arrow, or
   - Shortcut bar icons
3. Double-click 🅆, or select the filename and click Open.

Open a Document with Windows Explorer

Open Explorer, double-click the 🅆 icon next to the desired filename.

Open a New Blank Document

🗋 or (Ctrl+N) opens the document.
File, New opens the New dialog.

Create a New Document Based on a Template

1. File, New.
2. Select a template.
3. Replace, insert, and delete text.

Create a New Document with a Wizard

1. File, New.
2. Select a wizard.
3. Click Next between each dialog box, and then click Finish.
4. Replace, insert, and delete text.

Continued

Send Documents via E-mail

1. Open a document, and click 📧 E-mail.
2. Enter text for To: and Subject:.
3. Verify network connection.
4. Click <u>S</u>end a Copy.

CHAPTER 2

Saving a Document

In today's computer-centric world, a key element of any word processing package is its capability to save documents. Word 2000 offers a variety of ways to save documents, ranging from simply saving changes to an existing document to saving a document with a new name and format to a different location. On the MOUS Word 2000 exam, you will be required to demonstrate that you know the ins and outs of saving Word documents. This chapter presents all you need to know to pass core-level exam tasks instructing you to save documents. In this chapter, you'll review how to:

- Use Save
- Use Save As
- Manage Folders

OBJECTIVE 4

Use Save

You can use Word's basic Save feature to save changes to an existing document. After you open an existing document and make changes, you can save the changes by using any of these methods:

- Click the 💾 Save button on the Standard toolbar.
- Click the File menu and then click Save.
- Press Ctrl+S.

==When you save a document, you overwrite the existing version of the document with the currently displayed version of the document.== The new version of the document retains the same name and location as the earlier version. Attempting to save a new untitled document initiates the Save As command, as discussed in the next objective.

5 OBJECTIVE

Use Save As

The Save As command enables you to save any new or existing document with a new name, in a new location, or in a different file format. Implementing the Save As command opens the Save As dialog box, which assists you in renaming, relocating, or reformatting a document. To open the Save As dialog box click the File menu and select Save As, or execute any save command sequence within a new untitled document.

The Save As dialog box is similar to Word's Open dialog box.

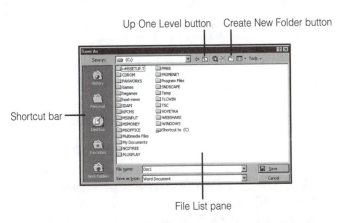

You can access the Save As feature from within both existing and new documents. Executing the Save As command within an existing document creates a new document based on the original and then closes the original document. After using the Save As command, your window displays a newly created copy of the original document. Any changes you make from that point forward are made to the new document—the original document remains unchanged.

17

Part 1 • Core Level

By default, the newly named document is saved in the same directory as the original document.

On a related note, when saving newly created documents, Word requires you to complete the Save As process automatically. Whenever you create a new document, Word temporarily names the new document Doc*n*.doc, where *n* represents the new document's number. (For example, if it's the third new document you've created during the current session, the document's name will be Doc3.doc.) When you save a new document, Word opens the Save As dialog box and prompts you to provide a name and location for the new document.

In the next few sections, you'll review how to save a document with a different name, in a new location, and as a different type. Keep in mind that you can simultaneously save a file with any combination of the described parameters within the Save As dialog box.

Save a Document with a Different Name

To save a document with a different name (including saving a Doc*n*.doc file with a new name), follow these steps:

1. Open a document, click the File menu, and select Save As. The Save As dialog box opens. By default, the file name in the File name text box is selected.
2. Type the new document name.
3. Click Save.

Save a Document in a Different Location

In addition to saving a document with a new name, you can also specify where to save a document. When you save an existing document to a new location, you are saving a copy of the document in its current state to a different directory—renaming the new document is optional. Any changes made to the newly created document (the document that resides in the new location) do not affect the original document, which retains its original state, location, and name. To save a copy of a document in a different location, open the Save As dialog box and navigate to the location where you want to save the current document using one or more of the following methods:

- Double-click drive and directory names in the File List pane
- Click the Save in drop-down list box

Objective 5 • Use Save As

- Click shortcut bar icons
- Click the Up One Level button

After you open the Save As dialog box and display the desired location for the new file, simply type a new file name (if desired) in the File name list box and click the Save button.

By default, all Word documents are saved as the Word Document type. However, you can save documents in a variety of formats, including Rich Text Format, Text Only, Document Template, Web page, and so forth. On the exam, you'll be required to save at least one document in a different file format.

Save a Document in a Different Format

To save a document in a different file format, follow these steps:

1. Open the Save As dialog box.
2. Click the Save as type drop-down arrow and select the desired file format from the list.
3. Click the Save button.

Saving a document as a Web page is highlighted in this chapter because it is a newer Word feature. Saving a Word document as a Web page is basically the same as saving a document in a different format with the added optional step of including a title for the Web page.

Save a Document as a Web Page

Saving a document as a Web page enables you to automatically generate HTML (Hypertext Markup Language) source code for a Word document. With this feature, you can convert text that you've formatted in Word into an HTML document containing formatted text that can be viewed on the Web or Web-like intranet.

The next two figures show a Word document saved as a Web page and the Word document's HTML source code. As you can see, a Word document saved as a Web page looks identical to a regularly saved Word document. On the other hand, the Word

Part 1 • Core Level

document's HTML source code view shows the "background" information that is incorporated into the document when it is saved as a Web page.

For the core-level exam, you will not need to interpret, edit, or otherwise work with HTML source code.

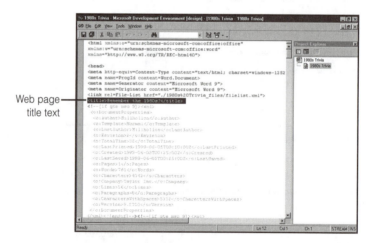

Web page title text

The following steps outline how to save a document as a Web page and how to view the Web page's source code:

1. In the Save As dialog box, click the Save as type drop-down arrow and then click Web page. Notice the Change Title button appears directly above the File name text box.

2. Click the Change Title button. The Set Page Title dialog box displays. This dialog box enables you to specify the text that you want to appear in the title bar of your Web page when it displays in a viewer's browser.

3. Type the Web page's title, then click OK.
4. Click Save. The document displays as a Web page.

At this point, you can view the document's HTML source code. Viewing HTML source code enables you to make custom changes to the HTML, including customizing header information, changing the Web page title, and hand-coding HTML commands.

To view the document's HTML source code, open the View menu, and click HTML Source. The HTML source code displays.

OBJECTIVE 6

Manage Folders

When you take the exam, you'll be asked to create a folder in which to save a document. Further, you might be asked to rename the folder you created. In the upcoming task, you'll practice creating and renaming folders in Word 2000.

Create a New Folder

Be prepared to create a new folder and then save a document into the newly created folder.

You can also create and rename folders in Word's Open dialog box.

Often, Word users need to create a folder when they save a document. Therefore, the exam requires you to create a new folder from within Word:

1. Open the Save As dialog box.

2. Navigate to the directory in which you want to create the new folder and click  Create New Folder. The New Folder dialog box opens.

3. In the Name text box, type the folder name, then click OK. By default, the Save As dialog box displays the contents of the new folder (which is empty).

4. Click Save to save the current document within the newly created folder.

Rename a Folder

After you create a folder, you need to know how to rename a folder from within Word. Renaming a folder within Word, is similar to renaming a folder in Windows Explorer:

1. Open either the Save As or the Open dialog box and display the folder in the File List pane.
2. Right-click the folder's name.
3. Select Rename from the shortcut menu.
4. Type the new folder name, and press Enter.

PRACTICE

TAKE THE TEST

Task 1

Objectives covered: 4, Use **S**ave; 5, Use Save **A**s; and 6, Manage Folders. Open the file named 1980s Trivia, which is stored in the Practice folder on the CD-ROM included with this book.

1. Save the document without changing the name, location, or file format.

2. Create a new folder named Trivia on your desktop by using the shortcut bar in the Save As dialog box.

3. Save the open document with the name Trivia Quiz, in the Web page format and in the Trivia folder.

4. View the HTML source code of the Trivia Quiz file, and then close the HTML source code window.

5. Rename the folder 1980s.

There is no solution file for this task.

Cheat Sheet

Save a Document

Click File, Save   (Ctrl+S)

Save a Document with a Different Name

1. Select File, Save As.
2. Type the new document name.
3. Click Save.

Save a Document in a Different Location

1. Select File, Save As.
2. Navigate to where you want to save your file.
3. Click Save.

Save a Document in a Different Format

1. Select File, Save As.
2. Click the Save as type drop-down arrow.
3. Select the desired file format.
4. Click Save.

Save a Document as a Web Page

1. Select File, Save As.
2. Click the Save as type drop-down arrow.
3. Select Web Page.
4. Click the Change Title button.
5. Type the Web page's title and click OK.
6. To view the HTML source code, click View, HTML Source.

Continued

Create a New Folder

1. Open the Save As or the Open dialog box.
2. Navigate to the directory in which you want to create a new folder.
3. Click 📁 Create New Folder.
4. In the Name text box, type the folder name and then click OK.

Rename a Folder

1. Open the Save As or the Open dialog box.
2. Display the folder in the File List pane.
3. Right-click the folder's name.
4. Select Rename.
5. Type the new folder name and press Enter.

CHAPTER 3

Working with Text

Not surprisingly, the MOUS Word 2000 exam focuses heavily on working with text. In one way or another, every task on the exam involves working with text to some extent. Sometimes, working with text is the main task; other times, you must work with text as a necessary subtask to completing a more complex task. Therefore, before taking the exam, ensure that you are extremely familiar with the steps necessary to:

- Add Text
- Select, Delete, and Move Text
- Find and Replace Text
- Undo, Redo, and Repeat Options
- Insert the Date and Time
- Insert Symbols
- Use AutoCorrect

OBJECTIVE 7

Add Text

Adding text to a document is straightforward, except for a small dogleg Microsoft throws into the exam. The dogleg is that ==you must be able to differentiate between inserting, overtyping, and using Click and Type to add text to a page.==

On the most basic level, when you create a new document, you add text to the document by typing, and then you save the document. The required skills to master this basic level of adding text to a document are described in earlier chapters. Specifically, Objective 2 describes how to open a new document; Objectives 4 and 5 explain how to save documents; and typing text at the cursor in a blank document is extremely intuitive. This chapter moves beyond that skill set to discuss how to use Microsoft's Insert, Overtype, and Click and Type features.

Insert Text

When you insert text, you add (or *insert*) characters or words between existing characters or words. For example, to change the word *crate* to *create*, you could insert an *e* between the *r* and *a* instead of deleting and retyping the entire word. When the exam instructs you to insert text, you *must* use the Insert feature. If you first delete the text and then type the correction or addition, you will miss the question.

By default, the Insert feature should be turned on. You can quickly tell if Word is in Insert or Overtype mode by looking at the status bar. If OVR is grayed-out, you are working in Insert mode. If OVR displays in black letters, you are working in Overtype mode (as described in the next section).

28

To toggle between Insert and Overtype mode, you can:

- Press the Insert key.
- Double-click the OVR button in Word's status bar.

To insert text, follow these steps:

1. Verify that the OVR button in the status bar is gray. If OVR is active, double-click the OVR button or press the Insert key.
2. Click where you want to begin inserting text.
3. Type the character(s) or word(s) you want to insert

When you are instructed to insert or overtype text, use the proper feature to ensure that you earn maximum points for the task.

Overtype Text

Overtyping text means typing over existing text. Overtyping text does *not* mean that you first delete existing text and then type new text. This might sound nit picky, but it's the small details like this that can trip you up on the exam.

As discussed in the preceding example, Microsoft tests your knowledge about inserting and overtyping text. You will be asked to work with text in both ways, and you must use the proper feature for each task. Therefore, at the risk of sounding slightly redundant, when the exam instructs you to overtype text, you must use the Overtype feature.

To determine whether you are currently working in Overtype mode, check Word's status bar. If the OVR button appears black (active), then Overtype is on. To toggle Overtype mode on and off, you can:

- Double-click the OVR button in Word's status bar.
- Press the Insert key.
- Click the Tools menu, select Options, click the Edit tab, and click the Overtype mode checkbox.

To overtype text, follow these steps:

1. Verify that the OVR button in the status bar is active. If OVR is inactive (gray), double-click the OVR button or press the Insert key.

Part 1 • Core Level

2. Click where you want to begin to type over existing text.

3. Type the new text.

Use Click and Type

Word's newest technique for adding text to a document is called *Click and Type*. The Click and Type feature enables you to quickly add text to a selected position on a page without having to press Enter a bunch of times, select an alignment option, reset margins, and so forth. Instead, you can display the document in Print Layout view, double-click where you want to add text, and then type the text you want to add. Click and Type automatically positions the item where you double-clicked.

By default, Click and Type is activated when you are in Layout view. You can tell whether Click and Type is on by watching the cursor as you move the cursor around a page in Layout View. If Click and Type is activated, the pointer's shape indicates whether the entered text will be left, center, or right aligned. If Click and Type is not on, you can activate it by clicking the Tools menu and selecting Options. On the Edit tab, click the Enable click and type checkbox as shown in the figure.

8 OBJECTIVE

Select, Delete, and Move Text

Selecting text expedites deleting and moving text, so you need to master text selection first. You should learn how to select the appropriate text as quickly as possible. Part of the score calculation process for the exams incorporates the speed in which you accomplish tasks.

After you review how to select text, you can review how to delete, move, cut, paste, and copy text. Most of these tasks involve storing text in the *Office Clipboard*. The Office Clipboard is a toolbar that stores up to 12 copied or cut items. You can use the Clipboard to copy and paste items among Office documents. When you save the 13th item to the Office Clipboard, you receive a dialog box stating that the most recently copied or cut item will be added to the end of the Clipboard and the first item on the Clipboard will be discarded. To view the Clipboard, open the <u>V</u>iew menu, click <u>T</u>oolbars, and then select Clipboard, or press Ctrl+C, Ctrl+C.

As always, when performing text modification tasks on the exam, ensure that you follow the instructions to the letter. If you're instructed to cut and paste text, do not copy, delete, and paste!

To view the contents of an item on the Clipboard, hover the cursor over the item.

31

Part 1 • Core Level

Select Text

Before you can cut, copy, or paste text, you must be able to select the text you want to work with. Selecting text entails highlighting text, as shown in the figure.

Selected text

While pressing and holding the Shift key or Shift+Ctrl key combination, you can use any arrow key to select text.

You can select text in a number of ways.

To select a character:

- Click before the character, and then drag to select a character (or characters).
- Position the cursor before the character; press Shift and the right-arrow key.

To select a single word:

- Double-click the word.
- Click before the word, and then drag to select the word.
- Position the cursor before the word; press Shift+Ctrl and the right-arrow key.

To select a series of words or characters:

- Double-click the first word, hold the mouse key down, and drag the cursor to select following words.
- Click before the first word that you want to select and then drag to select the following words.
- Position the cursor before the first word you want to select, press Shift+Ctrl, and then repeatedly press the right-arrow key for each word you want to select.

To select an entire line of text:

- Click in the left margin (in the area Microsoft refers to as the Selection bar) next to the line of text.

Objective 8 • Select, Delete, and Move Text

To select an entire sentence:

- Press and hold Ctrl, and then click within the sentence.

To select an entire paragraph:

- Triple-click anywhere within the paragraph.
- Double-click in the left margin.

To select a large block of text:

- Click before the first word of the text you want to select, press and hold Shift, and then click after the final word of the text you want to select.
- Click before the first word of the text you want to select, double-click EXT in the status bar, click after the final word of the text you want to select, and double-click EXT in the status bar.

To select an entire document:

- Press Ctrl+A.
- Triple-click in the left margin.
- Double-click Edit, then click Select All.

To select a vertical block of text:

- Press and hold Alt, and then drag the cursor to select the text block.

Delete Text

When you delete text, you remove text without saving it to the Clipboard for later use. To delete text:

- Click before the character you want to delete and press the Delete key.
- Click after the character you want to delete and press the Backspace key.
- Press Ctrl+Backspace to delete the preceding word.
- Press Ctrl+Delete to delete the following word.
- Select the text you want to delete, and press either the Backspace or the Delete key.

Part 1 • Core Level

Move Text

You can move text in a couple ways. One of the most common ways to move text involves dragging and dropping text.

You can drag and drop text from one Word document to another as long as both documents are open and visible on your desktop and the Drag and drop text editing option is selected. To turn on drag-and-drop text editing, click Tools, select Options, and select the Drag-and-drop text editing checkbox.

To drag-and-drop text:

1. Select the text you want to move.
2. Click within the selected text and hold the mouse button down.
3. Move your cursor to the location where you want the text to display, and then release the mouse button.

You can also move text by using the F2 key:

1. Select the text you want to move.
2. Click F2.
3. Click in the location where you want the text to display and press Enter.

Cut Text

When you cut text, you remove the text from a document and store it on the Office Clipboard. Storing text on the Clipboard enables you to paste the text elsewhere in the current document or in another document. Before you can cut text, you must first select the text. To cut selected text, you can:

- Click [✂] Cut in the Standard toolbar.
- Press Ctrl+X.
- Click the Edit menu and select Cut.
- Right-click the selected text and click Cut.

Objective 8 • Select, Delete, and Move Text

After you cut text, you can place (or *paste*) the text elsewhere in the current document or in another document. To paste text into a document, you must first specify where you want to paste the text. To specify the placement of pasted text, you can either click within the document to insert the text or highlight the text that you want to replace. After you specify where the pasted text should display, you can use any of the following procedures to paste the text:

Paste Text

- Click 📋 Paste in the Standard toolbar.
- Press Ctrl+V.
- Click the Edit menu and select Paste.
- Right-click, and click Paste.
- Click the View menu, point to Toolbars, and select Clipboard, or press Ctrl+C, Ctrl+C; then, click the item you want to paste from the Clipboard.

Copying text means that you place duplicate text on the Clipboard without removing existing text from a document. Copying text to the Clipboard enables you to repeat existing text elsewhere in the current document or in another document. Before you can copy text, you must select the text. Then, to copy text, you can:

Copy Text

- Click 📋 Copy in the Standard toolbar.
- Press Ctrl+C.
- Click the Edit menu and select Copy.
- Right-click the selected text and click Copy.

You can quickly copy and paste text using drag-and-drop if the drag-and-drop editing option is activated. To do so, press and hold Ctrl, highlight the text you want to copy, then drag the selected text to the location where you want to insert the copied text.

Part 1 • Core Level

Use Paste Special

Paste Special is a Word feature that enables you to paste items stored on your Clipboard in a different format from the original. For example, you can paste text into your Word document like a picture. Then, you can resize and place the text just as you can resize and place pictures within a document. To use Word's Paste Special feature:

1. Click where you want to paste an item.

2. Click the Edit menu and select Paste Special. The Paste Special dialog box opens.

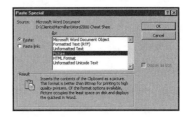

3. Click the format in which you want to paste the copied item.

4. Click OK.

9 OBJECTIVE

Find and Replace Text

Two of Word's commonly accessed text-management features are the Find and Replace tools. The Find and Replace tools enable you to locate and change text quickly by moving directly to characters or text that matches your search criteria. The exam tests your skill in using both of these techniques.

Find

You can find occurrences of particular words or phrases in a document by using the Find tab in Word's Find and Replace dialog box, as shown in the figure.

There are a number of ways to open the Find and Replace dialog box:

- Press Ctrl+F.
- Click Edit, Find.
- Click Select Browse Object in the right-side scrollbar, and then click 🔍 Find on the Browse pop-up menu.

Further specify text attributes by clicking the More button and selecting additional criteria for the search text.

37

Part 1 • Core Level

After you open the Find and Replace dialog box, you simply type the word, phrase, or other character (including special characters, such as tabs, double-spaces, and so forth) in the Find what text box. Then, click the Find Next button. Word will highlight the first instance of the specified text that appears after the cursor's current position within the document. To find the next instance of the text, click the Find Next button again.

Replace

Word's Replace feature is similar to the Find feature. The difference is that when you use Replace, you can specify the text you want to insert in place of the existing text. For example, you could use the Replace feature to replace all instances of the word *blue* with the word *green*. The figure shows the Replace tab in the Find and Replace dialog box.

You can click on the document and modify text that you've found without closing the Find and Replace dialog box.

You can display the Replace tab in the Find and Replace dialog by executing any of the following commands:

- Press Ctrl+H.
- Click the Edit menu and select Replace.
- Click [✂] Select Browse Object in the right-side scrollbar, click [🔍] Find on the Browse pop-up menu, and then click the Replace tab.

To indicate the text you want to find and replace, enter text into the Find what and Replace with text boxes.

You can use Word's Replace feature in two ways. You can replace selected text on a case-by-case basis, or you can replace all instances of specified text.

When you view each instance of a text change, you can determine on a case-by-case basis whether you want to replace the existing text. To change text, click Replace; Word changes the selected text and highlights the next instance of the Find what text. To keep the existing text, click Find Next.

Objective 9 • Find and Replace Text

You can choose to replace all instances of the text specified in the Fi*n*d what text box with the text in the Replace w*i*th text box by clicking the Replace *A*ll button. Be careful when using the Replace *A*ll button—you can easily make unintended changes. For example, let's say you have a document that contains the sentence:

```
Mix the mixture.
```

If you replace all instances of the word *mix* with the word *beat*, you will get:

```
Beat the beatture.
```

To avoid this error, you can include a space after the word *mix* in the Fi*n*d what text box and a space after the word *beat* in the Replace w*i*th text box.

OBJECTIVE 10

Undo, Redo, and Repeat Options

You can easily undo actions in Word, as well as redo and repeat actions. In the next three sections, you'll review how to use Word's Undo, Redo, and Repeat features.

Undo

The Undo feature is a popular word processing feature. It's literally a safety net for your actions. You can edit and change text freely. If you make a move that doesn't satisfy you, you can undo your action with a click of a button. For example, let's say you've selected an entire document and then accidentally press Delete. Suddenly, you're faced with a perfectly blank page! Fortunately, you can retrieve your document's contents easily by clicking the ⤺ Undo button in the Standard toolbar. When you click ⤺ Undo, your previous action is reversed. Furthermore, you can undo a series of actions by clicking Undo a number of times. To execute the Undo command:

- Click ⤺ Undo.
- Press Ctrl+Z.
- Click the Edit menu and select Undo Typing.

Redo

Redo is literally the antithesis of Undo. Redo enables you to change your mind after you undo an action. To redo an action that you've undone, you can:

- Click ⤻ Redo.
- Press Ctrl+Y.
- Click the Edit menu and select Repeat Typing.

Similar to the Redo feature, you can use Word's Repeat feature to redo an action. ==The difference between the Repeat and Redo commands is that the Repeat feature can redo an action multiple times.== For example, if you type *On Sale!*, you can use Word's Repeat feature to insert the same text any number of times within your document. If Word cannot repeat your previous action, the Repeat Typing option on the Edit menu will appear grayed-out. To use the Repeat feature:

1. Type the first instance of the text you want to repeat.
2. Click where you want the repeated text to display.
3. Press Ctrl+Y or click the Edit menu and select Repeat Typing.
4. Click in the next position where you want the repeated text to display.
5. Press Ctrl+Y or click the Edit menu and select Repeat Typing.

Repeat

The drop-down arrows next to the Undo and Redo buttons on the Standard toolbar display lists of changes you can choose from to undo or redo actions.

OBJECTIVE 11

Insert the Date and Time

Word enables you to quickly and easily insert the date and time into a document. Word draws the date and time information from the computer's system clock. To insert the date and/or the time into a document:

1. Click where you want to insert the date and/or time information.

2. Click the Insert menu and select Date and Time. The Date and Time dialog box opens.

Do not select this option if you are inserting the date and time into a time-sensitive document, such as a letter or contract.

3. Choose the date and time format you want to use. If you activate the Update automatically checkbox, the date and time will be inserted as a field, which means the date and time information will be updated automatically to the current date and time each time the document is opened.

4. Click OK. The date and time displays in the document.

You can insert a date field by pressing Alt+Shift+D. This option inserts a date in the format selected in the Control Panel's Regional Settings, and it automatically updates each time the document is opened.

42

12 OBJECTIVE

Insert Symbols

You can insert symbols—such as accent marks, copyright symbols, arrows, Greek letters, and so forth.

The following steps illustrate how to insert a symbol into a document:

1. Click where you want to insert a symbol.

2. Click the Insert menu and select Symbol. The Symbol dialog box opens.

3. In the Font list, click the drop-down arrow, and then click a font. The symbols available with the selected font display in the Symbols palette.

4. Click a symbol. A larger view of the symbol displays. Notice that the shortcut keyboard combination displays in the dialog box.

5. Click the Insert button to insert the symbol into the document.

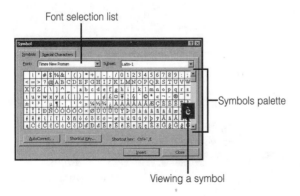

43

OBJECTIVE 13

Use AutoCorrect

The AutoCorrect feature automatically finds and corrects typographical, spelling, grammatical, and capitalization errors. For example, if you type *adn* plus a space, AutoCorrect replaces the mistyped word with *and*. Alternatively, if you type a lowercase letter after a period, AutoCorrect automatically changes the letter to uppercase. AutoCorrect can also be used to quickly insert text, graphics, and symbols. For example, AutoCorrect is configured, by default, to insert © when you to type *(c)*. The key to managing AutoCorrect's features lies in the AutoCorrect dialog box, as shown in the following figure.

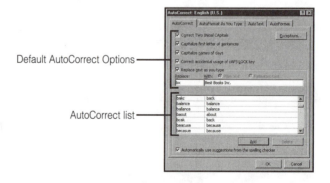

Default AutoCorrect Options

AutoCorrect list

Notice in the AutoCorrect dialog box that you can use checkboxes to turn on and off basic features, such as automatic capitalization. You can also scroll through the list of AutoCorrect words and edit the spelling and the correction of any AutoCorrect item. Further, you can customize AutoCorrect to insert specific text whenever you press particular keys. For example, you can specify AutoCorrect to insert a company name each time you type a short two or three letter combination, as described here:

1. Click the Tools menu and select AutoCorrect. The AutoCorrect dialog box opens.

2. Click in the Replace text box and type the two or three letters that will represent the company's name.

3. Click in the With text box and type the company's full name.

4. Click Add, and click OK. The new AutoCorrect item is created and added to the AutoCorrect list.

5. In your document, type the short letter combination. The letters are automatically replaced by the company name text.

To delete the AutoCorrect entry:

1. Click the Tools menu and select AutoCorrect. The AutoCorrect dialog box opens.

2. Click in the Replace text box and type the letter combination.

3. Highlight the entry in the AutoCorrect list, and then click Delete. The AutoCorrect item is deleted.

4. Click OK. Type the letter combination in your document. The letters remain unchanged.

PRACTICE

TAKE THE TEST

Task 1   Objectives covered: 7, Add Text; 8, Select, Delete, and Move Text; 10, Undo, Redo, and Repeat Options; and 13, Use AutoCorrect. Open the file named `Ingredients`, which is stored in the `Practice` folder on the CD-ROM included with this book.

1. Use the Insert feature to change *sugr* to *sugar*.
2. Use Overtype mode to change the word *green* to *brown*.
3. Use Click and Type to insert the text *Chocolate Chip Cookies* as a centered title about the word *Ingredient*.
4. Select and delete the word *ostrich*.
5. Move *6 ounces of milk chocolate chips* to the bottom of the list.
6. Copy the word *cup* and paste it before the word *lard*.
7. Cut the word *Ingredient*.
8. Undo the cut.
9. Create an AutoCorrect entry that changes *tsp* to the word *teaspoon*.
10. Use AutoCorrect to insert the word *teaspoon* before the words *salt, vanilla,* and *baking soda*.

Hint: Ensure that Insert mode is active when inserting the word teaspoon *in Step 10.*

Check your work against solution file `1147B`.

Task 2

Objectives covered: 8, Select, Delete, and Move Text; 9, Find and Replace Text; 11, Insert the Date and Time; and 12, Insert Symbols. Open the file named Procedure, which is stored in the Practice folder on the CD-ROM included with this book.

1. Find the text *last updated*.
2. Delete the existing date of the previous update.
3. Insert today's date and time using the format **M/D/YY hour:minute:seconds AM** (or PM)
4. Replace all instances of *Beat* with the word *Mix*.
5. Delete the word degrees and replace the word with the degree symbol (°).

Check your work against solution file 1147C.

Cheat Sheet

Insert vs. Overtype

Overtype replaces existing text while you type. Insert pushes text to the right while you type.

Toggle OVR on and off by pressing Insert.

Use Click and Type

1. 🔲 View, Print Layout.
2. Double-click to place the insertion point.

Select Text

- Click, double-click, or triple-click on the text or within the left margin.
- Click-and-drag to select text.

Delete Text

Press Delete or Backspace.

Move Text

- Drag selected text to another location.
- Select text, press F2, click the location where you want the text to display, and press Enter.

Cut Text

1. Select text.
2. ✂ Edit, Cut (Ctrl+X), or Right-click selected text, and click Cut.

Paste Text

- Click 📋 Edit, Paste (Ctrl+V).
- Right-click and click Paste.
- Press Ctrl+C, Ctrl+C, and then click the item you want to paste from the Clipboard.

Copy Text

1. Select text.
2. Click 📋 Edit, Copy (Ctrl+C), or Right-click the selected text and click Copy.

Use Paste Special

To paste a copied element in a different file format, click Edit, Paste Special.

Find Text

1. Click Edit, Find (Ctrl+F) or ✂, 🔍.
2. Type text into the Find what text box.
3. Click Find Next.

Replace Text

1. Edit, Replace (Ctrl+H) or ✂, 🔍, and then click the Replace tab.
2. Type text into the Find what text box.
3. Type text into the Replace with text box.
4. Click Find Next and Replace; or Replace All.

Continued

Undo Actions

Click 🔁 Edit, Undo Typing (Crtl+Z).

Redo Actions

Click 🔁 Edit, Repeat Typing (Crtl+Y).

Repeat Actions

Click Edit, Repeat Typing (Ctrl+Y).

Insert the Date and Time

1. Click Insert, Date and Time.
2. Choose a format.
3. Click OK.

Insert Symbols

1. Click Insert, Symbol.
2. Select a font in the Font list.
3. Click a symbol, click Insert, and click Close.

Use AutoCorrect

1. Click Tools, AutoCorrect.
2. Click in the Replace text box, and type the text you want AutoCorrect to change.
3. Click in the With text box, and type the replacement text.
4. Click Add, and click OK.

CHAPTER 4

Formatting Text

After awhile, basic text formatting usually becomes second nature to Word users. However, because Word offers so many ways to format text, you are bound to need to brush up on some text-formatting skills before taking the Word exam. Therefore, this chapter reviews how to:

- Apply Character Effects
- Apply Advanced Character Effects
- Change Font Color
- Select and Change Font and Font Size
- Add a Hyperlink
- Highlight Text
- Use Format Painter

OBJECTIVE 14

Apply Character Effects

A brief visit to the Font dialog box serves as a good place to start a review of Word's character formatting options. ***To display the Font dialog box, select the F̲ormat menu and click F̲ont.*** As you can see in the following figure, a large selection of Word's character-formatting commands can be controlled in the Font dialog box.

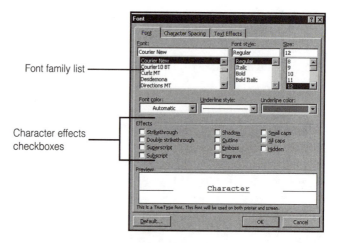

Font family list

Character effects checkboxes

Although the Font dialog box serves as a prime review tool, ==you'll gain greater benefits from memorizing as many toolbar icons and keyboard shortcuts as possible.== By using toolbar icons and keyboard shortcuts during the test, you'll conserve time for more-complex tasks. The main character-formatting icons display in the Formatting toolbar, as shown in the following figure.

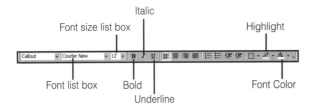

In the upcoming sections, you'll review the various ways you can display bold, italic, and underlined text.

Apply Bold

You probably know that bold text is text that appears darker and thicker than regularly formatted text—**like this.** What you might not know is that bold text actually comes in two strains—bold font families and bold format. In other words, some bold text is bold because the entire font family is designed as dark, boldfaced text (such as Helvetica Bold and Arial Bold). You can find evidence of bold-styled font families by clicking the Font drop-down arrow on the Format toolbar or by scrolling through the Font style list in the Font dialog box.

In contrast to those designed-to-be-bold font families, you can apply bold formatting to selected characters within non-bold font families. On the Word exam, you'll primarily be required to apply bold formatting to non-bold font family text. For example, you might be instructed to bold all instances of the word *Start*.

When the Word exam instructs you to bold text, *do not* reformat the text with a bold font. Instead, apply bold formatting to selected text using one of the following methods:

- Click **B** Bold on the Formatting toolbar.
- Press Ctrl+B.
- Open the F_ormat menu and click _Font or right-click and select _Font to display the Font dialog box, click Bold in the Font st_yle list, and then click OK.

53

Part 1 • Core Level

Italicize Text

Italic text is text that appears emphasized by taking on a slanted appearance—*like this*. Similar to bold text, italic text comes in two varieties—italic font families and italic formatting. On the exam, you'll primarily deal with italicizing standard fonts as opposed to typing text designed as an italic font. To apply italics to selected text:

- Click *I* Italic on the Formatting toolbar.
- Press Ctrl+I.
- Open the F_o_rmat menu and click _F_ont or right-click text and select _F_ont to display the Font dialog box, click Italic in the Font st_y_le list, and then click OK.

Add Underlines

You can apply Bold and Italic attributes to text at once by choosing Bold Italic in the Font dialog box's Font style list.

By default, underlining text in Word results in underlining text and spaces with a single text-colored line—like this. To format text using Word's default underline scheme, you can:

- Click U Underline on the Formatting toolbar.
- Press Ctrl+U.

You can also opt to add decorative underlines within your document. In other words, you can create dashed, double, extra thick, dotted, wavy, and other types of underlines, as shown in the following figure.

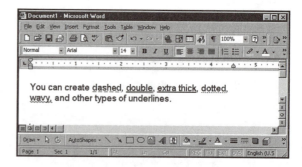

Objective 14 • Apply Character Effects

Furthermore, you can apply color to underlines for added emphases. ==You must open the Font dialog box to apply underline attributes to text.== To add a custom underline to text, follow these steps:

1. Open the F<u>o</u>rmat menu, and click <u>F</u>ont to display the Font dialog box.

2. Click the <u>U</u>nderline style drop-down arrow, and select an underline style.

3. If desired, click the Under<u>l</u>ine color drop-down arrow, and select an underline color.

4. Click OK.

Press Ctrl+Shift+W to underline words but not spaces or press Ctrl+Shift+D to double-underline text.

OBJECTIVE 15

Apply Advanced Character Effects

Along with bolding, italicizing, and underlining text, the Word exam requires you to apply more-advanced (and less-often-used) character-formatting effects. Namely, you'll need to format characters as subscripts, superscripts, strikethrough text, small caps, and outlined, as shown in the following figure.

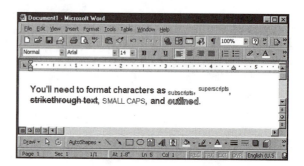

As you can see in the figure of the Font dialog box (shown earlier in this chapter), many advanced character effects are accessible in the Font dialog box.

Generally, when you apply advanced text formatting options (such as subscripts, strikethroughs, small caps, and outlines), you should type text beyond the text you want to format. Then, go back and apply the formatting effect. If you apply the formatting while you type, you'll double your workload. This is because you would need to stop typing, open the Font dialog box to turn on the effect, type the formatted text, and then open the Font dialog box a second time to turn the effect off. Therefore, the following sections briefly describe the recommended ways to add advanced character effects.

Create Subscripts and Superscripts

Applying the subscript and superscript formats to selected text displays the text below and above the text line's baseline and in a smaller font size—like $_{this}$ Or like ^{this}. Usually, subscripts and superscripts are used in mathematical and scientific notation. The recommended way to format subscripted and superscripted text is to select the text you want to format and then do one of the following:

- Click the Su*b*script or Su*p*erscript checkbox in the Font dialog box.
- Press Ctrl+= for subscripting or Ctrl+Shift+= for superscripting.

Format Strikethrough Text

Strikethrough text is text that appears with a line drawn through it. Generally, strikethrough text is used to show edited text, such as in a contract or legal proceeding. Creating strikethrough text is similar to creating subscripts. To strike through text, click the Stri*k*ethrough checkbox in the Font dialog box.

Create Small Caps

Similar to creating subscripts and strikethrough text, you can create SMALL CAPS using either of the following methods:

- Click the S*m*all caps checkbox in the Font dialog box.
- Press Ctrl+Shift+K.

Apply Outlined Formatting

Finally, the exam requires you to know how to create outlined text. To outline text, click the *O*utline checkbox in the Font dialog box.

57

OBJECTIVE 16

Change Font Color

The Format toolbar (as well as the Drawing toolbar) enables you to quickly select and re-color text using the A Font Color button. To change text color, select the text you want to color, click the A Font Color drop-down arrow, and click on a color patch on the pop-up color palette. After you perform this action, the selected text and the color on the A Font Color button reflect the color you selected on the color palette.

You can also change the color of selected text by opening the Font dialog box and selecting a color on the Font color drop-down list.

You can change text to the color displayed on the A Font Color button by selecting the text and clicking A Font Color without opening the color palette.

17 OBJECTIVE

Select and Change Font and Font Size

On the Word core-level exam, you will be required to change the font style and size of selected text. For example, you might be asked to change a heading appearing as Times 14 point text to Arial 16 point text. In the next two sections, you'll review how to change the font families and sizes of selected text.

Change Font Families

Each font has its own typeface, or *font family*, which determines how the font's letters display. Font families are represented by font names, such as Arial, Courier, Times New Roman, and so forth. You can easily reformat selected text to display in another font in a couple ways:

- Click the Font drop-down arrow on the Formatting toolbar, and click a font in the font list box.

- Open the Font dialog box, click a font in the Font list box, and click OK.

Change Font Sizes

Fonts sizes are measured in points, and 72 points are in 1 inch. Most documents' body text falls within the 8 through 14 point range. Larger font sizes are usually reserved for headings, and smaller font sizes are often applied to notes and footnotes.

Changing the size of selected text is similar to changing the selected text's font family. To change the size of selected text, follow any of these procedures:

- Click the Size drop-down arrow on the Formatting toolbar, and click a size in the font size list box or type a size in the Size text box.

Part 1 • Core Level

To change the font or font size for all the text in a document, press Alt+A to select the entire document before applying a new font family or size.

- Press Ctrl+] or Ctrl+Shift+> to increase font size, and press Ctrl+[or Ctrl+Shift+< to decrease font size.

- Open the Font dialog box, click a size in the Size list box or type a size in the Size text box, and click OK.

18 OBJECTIVE

Add a Hyperlink

For a few years now, Microsoft has been hot on the idea of integrating users' desktops with the Internet. The goal is to create a smooth interaction among Office applications, the Windows interface, and the Internet—so smooth that users hardly notice whether they're working on a document stored locally or halfway around the world. Obviously, computing still has a ways to go to make complete integration a reality, but Word implements a few Web-friendly features to help you to narrow the gap a little. For example, as you saw in Objective 6, you can save Word documents as Web pages.

In addition to saving documents as Web pages, you can insert *hyperlinks* into your documents. A hyperlink is text that is formatted to open another document when you click the linked display text. The other linked document can be located on your desktop, an intranet, a network, or the Internet. A hyperlink might also go to an email address or to another area within the same document. You can display hyperlinks in two ways within your documents:

- As Web addresses, such as www.mcp.com
- As linked text in which the Web address or other location is hidden from view, such as Macmillan's home page.

In either case, you can display the Insert Hyperlink dialog box to format text as a hyperlink. Furthermore, if you simply want to create a hyperlink that displays as a Web address, you can type the address directly into your document, and, by default, Word will format it as a hyperlink.

61

Part 1 • Core Level

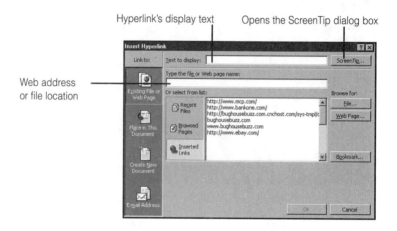

You can use any of the following methods to open the Hyperlink dialog box:

- Click ![icon] Insert Hyperlink on the Standard toolbar.
- Press Ctrl+K.
- Right-click and select Hyperlink on the pop-up menu.
- Open the Insert menu, and click Hyperlink.

To create a hyperlink within a document, you can type a Web address in your document or follow these steps:

1. Click ![icon] Insert Hyperlink on the Standard toolbar.
2. Type the file address or Web page that you want the hyperlink to point to. By default, the cursor is positioned in the Type the file or Web page name text box.
3. Click in the Text to display text box, and type the hyperlink text that you want to display in the current document.
4. Click the ScreenTip button. The Set Hyperlink ScreenTip dialog box opens, as shown in the figure.

Objective 18 • Add a Hyperlink

5. Type the pop-up text you want to display when users hover their cursor over the hyperlink.

6. Click OK, and then click OK in the Insert Hyperlink dialog box to complete the task. An active hyperlink is inserted into the document.

You can also create a hyperlink from existing text. To do so, highlight the existing text, and open the Insert Hyperlink dialog box. Or, if you are displaying the Web address as the hyperlink (such as www.mcp.com), you can create hyperlinks in an instant:

1. Select the Web address text in your document.

2. Click ![icon] Insert Hyperlink in the Standard toolbar.

Most likely, the exam will require you to convert a plain text Web address (also called a URL) into a hyperlink. Thus, you'll be able to use the select+![icon] Insert Hyperlink quick combination to create a hyperlink.

To change an existing hyperlink to plain text, right-click it, click Hyperlink, and select Remove Hyperlink.

To control whether Word automatically formats addresses as hyperlinks, click Tools, AutoCorrect, AutoFormat As You Type, and check Internet and network paths with hyperlinks.

63

OBJECTIVE 19

Highlight Text

<mark>You can highlight text to draw attention to important concepts and ideas within a document</mark> (as you can see in this book!). Luckily (especially for everyone involved in pulling Cheat Sheet books together!), highlighting text is quick and easy. To highlight text:

- Select the text you want to highlight, and click Highlight on the Standard toolbar.

You can change the highlight color by clicking the drop-down arrow on the Standard toolbar's Highlight button and clicking a color patch on the color palette, as shown in the following figure.

Removes highlighting from selected text
Currently selected highlight color

To hide all highlighting, open the Tools menu, click Options, and clear the Highlight checkbox on the View tab.

To remove highlighting:

1. Select the highlighted text.
2. Click the Highlight drop-down arrow.
3. Click None on the color palette.

64

20 OBJECTIVE

Use Format Painter

Now that you've reviewed a variety of ways to format text, a logical progression is to review how to use Word's *Format Painter*. The Format Painter tool enables you to copy text-formatting attributes.

Don't be fooled into thinking the Format Painter is just another clever tool—you'll need to know how to use Word's Format Painter during the exam. For example, at one point, you will be instructed to apply one heading's format to an unformatted heading. Of course, you *could* decipher the formatted heading's settings and manually apply the effects to the unformatted heading over the course of a few minutes. In contrast, you could manage your time more efficiently by using Word's Format Painter to complete the task in 5 seconds and move on to the next task.

Using the Format Painter is a matter of performing three easy steps:

1. Select the text that contains the formatting you want to copy.

2. Click ![] Format Painter on the Standard toolbar. The cursor changes to a paintbrush and an I-mark. (If you change your mind at this point, you can re-click ![] Format Painter or press the ESC key to dispel the Format Painter icon.)

3. Drag the cursor over the text you want to format.

To copy formatting to several locations, double-click the Format Painter icon to toggle it on; click again to toggle off.

TAKE THE TEST

Task 1

Objectives covered: 14, Apply Character Effects; 17, Select and Change Font and Font Size; and 19, Highlight Text. Open the file named `Baseball`, which is stored in the `Practice` folder on the enclosed CD-ROM.

1. Format the text *Summer League Baseball* to Arial font size 18, Bold with a double underline.

2. In the first paragraph, italicize the text *every child plays at least half the game*.

3. Strike out the text *Lakes Park* in the Playing Locations list.

4. Highlight the fee amount, $35.00, in yellow.

Check your work against solution file `1147D`.

Task 2

Objectives covered: 15, Apply Advanced Character Effects; 16, Change Font Color; 18, Add a Hyperlink; and 20, Use Format Painter. Open the file named `Baseball_2`, which is stored in the `Practice` folder on the enclosed CD-ROM.

1. Change the *Fee:* and *Playing Locations:* headings so that they are formatted in the same manner as the *Volunteer Assistant Coaches Needed* heading.

2. Color *H20* as blue text, and change the *2* to a subscript.

3. Format the entire sentence beginning with the words *Special Note:* as small caps.

4. In the last sentence, change the word *here* to a hyperlink that points to the fictitious Web page www.baseballdays.com. Use the ScreenTip text *Sign up Today!*

Check your work against solution file 1147E.

Cheat Sheet

Apply Bold

- **B** Bold.
- Ctrl+B.
- Open the Font dialog box, and click Bold in the Font style list.

Italicize Text

- *I* Italic.
- Ctrl+I.
- Open the Font dialog box, and click Italic in the Font style list.

Add Underlines

- U Underline.
- Ctrl+U, Ctrl+Shift+W, or Ctrl+Shift+D.
- Open the Font dialog box, select an underline format in the Underline style drop-down list.

Create Subscripts and Superscripts

- Open the Font dialog box, click the Subscript checkbox or the Superscript checkbox.
- Press Ctrl+= or Ctrl+Shift+=.

Format Strikethrough Text

- Open the Font dialog box, click the Strikethrough checkbox.

Create Small Caps

- Open the Font dialog box, click the Small caps checkbox.
- Press Ctrl+Shift+K.

Apply Outline Formatting

- Open the Font dialog box, click the Outline checkbox.

Change Font Color

- [A] Font Color.

Change Font Families

- Click the Font drop-down arrow on the Formatting toolbar, and select a font.
- Open the Font dialog box, and click a font in the Font list box.

Change Font Sizes

- Click the Size drop-down arrow on the Formatting toolbar, and select a size or type a size in the Size text box.
- Press Ctrl+], Ctrl+Shift+>, Ctrl+[or Ctrl+Shift+<.
- Open the Font dialog box, and click a size or type a size in the Size text box.

Add a Hyperlink

- Insert Hyperlink (Ctrl+K).
- Type a Web address in your document.
- Right-click and select Hyperlink.
- Open the Insert menu, and click Hyperlink.

Highlight Text

1. Select the highlighted text.
2. Click the Highlight drop-down arrow.
3. Click None on the color palette, or clear the Highlight checkbox on the View card in the Options dialog box.

Continued

Use Format Painter

1. Select text that contains the formatting you want to copy.
2. Click the ![icon].
3. Drag the cursor over the text you want to format.

CHAPTER 5

Formatting Paragraphs

Knowing how to format text characters is a required skill for the Word exam, but that knowledge alone is not enough to pass—you also need to know how to format paragraphs. Although formatting paragraphs can equate to simply applying a font style to a group of four or five sentences that support a main theme, this is not Microsoft's definition of formatting paragraphs. In Word, any text offset by paragraph marks (¶) is considered a paragraph (including list items, headings, and so forth). Paragraph marks are inserted each time you press Enter. Therefore, formatting paragraphs relates to formatting elements that don't always appear as paragraphs in the traditional sense. To pass the exam, you'll need to be able to:

- Create Bulleted Lists
- Create Numbered Steps
- Work in Outline View
- Align Text in Paragraphs
- Adjust Paragraph Spacing
- Add Borders to Paragraphs
- Apply Shading to Paragraphs
- Indent Paragraphs
- Place Tabs
- Use Tab leaders

OBJECTIVE 21

Create Bulleted Lists

This chapter starts with formatting one of the smaller paragraph types—bulleted list items. At first glance, creating bulleted lists might not seem like a paragraph-formatting task. But, as mentioned in the introduction, any text in Word offset by paragraph marks (¶) is considered a paragraph as far as formatting commands are concerned.

Typically, when you create a list, you type a list item, press Enter, type another list item, press Enter, and so forth. As you can see, this process essentially creates a series of paragraphs. You can think of bulleted lists as a series of short paragraphs, as shown in the following figure. Notice that each bulleted list item ends with a paragraph mark.

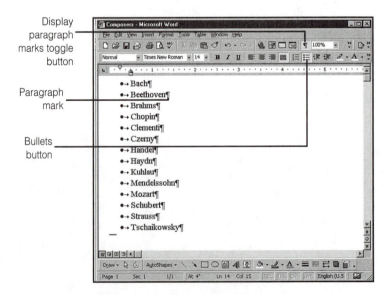

Display paragraph marks toggle button

Paragraph mark

Bullets button

72

Generally, paragraph marks remain hidden while you work. When you are formatting paragraphs, you might find it helpful to show paragraph marks (¶). To toggle the display of paragraph marks, click ¶ Show/Hide ¶ in the Standard toolbar.

To format a bulleted list, ensure that each list item is separated by a paragraph mark, select all the list items, and then perform one of the following actions:

- Click ≡ Bullets in the Standard toolbar. The ≡ Bullets button is a toggle button that applies and removes Word's default bulleted list settings.

- Open the Format menu, and click Bullets and Numbering; or right-click and select Bullets and Numbering on the pop-up menu. The Bullets and Numbering dialog box appears, as shown in the following figure. Select a bullet style, and click OK.

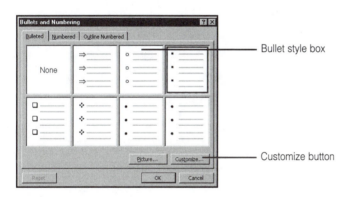

You can use the Bullets and Numbering dialog box to further customize your bulleted list. For example, you can click the Customize button to open the Customize Bulleted List dialog box, which allows you to adjust the bullet character, bullet position, and text position.

Part 1 • Core Level

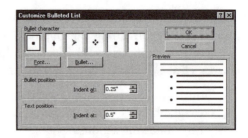

Finally, keep in mind that you can also turn on the bulleted list feature before you type list items to automatically format a list as you type. To do this:

1. Click the 📋 Bullets button in the Standard toolbar.
2. Type a list item, and press Enter.
3. Continue to type list items, pressing Enter between each item.
4. Click the 📋 Bullets button to turn off the formatting.

22 OBJECTIVE

Create Numbered Steps

Creating numbered lists is similar to creating bulleted lists. The difference is that Word's Numbering feature automatically adds numbers instead of bullets to list items, as shown in the following figure.

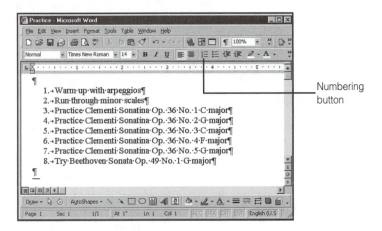

As with bulleted items, each item in a numbered list is usually offset by paragraph marks. The paragraph marks indicate to Word the beginning and end of entries. To add automatically incrementing numbers to a list, ensure that the items are separated by paragraph marks, select the text, and then perform one of the following actions:

- Click ▤ Numbering in the Standard toolbar. The ▤ Numbering button is a toggle button that applies and removes Word's default Numbering settings.

75

Part 1 • Core Level

- Open the Format menu, and click Bullets and Numbering; or right-click and select Bullets and Numbering on the pop-up menu. The Bullets and Numbering dialog box appears. Click the Numbered tab, as shown in the following figure. Select a numbered style, and click OK.

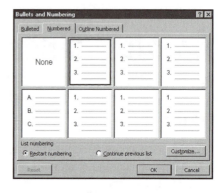

To add an entry to a bulleted or numbered list, click before the preceding item's paragraph mark and press Enter.

Notice that the Numbered tab in the Bullets and Numbering dialog box includes radio button options enabling you to specify whether to continue an existing list or to start a new numbered list.

If want to create two or more numbered lists immediately after one another, you need to specify where each new numbered list begins. To do so, open the Bullets and Numbering dialog box, and click the Restart Numbering bullet. In contrast, if unnumbered text or another element separates a continuing series of numbered items, you need to specify where to continue the numbered list. To do this, you click the Continue previous list checkbox.

Finally, keep in mind that you can also turn on the Numbering list feature before you type list items to automatically format the list as you type. To do this, click the ⊟ Numbering button in the Standard toolbar, create the list, and then click the ⊟ Numbering button to turn off the formatting tool.

23 OBJECTIVE

Work in Outline View

You can use Word's Outline feature to view a document's structure, as shown in the following figure.

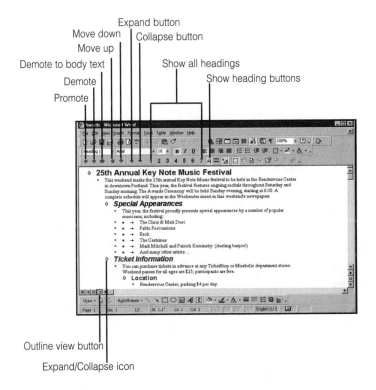

The figure shows how Outline view indents text based on Word's default styles, including Heading 1, Heading 2, Heading 3, and so forth. In the following figure, the Heading 1 ("25th Annual Key Note Music Festival") aligns flush left, the

77

Part 1 • Core Level

Heading 2 elements ("Special Appearances" and "Ticket Information") display slightly indented, and the Heading 3 ("Location") is further indented. This indentation applies only within Outline view. The corresponding document appears with the heading styles' settings, which are left-aligned as shown in the next figure.

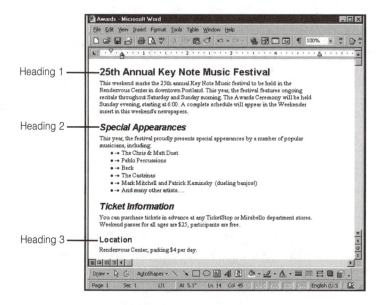

Word's outline feature offers a wide variety of capabilities to users, some of which can be quite advanced. ==For the core-level exam, you only need to know the outlining basics, such as displaying a document in outline view, hiding and displaying section information, and moving sections.==

Display a Document in Outline View

Word creates outlines based on documents that use Word's default styles, such as Heading 1, Heading 2, Normal, and so forth. Documents not using these styles can display as outlines if document elements are assigned outline levels using the Paragraph dialog box (Format, Paragraph). The document you are provided on the exam will be pre-formatted to show outline levels.

Objective 23 • Work in Outline View

To show a document in outline view, you can:

- Click ▦ Outline View on the horizontal scroll bar.
- Open the <u>V</u>iew menu, and click <u>O</u>utline.

You can hide and display outline information in Outline view to simplify working with the outline structure. To control whether text displays below a heading, you can:

- Click the ➕ Expand and ➖ Collapse buttons on the Outline toolbar.
- Double-click the expand/collapse (plus sign) marker next to a heading.

Click the Show Heading buttons. Each Show Heading number represents how many levels of headings should display. For example, clicking the number 3 Show Heading button shows only the first three heading levels without text. In contrast, ==clicking the All button shows all headings and all text.==

You can use Outline view to change heading levels and drag-and-drop sections to other areas in the document. To move sections in Outline view:

- Drag the expand/collapse plus sign right, left, up, and down.
- Click within a heading or body text, and then click the Promote, Demote, Move Up, and Move Down buttons in the Outlining toolbar.

Hide and Display Outline Information

To return to Normal view from Outline view, click the Normal View button in the horizontal scroll bar.

Move Sections

Clicking on the expand/collapse marker next to a heading selects the heading and its contents.

79

OBJECTIVE 24

Align Text in Paragraphs

Now that you've reviewed some of the not-so-traditional types of paragraph formatting, you might be relieved to learn that the remainder of the chapter deals with more typical paragraph formatting issues, including alignment and spacing. Many of the upcoming sections reference the Paragraph dialog box, as shown in the following figure.

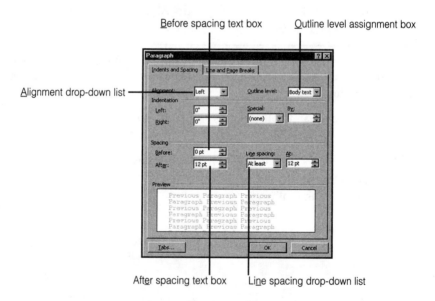

You can use either of the following methods to open the Paragraph dialog box:

- Open the Format menu, and click Paragraph.
- Right-click in a paragraph, and click Paragraph on the pop-up menu.

80

The paragraph dialog box contains the Indents and Spacing tab and the Line and Page Breaks tab. The first feature on the Indents and Spacing tab is the Alignment list box. ==Word enables you to align paragraph text in four ways: left, center, right, and justified.== The following list discusses the effects of each alignment option:

- **Align Left**—Aligns the left edge of the paragraph with the page's left margin. This alignment creates a straight left edge and a jagged right edge.

- **Center**—Situates the paragraph in the horizontal center between the page's margins. This alignment creates a jagged edge on both sides of the paragraph.

- **Align Right**—Aligns the right edge of the paragraph with the page's right margin. This alignment creates a jagged left edge and a straight right edge.

- **Justify**—Forces the paragraph text to align along the page's left and right margins. This alignment creates straight edges along both the left and right edges.

The following figure shows samples of each text alignment.

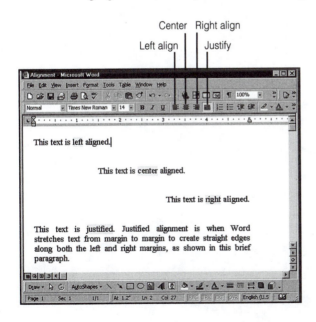

81

Part 1 • Core Level

To align paragraph text, you can:

- Use the <u>A</u>lignment drop-down list in the Paragraph dialog box

- Click the ▤ Align Left, ▤ Center, ▤ Align Right, and ▤ Justify buttons on the Formatting toolbar.

- Press Ctrl+L (left align), Ctrl+E (center), Ctrl+R (right align), and Ctrl+J (justify).

When you align paragraph text, you simply click anywhere within the paragraph and then apply the alignment setting—you do not have to select the entire paragraph.

25 OBJECTIVE

Adjust Paragraph Spacing

Often, spacing within and around paragraphs needs to be adjusted. You need to know how to adjust spacing between characters and lines, as well as the spacing above and below paragraphs. In the next few sections, you'll review how to adjust paragraph spacing within Word.

To view a paragraph's current formatting settings, click Help, What's This?, or press Shift+F1 and click within the paragraph. A callout box displays the paragraph's formatting. To close the callout box, click Esc or click outside the paragraph text.

	Set Character Spacing
You might need to adjust character spacing if you're trying to squeeze the last few words onto a page or fill up some unwanted white space. You might also want to adjust character spacing when you're flowing text around images and other embedded objects.	

Changing character spacing means to move words and characters closer together or spread words and characters apart.
To change character spacing, follow these steps:

1. Select the text you want to modify.

2. Open the Format menu, and click Font; or right-click on the selected text, and click Font.

3. In the Font dialog box, click the Character Spacing tab. The Character Spacing tab appears as shown in the following figure.

To compress or stretch the character horizontal width, change the Scale percentage on the Character Spacing tab.

83

Part 1 • Core Level

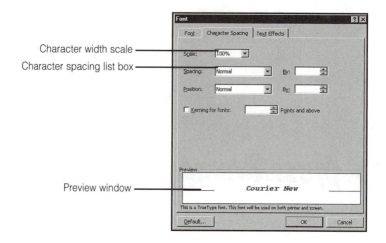

4. Click the Spacing drop-down arrow, and specify whether you want to expand or condense the space between selected text.

5. Click in the By text box and specify the amount of space, in points, to expand or condense the character spacing. The Preview window shows you how the text will display with the modified character spacing.

6. Click OK.

Adjust Line Spacing

Line spacing refers to the amount of vertical space between each line within a paragraph. Common line spacing settings are single, double, and 1.5. To change a paragraph's line spacing setting, click within the paragraph you want to reformat, and then:

- Open the Paragraph dialog box, select an option on the Line Spacing drop-down list, and enter information into the At box, if necessary.

- Press Ctrl+1 (single-spaced), Ctrl+5 (1.5-spaced), or Ctrl+2 (double-spaced).

Objective 25 • Adjust Paragraph Spacing

In addition to character and line spacing, you can modify spacing above and below paragraphs. Modifying a paragraph's surrounding spacing can offset a paragraph to make it stand out or make the paragraph fit more snugly within the document (such as reducing the space before the first paragraph following a heading). To change spacing above and below paragraphs, follow these steps:

1. Select a paragraph, open the Paragraph dialog box and click in the Before list box.

2. Enter the amount of space you want to insert before the selected paragraph.

3. Click in the After text box.

4. Enter the amount of space you want to insert after the selected paragraph.

5. Click OK.

Modify Spacing Above and Below Paragraphs

To quickly add a single line space above a paragraph, press Ctrl+0 (zero).

Click the arrows in the Before and After text boxes to change a paragraph's before and after spacing.

85

OBJECTIVE 26

Add Borders to Paragraphs

> Word enables you to add borders to paragraphs similar to the border drawn around this paragraph. Keep in mind that adding borders can mean simply adding a line along one or two edges of a paragraph—a border is not always a box. If you see task instructions to "add a border" on the exam, read the remainder of the question carefully so that you'll know what type of border you need to add.

You can add a border to a paragraph by clicking within the paragraph and then executing one of the following procedures:

- Open the Format menu and click Borders and Shading. The Borders and Shading dialog box appears, as shown in the following figure.

- Click ▪ Border in the Formatting toolbar. The ▪ Border button applies a border style based on the most-recent border style configured in the Borders and Shading dialog box.

- Click View, Toolbars, Tables and Borders; right-click a toolbar and click Tables and Borders; or open the Borders and Shading dialog box and click the Show Toolbar button.

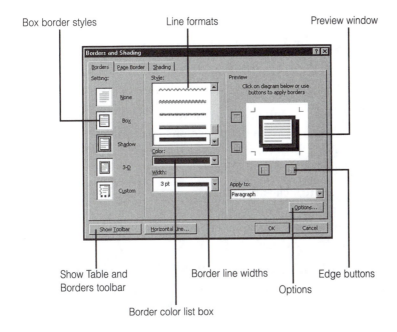

Box border styles — Line formats — Preview window

Show Table and Borders toolbar — Border line widths — Edge buttons
Border color list box — Options

Clicking the ■ Border button automatically applies the border style currently shown on the button face. You can change the ■ Border button face by clicking on the button's drop-down arrow and selecting a border option on the pop-up menu. The figure shows the border options available on the ■ Border pop-up list.

Creating borders with the Borders and Shading dialog box grants you added control over the border's style and color. To create a customized paragraph border, follow these steps:

1. Open the Format menu, and click Borders and Shading. Then click the Borders tab.

2. If you want to enclose the entire paragraph in a border, select a border style. If you only want to add a border to selected edges of the paragraph, click Custom and click the appropriate edge icons in the Preview area.

3. In the Style list, select a line style.

4. Specify Color and Width settings using the corresponding drop-down list arrows.

5. Ensure that *Paragraph* displays in the Apply to text box.

6. Click the Options button if you want to customize the distance between the paragraph's text and border line(s). Click OK to close the Border and Shading Options dialog box.

7. If desired, click the Horizontal Line button to open the Horizontal Line dialog box. The Horizontal Line dialog box enables you to select and add lines and borders to Web page documents.

8. Click OK to create a border based on your settings.

27 OBJECTIVE

Apply Shading to Paragraphs

You can customize paragraphs by adding shading behind the text like this paragraph. You can add any color of shading to a document using Word. To add shading, click in the paragraph you want to shade, and then follow these steps:

1. Open the View menu, click Toolbars, and select Tables and Borders; or open the Format menu, and click Borders and Shading, and then click the Shading tab. The next two figures show the Table and Borders toolbar and the Shading tab in the Borders and Shading dialog box.

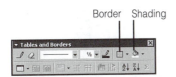

Border   Shading

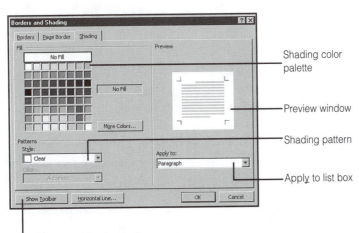

Shading color palette
Preview window
Shading pattern
Apply to list box

Show Tables and Borders toolbar

Part 1 • Core Level

2. In the Tables and Borders dialog box, click the Shading Color drop-down list arrow, and click a color on the color palette; or, on the §hading tab, click a fill color on the color palette, click a fill pattern. (If you select a pattern other than a solid shade, you will be given the option to use the Color drop-down list to select a color to apply over the pattern's fill color). Click OK.

==You can shade more than one paragraph at a time by clicking within the first paragraph you want to shade, dragging to select text within the next paragraph you want to shade, and then applying the shading in the same manner you apply shading to a single paragraph.==

28 OBJECTIVE

Indent Paragraphs

Indenting paragraphs is a common word processing action, and the exam will test you in a few areas of text indentation. Therefore, be prepared to complete tasks requiring you to increase and decrease indents, indent first lines, and create hanging indents. In most cases, you can drag horizontal ruler markers to change indention settings. To display Word's horizontal ruler, click View, Ruler.

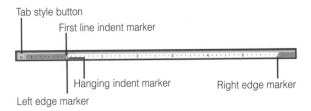

Tab style button
First line indent marker
Hanging indent marker
Right edge marker
Left edge marker

Dragging horizontal ruler markers applies the indentation settings to the current paragraph or selected paragraphs. Alternatively, you can click where you want to add or insert text, adjust the ruler, and then type text using the new ruler settings.

Increase and Decrease Indents

Increasing and decreasing a paragraph's indents involves moving the entire paragraph to the right or left by one tab space. Word makes increasing and decreasing indents quick and easy by including the ⬛ Decrease Indent and ⬛ Increase Indent buttons on the Formatting toolbar. You can also open the Paragraph dialog box or press keyboard commands to change paragraph indents.

91

Part 1 • Core Level

To increase an indent (shift the paragraph to the right), you can take any of the following actions:

- Click ![icon] Increase Indent.
- Press Ctrl+M.
- Drag the Left Indent marker on the horizontal ruler.
- Open the Paragraph dialog box and adjust the Left indentation settings.

To decrease an indent (shift the paragraph to the left), you can take any of the following actions:

To format a bulleted list flush left, select text, click Bullets on the Formatting toolbar, and click Decrease Indent.

- Click ![icon] Decrease Indent.
- Press Ctrl+Shift+M.
- Drag the Left Indent marker on the horizontal ruler.
- Open the Paragraph dialog box and adjust the Left indentation settings.

You can also change the right indent for paragraphs by using either of the following methods:

- Drag the Right Indent marker on the horizontal ruler.
- Open the Paragraph dialog box and adjust the Right indentation settings.

Indent the First Line

To change the indent settings for all paragraphs in a document, press Ctrl+A and apply the settings.

Many paragraphs begin with the first line indented—like this paragraph. Instead of pressing tab to indent the first line, you can format your paragraph to indent the first line according to your specifications. To indent the first line of a paragraph:

- Drag the First Line indent marker on the ruler.
- Open the Paragraph dialog box, select First Line in the S̲pecial drop-down list, and then type the measurement (in points) of the first-line indent in the B̲y list box.

Create Hanging Indents

==Hanging indents are the reverse of first-line indents—like this paragraph.== When a paragraph has a hanging indent, the first line starts further left than the body of the paragraph.

You can create a hanging indent in several ways:

- On the Ruler, drag the Left Indent marker to right and position the marker where the body text of the paragraph should display. Then, drag the First Line Indent marker to the left and position the marker where the first-line should begin.

- Open the Paragraph dialog box, select Hanging in the Special drop-down list, and then type the measurement (in points) of the first-line indent in the By list box.

- Press Ctrl+T

To remove paragraph formatting, click Ctrl+Q.

OBJECTIVE 29

Place Tabs

Placing tabs enables you to manage tables, columns, and other layout design needs. You can place tabs in a couple of ways. The two most common ways to create tabs entail using the horizontal ruler and the Tabs dialog box. You worked with the horizontal ruler in the previous sections, and so you should be feeling familiar with that tool. The Tab dialog box is shown in the following figure.

To open the Tabs dialog box, open the Format menu, and click Tabs; or, open the Paragraph dialog box, and click the Tabs button. The Tabs dialog box is useful for precisely placing tabs, inserting tab leaders, and clearing existing tabs.

When you work with tabs, you might want to display tab marks (which display as arrows) in body text. To control the display of tab marks, click Tools, Options, and check or uncheck the Tab characters check box on the View tab. Also, you can use the Hide/Show toggle button in the Standard toolbar to display and hide tab marks.

For tab placement, the horizontal ruler is the quickest, easiest way to create standard tab stops. For the exam, consider using the ruler to create basic tabs, such as left, right, center, and decimal tabs. If you need to create tabs with leaders, use the Tabs dialog box (as described later in this chapter).

To place tabs with the horizontal ruler (remember, to display the ruler, click <u>V</u>iew, <u>R</u>uler), you must first show the type of tab you want to place on the Tab style button (located on the left corner of the horizontal ruler). To change the tab style, simply click the Tab style button until you see the tab style you want to use. Each graphic represents a tab style:

- Left tab—Aligns text along left edge.
- Right tab—Aligns text along right edge.
- Center tab—Aligns text along center axis.
- Decimal tab—Aligns text by decimal (such as a column of numbers).
- Bar tab—Inserts a vertical bar at the tab stop.

The following figure demonstrates the basic tab-alignment settings.

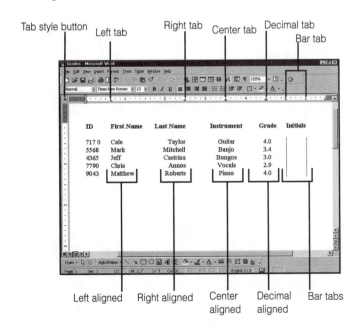

95

Part 1 • Core Level

To place a tab using the horizontal ruler, place your cursor where you want to apply the tab settings or select the text you want to be affected, then follow these steps:

1. Click the Tab style button in the horizontal ruler to display the type of tab (right, left, center, or decimal) you want to place.

To move a ruler tab, click the tab and drag it left or right. To remove a tab, drag it off the ruler.

2. Click the ruler where you want to place the tab or display the document in Print Layout View and double-click where you want to insert a tab.

30 OBJECTIVE

Use Tab Leaders

Often documents require the use of leading tabs. Leading tabs are tab stops that automatically insert characters, such as periods, within the space preceding the tab. For example, table of contents documents often use dotted tab stops between chapter names and page numbers.

To use a tab leader, follow these steps:

1. Open the Format menu and click Tabs to open the Tabs dialog box.

2. In the Tab stop position text box, type a new tab stop's position and select a tab style; or click an existing tab stop in the Tab stop position list box.

3. Select an Alignment setting.

4. Click a tab leader style in the Leader area, click Set, and click OK.

You can open the Tabs dialog box by double-clicking the horizontal ruler.

TAKE THE TEST

Task 1

Objectives covered: 24, Align Text in Paragraphs; 26, Add Borders to Paragraphs; 27, Apply Shading to Paragraphs; and 28, Indent paragraphs. Open the file named Alignment, which is stored in the Practice folder on the enclosed CD-ROM.

1. Align each paragraph according to the text's description.
2. Increase the indent for the justified paragraph.
3. Add a double-line border box around the first three paragraphs.
4. Apply any color of shading within the border box.

Check your work against solution file 1147F.

Task 2

Objectives covered: 21, Create Bulleted Lists; 23, Work in Outline View; 25, Adjust Paragraph Spacing; and 28, Indent Paragraphs. Open the file named Awards, which is stored in the Practice folder on the enclosed CD-ROM.

1. Create a bulleted list for the special appearance guests.
2. Decrease the bulleted list's indent so that the list is flush left with the text.
3. View the document in Outline view.
4. While in Outline view, change the Location heading to a Heading 2.
5. Return to Normal view.
6. Remove the first-line indent in the first paragraph.

Check your work against solution file 1147G.

Objectives covered: 22, Create Numbered Steps; 29, Place Tabs; and 30, Use Tab Leaders. Open the file named `Grades`, which is stored in the `Practice` folder on the enclosed CD-ROM.

Task 3

1. Format the five lines of text following the Check ID numbers line as numbered steps 2 through 6.

2. Select the student information and use the Ruler to format the information so that first names align left, last names align right, instruments align center, Grades align by decimal, and two bar tabs create lines below the Initials heading.

3. Add a solid underline leader to the tab between the words Signature and Date (position .4), and the tab from Date to the edge of the document (position 5.5).

Check your work against solution file `1147H`.

Cheat Sheet

Create Bulleted Lists

- Bullets.
- Click F̲ormat, Bullets and N̲umbering; or right-click and select Bullets and N̲umbering on the pop-up menu. Select a bullet style, and click OK.

Create Numbered Steps

- Numbering.
- Click F̲ormat, Bullets and N̲umbering; or right-click and select Bullets and N̲umbering on the pop-up menu. Click the N̲umbered tab. Select a numbered style and click OK.

Display a Document in Outline View

- Outline View.
- V̲iew, O̲utline.

Hide and Display Outline Information

- Expand and Collapse
- Double-click the expand/collapse (plus sign) marker next to a heading.
- Click the Show Heading buttons.

Move Sections

- Drag the expand/collapse plus sign right, left, up, and down.
- Click the expand/collapse plus sign, and then click the Promote, Demote, Move Up, and Move Down buttons in the Outlining toolbar.

Align Text in Paragraphs

- Click the Alignment drop-down list in the Paragraph dialog box.
- ▤ Align Left, ▤ Center, ▤ Align Right, and ▤ Justify.

Set Character Spacing

1. Select the text you want to modify.
2. Click F*o*rmat, *F*ont; or right-click on the selected text, and click *F*ont.
3. Click the Cha*r*acter Spacing tab.
4. Click the *S*pacing drop-down arrow, and specify Expanded or Condensed.
5. In the B*y* text box, specify the amount of space, in points, to expand or condense the character spacing.
6. Click OK.

Adjust Line Spacing

- In the Paragraph dialog box, select a Li*n*e Spacing drop-down list option, and enter information into the B*y* box, if necessary.
- Press Ctrl+1 (single spaced), Ctrl+5 (1.5 spaced), or Ctrl+2 (double spaced).

Modify Spacing Above and Below Paragraphs

1. Select a paragraph, open the Paragraph dialog box, and click in the *B*efore list box.
2. Enter the amount of space you want to insert before the selected paragraph.
3. Click in the Aft*e*r text box.

Continued

4. Enter the amount of space you want to insert after the selected paragraph.
5. Click OK.

Add Borders to Paragraphs

1. Click F*o*rmat, *B*orders and Shading.
2. Select a border style, or click edge icons.
3. Select a line style.
4. Specify *C*olor and *W*idth settings.
5. Ensure that *Paragraph* displays in the Appl*y* to text box.
6. Click OK.

Apply Shading to Paragraphs

1. Click *V*iew, *T*oolbars, and select Tables and Borders; or open the F*o*rmat menu, click *B*orders and Shading, and then click the *S*hading tab.
2. ▦ Shading Color drop-down list arrow, and click a color on the color palette; or, on the *S*hading tab, click a fill color, click a fill pattern, and click OK.

Increase and Decrease Indents

- ▦ Increase.
- Press Ctrl+M.
- Drag the Left Indent marker on the horizontal ruler.
- Open the Paragraph dialog box and adjust the Left indentation settings.

- ![icon] Decrease.
- Press Ctrl+Shift+M.
- Drag the Left Indent marker on the horizontal ruler.
- Open the Paragraph dialog box and adjust the Left indentation settings.
- Drag the Right Indent marker on the horizontal ruler.
- Open the Paragraph dialog box, and adjust the Right indentation settings.

Indent the First Line

- Drag the First Line indent marker on the ruler.
- Open the Paragraph dialog box, select First Line in the Special drop-down list, and then type a measurement in the By list box.

Create Hanging Indents

- On the Ruler, drag the Left Indent marker to right, and drag the First Line Indent marker to the left.
- Open the Paragraph dialog box, select Hanging in the Special drop-down list, and type a measurement in the By list box.
- Press Ctrl+T

Place Tabs

1. Click the Tab style button in the horizontal ruler to select a tab style.
2. Click the ruler where you want to place the tab.

Continued

Use Tab Leaders

1. Click Format, Tabs.

2. Type a new tab stop's position and select a tab style; or click an existing tab stop in the Tab stop position list box.

3. Select an alignment setting.

4. Click a tab leader style, and click OK.

CHAPTER 6

Working with Documents

Word comes with a number of features designed to help you when you're working with documents, and Microsoft requires Office User Specialists to know how to use these features. Therefore, to pass the exam, you'll need to master the art of working with documents. This means that you'll need to know how to quickly reposition your cursor as well as how to reference Word's versions of traditional writing resources, such as a dictionary, thesaurus, and grammar guide. In addition, you'll need to know how to create and modify page numbers, headers, and footers. This chapter reviews the following document fundamentals to prepare you to meet the exam's objectives:

- Navigate through Documents
- Run the Spelling Feature
- Access the Thesaurus Feature
- Run the Grammar Feature
- Work with the Office Assistant
- Run the Go To Feature
- Configure Page Numbers
- Use Headers and Footers

OBJECTIVE 31

Navigate through Documents

Word provides a number of navigational tricks that you can use to move around within a document. When working with Word documents, you will often need to navigate to a different section to edit and update information. To quickly navigate within a document, you can use three basic techniques: keyboard commands, scroll bar actions, and the Document Map. The navigational keyboard commands are shown in the following table.

Navigating Documents Using Keyboard Commands

To Move	Press This
One character to the left or right	Left or Right Arrow
One word to the left or right	Ctrl+Left Arrow or Ctrl+Right Arrow
Up or down one line	Up Arrow or Down Arrow
Up or down one paragraph	Ctrl+Up Arrow or Ctrl+Down Arrow
To the end of a line	End
To the beginning of a line	Home
To the top or bottom of the window	Alt+Ctrl+Page Up or Alt+Ctrl+Page Down
Up or down one screen	Page Up or Page Down

To Move	Press This
To the top of the next page	Ctrl+Page Down
To the top of the previous page	Ctrl+Page Up
To the end of a document	Ctrl+End
To the beginning of a document	Ctrl+Home
To a specified page in the document	Ctrl+G
To the location of the cursor when the document was closed	Shift+F5

Next, you can review the scroll bar options used to navigate in a document. Keep in mind that when you navigate to a new position in a document using the scroll bars, you only change your view of the document—not your cursor location. You need to click on your new page to move your cursor to the current screen; otherwise, your typed changes and arrow key movements will be executed at the original cursor location.

Navigating Documents Using the Scroll bar

To Scroll	Do This
Up one line	Click ▲ Up scroll arrow
Down one line	Click ▼ Down scroll arrow
Up or down one screen	Click above or below the Scroll box
To a specific page	Drag the Scroll box
Left	Click ◄ Left scroll arrow

continues

107

Part 1 • Core Level

Continued

To Scroll	Do This
Right	Click ▶ Right scroll arrow
Left beyond the margin	Press and hold Shift, and click ◀ Left scroll arrow.
Down or up one page	Click ⊙ Select Browse Object, and click ▫ Browse by Page. Then, click ▼ Next Page or ▲ Previous Page scroll bar buttons.

Finally, Word's Document Map offers a quick way to move to specific sections in a document. ==The Document Map shows an outline of a document's headings in a vertical pane along the left edge of the window,== as shown in the following figure.

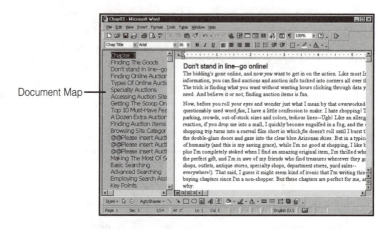

Document Map

Objective 31 • Navigate through Documents

To open the Document Map you can take either of the following actions:

- Click 🔍 Document Map in the Standard toolbar.
- Open the <u>V</u>iew menu and click <u>D</u>ocument Map.

To display document sections:

- Click a heading in the Document Map.

To close the Document Map:

- Click 🔍 Document Map in the Standard toolbar
- Double-click the right edge of the Document Map pane.
- Open the <u>V</u>iew menu and click <u>D</u>ocument Map.

109

OBJECTIVE 32

Run the Spelling Feature

You can (and should!) spell check your documents using Word's Spelling feature. Word's spell checker compares the words in your document to a standard dictionary. When the application encounters a word in a document that doesn't appear in the dictionary, the spell checker displays the Spelling and Grammar dialog box.

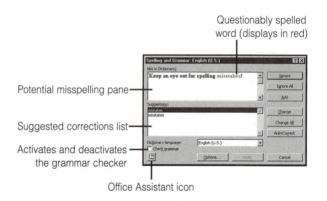

Questionably spelled word (displays in red)

Potential misspelling pane

Suggested corrections list

Activates and deactivates the grammar checker

Office Assistant icon

When you run the spell checker, you can check a block of selected text or you can check the entire document. If you choose to check an entire document, Word's spell checker checks text beginning at the current cursor location.

To run Word's spell checker, use any of the following options:

- Click the [ABC] Spelling and Grammar button on the Standard toolbar.
- Press F7.

110

- Open the Tools menu and click Spelling and Grammar.
- Right-click a flagged spelling error and click Spelling.

After you start the spell checker and the Spelling and Grammar dialog box appears identifying a possible misspelling or error (such as two consecutive instances of the same word), you can take any of the following actions:

- Click the Ignore button to leave the questionable word unchanged and move on to the next spelling issue.
- Click Ignore All to ignore all instances of the unidentified word. Clicking this option ensures that you won't have to continually press the Ignore button for the same words throughout a document.
- Click Add to add the questionable word to the dictionary, thereby avoiding having to ignore the word in future documents.
- Click Change after either selecting an option in the suggested corrections list or editing the questionable word in the Not in Dictionary window. This action will correct the text.
- Click Change All after either selecting one of the options in the suggested corrections list or editing the questionable word in the Not in Dictionary window. This action changes all instances of the questionable word.
- Click AutoCorrect to add a spelling error and its correction to the AutoCorrect list. This action configures Word to correct the error automatically as you type.
- Click Options to open the Spelling & Grammar options dialog box, which you can use to set specific spelling and grammar preferences.

In addition to opening the Spelling and Grammar dialog box, Word can check spelling as you type. By default, Word is configured to verify your spelling as you type. To see if this feature is active, open the Tools menu, click Options, and display the Spelling and Grammar tab (or click Options in the Spelling and

111

Part 1 • Core Level

Grammar dialog box). The Check spelling as you type checkbox should be checked.

When Word automatically checks spelling as you type, potentially misspelled words are flagged with a wavy red underline. You can right-click a flagged term to open a pop-up menu containing suggested spellings, as shown in the following figure.

33 OBJECTIVE

Access the Thesaurus Feature

Another writing tool included with Word is the Thesaurus feature. The purpose of Word's Thesaurus is the same as Roget's (and any other) thesaurus—to provide synonyms and antonyms.

The quickest way to take advantage of Word's Thesaurus feature is to right-click within the text you want to rephrase and click Synonyms to view a list of suggestions. Occasionally, the synonyms list will be empty; in which case, you can click the pop-up menu's Thesaurus option to open the Thesaurus dialog box. The figure shows synonyms suggested for the word *list*.

You can also use Word's Thesaurus feature by opening the Thesaurus dialog box. Perform any of the following actions to open the Thesaurus dialog box:

- Open the Tools menu, click Language, and then select Thesaurus.
- Press Shift+F7.
- Right-click a word, click Synonyms, and click Thesaurus.

Part 1 • Core Level

The following figure shows the Thesaurus opened when the word *huge* is selected.

If no text is selected when you open the Thesaurus, the word nearest the cursor is selected.

Notice in the figure that the Replace with Synonym list box displays synonyms and sometimes antonyms for the original term. You can click any suggested synonym or antonym and click Look Up to view synonyms and antonyms for suggested words. Further, you can click entries in the Meanings list box to clarify the context of the originally selected word.

34 OBJECTIVE

Run the Grammar Feature

Run-on sentences, subject-verb agreement, incorrect capitalization, and more—Word's grammar feature is like having your high school English teacher look over your shoulder while you write. The grammar feature flags potential grammatical errors and offers suggestions for improving the text.

Word's grammar feature is integrated with the spelling feature, so the procedures required to run these tools are similar. Similar to Word's spelling feature, Word's Grammar checker can be configured to check grammar automatically while you type. To specify whether you want to check automatically grammar as you type, open the Tools menu, click Options, and display the Spelling and Grammar tab (or click Options in the Spelling and Grammar dialog box). The Check grammar as you type check box should be checked.

The Check grammar as you type feature flags potentially incorrect grammar with a wavy green underline.

- Click the ![] Spelling and Grammar button on the Standard toolbar, and select the Check grammar checkbox in the Spelling and Grammar dialog box.

- Press F7 and select the Check grammar checkbox in the Spelling and Grammar dialog box.

- Open the Tools menu, click Spelling and Grammar, and select the Check grammar checkbox in the Spelling and grammar dialog box.

- Right-click a flagged grammatical error and click Grammar.

By default, Word checks spelling and grammar at the same time.

115

Part 1 • Core Level

When the Spelling and Grammar dialog box addresses a grammatical error (as opposed to a spelling error), the dialog box displays a different set of buttons related to correcting the grammar problem. Further, you can view grammatical rules related to text marked as ungrammatical by clicking the Office Assistant icon in the Spelling and Grammar dialog box, as shown in the following figure. The Office Assistant will open and give a quick review of basic grammatical rules.

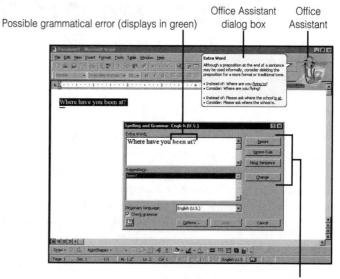

When the Spelling and Grammar dialog box displays a suspected grammatical error, you can change your text by selecting an entry in the Suggestions list box and clicking Change. Alternatively, you can bypass the change by clicking the Ignore or Ignore Rule button.

35 OBJECTIVE

Work with the Office Assistant

The Office Assistant is Word's user-friendly Help dialog box. The Office Assistant is an animated character that sits on your desktop ready and waiting to respond to your queries. To open the Office Assistant, take one of the following actions:

- Click [?] Microsoft Word Help on the Standard toolbar.
- Press F1.
- Open the Help window and click Show the Office Assistant (this option shows the Office Assistant icon without opening the Office Assistant dialog box).
- Open the Help window and click Microsoft Word Help.

You can configure several options related to the Office Assistant, including whether you can drag the assistant around your desktop. To view the assistant's options, right-click the assistant, and click Options or click Options in the Office Assistant's dialog box. Notice that the Office Assistant dialog box also offers a Gallery tab, which enables you to choose a new assistant character.

Double-clicking the office assistant hides and displays the Help dialog box.

To glean information from the assistant, follow these steps:

1. Display the Office assistant. If the graphic displays without the Help dialog box, you can display the Help dialog box by clicking [?] Microsoft Word Help, double-clicking the assistant icon, pressing F1, or clicking Microsoft Word Help on the Help menu.

2. Type a word, phrase, or question in the text box.

117

Part 1 • Core Level

3. Press Enter or click Search. A bulleted list of possible topics displays.

4. Click a bulleted topic item, and a Microsoft Word Help dialog box opens, as shown in the following figure. When you close the Microsoft Word Help dialog box, the Office Assistant's dialog box closes, although the icon remains on your desktop.

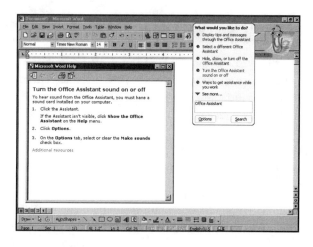

To hide the Office Assistant, take one of the following actions:

- Open the Help menu and click Hide the Office Assistant
- Right-click the character and click Hide

118

36 OBJECTIVE

Run the Go To Feature

Similar to the navigation techniques presented earlier in this chapter, the Go To feature can be used to quickly locate specific elements in a document. The Go To feature can be found on the G̲o To tab in the Find and Replace dialog box.

To access the Go To feature:

- Press Ctrl+G.
- Press F5.
- Open the E̲dit menu and click G̲o To.
- Click ⊙ Select Browse Object in the scroll bar and click → Go To.

To use the Go To feature, display the G̲o To tab in the Find and Replace dialog box and then follow these steps:

1. In the G̲o to what list box, select the type of element to which you want to go.

2. Click Nex̲t or Previou̲s; or, click in the E̲nter text box, type the go to occurrence, and click Go T̲o. For example, if you want to go to every other page, type +2.

119

OBJECTIVE 37

Configure Page Numbers

The usefulness of page numbers does not need to be recounted here—everyone has experienced the frustration of working with a document that lacks page numbers. Fortunately, Word makes adding page numbers a snap, and the exam will test your knowledge of this basic task in two ways. First, you'll be required to know how to add page numbers to a document. Then, you'll need to know how to modify existing page numbers.

Add Page Numbers

You can add page numbers in two ways: by using the Page Numbers dialog box and by using the Header and Footer option. The Header and Footer option is discussed in more detail in Objective 38—this section focuses on using the Page Numbers dialog box, as shown in the figure. To open the Page Numbers dialog box, open the Insert menu, and click Page Numbers.

To add page numbers to the current document, follow these steps:

1. Open the Insert menu and click Page Numbers.

2. Click the Position drop-down arrow and select either Top of page or Bottom of page.

120

3. Click the Alignment drop-down arrow and select Left, Center, Right, Inside, or Outside.

4. Clear the Show number on first page check box if you prefer.

5. Click the Format button to open the Page Number Format dialog box and access further page numbering options, such as Number format.

6. Click OK in both the Page Number Format and the Page Numbers dialog boxes.

If you inserted page numbers using the Page Numbers dialog box, you can modify your page number settings as follows:

- Reopen the Page Numbers dialog box and change existing settings.

- Double-click the page number while in Print Layout View and change existing settings.

Modify Page Numbers

121

OBJECTIVE 38

Use Headers and Footers

Headers and Footers enable you to add repeating information within the top and bottom margins of your documents. Typically, Headers and footers are used for printed documents, and they are commonly used to supply information, such as chapter names and numbers, dates of publication, and so forth. For the Word exam, you'll need to know how to create and modify headers and footers.

Create Headers and Footers

To create headers and footers, you must first change to the Header and Footer view by opening the View menu and then clicking Header and Footer. Header and Footer view displays as shown in the figure.

Header and footer text displays only in Print Layout View and on printed documents.

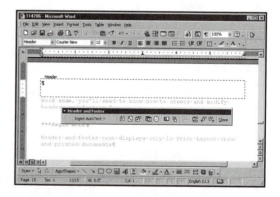

In Header and Footer view, the only components you need to work with are the Header pane (delimited by a dotted outline), the Footer pane, and the Header and Footer toolbar.

122

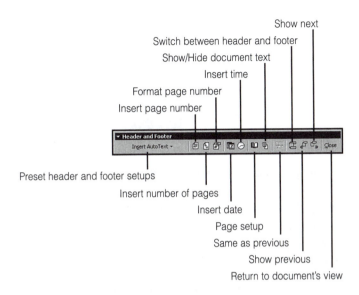

To create headers and footers, follow these steps:

1. Open the View menu and click Header and Footer. The header text box is activated and the Header and Footer toolbar opens automatically.

2. To insert header information, select an option on the Insert AutoText drop-down list, click toolbar buttons to enter elements, or type header text into the Header pane.

3. Click 🗐 Switch Between Header and Footer to view the footer text box.

4. To insert footer information, select an option on the Insert AutoText drop-down list, click toolbar buttons to enter elements, or type footer text into the Footer pane.

5. Click the Close button on the Header and Footer toolbar.

To create alternating headers and footers, click 🗐 Page Setup on the Header and Footer toolbar to open the Page Setup dialog box.

Part 1 • Core Level

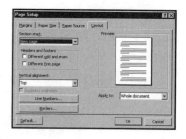

In the Page Setup dialog box, the Header and Footer area includes a Different odd and even check box. Select the Different odd and even check box to format your document with alternating headers or footers. Click OK. Then, use the Show Previous and Show Next buttons on the Header and Footer toolbar to format the alternating headers and footers.

Modify Headers and Footers

You can modify headers and footers by displaying the document's Header and Footer view in either of the following ways:

- Open the View menu and click Header and Footer.

- Double-click a header or footer element while in Print Layout View.

You can use click and type to automatically position text within footer and header text boxes.

After you are in Header and Footer view, you can click Header and Footer toolbar buttons to change the settings or you can type text directly into the text boxes. You can format header and footer text just as you format text in a document. For example, you can highlight text and change the text's alignment using Standard toolbar buttons. When you finish making changes, click the Close button on the Header and Footer toolbar to return to the document.

TAKE THE TEST

Task 1

Objectives covered: 31, Navigate through Documents; 32, Run the Spelling Feature; 34, Run the Grammar Feature; and 37, Configure Page Numbers. Open the file named `Auctions1`, which is stored in the `Practice` folder on the enclosed CD-ROM.

1. Use keyboard commands to move to the end of the line and then to the end of the document. Use the scroll bar to display the beginning of the document.

2. Check the document's spelling and grammar.

3. Add page numbers to the document and position them in the bottom-left area of the document.

4. Change the page number display to center at the bottom of the page.

Check your work against the solution file 1147I.

Task 2

Objectives covered: 33, Access the Thesaurus Feature; 35, Work with the Office Assistant; 36, Run the Go To Feature; and 38, Employ Headers and Footers. Open the file named `Auctions2`, which is stored in the `Practice` folder on the enclosed CD-ROM.

1. At the beginning of the second paragraph, use the thesaurus to replace the word *Recently*.

2. Open the Office Assistant and find a list of keyboard shortcut commands.

3. Use the Go To feature to move the cursor to the third line, fifth line, ninth line, and then the seventeenth line.

4. Create a header that includes the word *Confidential*, the page number, and today's date.

5. Switch to the Footer dialog box, add page numbers in the format *Page X of Y*, and center the element.

6. Reformat the header to only display the word *Confidential* and align the word along the right margin.

Check your work against the solution file 1147J.

Cheat Sheet

Navigate through Documents

- Press keyboard commands, click scroll bar buttons, open the Document Map, or access the Go To feature.

Run the Spelling Feature

- Click [ABC✓] Spelling and Grammar.
- Press F7.
- Open the Tools menu and click Spelling and Grammar.
- Right-click a flagged spelling error and click Spelling.

Access the Thesaurus Feature

- Open the Tools menu, click Language, and then select Thesaurus.
- Press Shift+F7.
- Right-click a word, click Synonyms, and click Thesaurus.

Use the Grammar Feature

- [ABC✓] Spelling and Grammar and select the Check grammar checkbox.
- Press F7, and select the Check grammar checkbox.
- Open the Tools menu, click Spelling and Grammar, and select the Check grammar check box.
- Right-click a flagged grammatical error and click Grammar.

Use the Office Assistant

1. [?] Microsoft Word Help, press F1, or click Microsoft Word Help.
2. Type a word, phrase, or question in the Office Assistant dialog box.
3. Press Enter or click Search.
4. Click a bulleted topic item.

Continued

Use the Go To Option

1. Press Ctrl+G, Press F5, or click Edit, Go To.
2. Select the type of element to which you want to go.
3. Click Next or Previous; or, click in the Enter text box, type the go to occurrence, and click Go To.

Add Page Numbers

1. Click Insert, Page Numbers.
2. Select a number position option.
3. Select a number alignment option.

Modify Page Numbers

- Reopen the Page Numbers dialog box.
- Double-click the page number while in Print Layout View.

Create Headers and Footers

1. Click View, Header and Footer.
2. Select an option on the Insert AutoText drop-down list, click toolbar buttons, or type text into the Header pane.
3. Click Switch Between Header and Footer to access the footer text box.
4. Click the Close button on the Header and Footer toolbar.

Modify Headers and Footers

- Open the View menu and click Header and Footer.
- Double-click a header or footer element while in Print Layout View.

CHAPTER 7

Formatting a Document

In this chapter, you step back from the text and look at formatting document pages. Turning your attention to page formatting details pays off when you print your document or upload it to a network. For the exam, you'll need to demonstrate your proficiency with Word's page layout commands. Namely, you'll need to:

- Set Page Orientation
- Set Margins
- Align Text Vertically
- Insert a Page Break
- Create Sections
- Apply a Style

OBJECTIVE 39

Set Page Orientation

The first order of business when formatting a document is to specify the text's orientation on the paper. Understandably, you're limited to two options: Portrait and Landscape. Portrait represents the standard page layout style in which the text displays taller than wide. Landscape prints text wider than it is tall. Portrait is the default because it is the most common page layout choice. You can change the default setting by clicking a radio button on the Paper Size tab in the Page Setup dialog box, as shown in the figure. In the figure, the Portrait radio button is selected and the Preview window shows how the document will print on the page.

To specify a document's page orientation, follow these steps:

1. Open the File menu and click Page Setup, or click Page Setup while in Header and Footer view.
2. Click the Page Size tab.
3. Click the Portrait or the Landscape radio button.

130

40 OBJECTIVE

Set Margins

After you determine a document's page orientation, your next decision regards how to position the text within the page orientation's boundaries. In other words, you need to assign margins to your documents. Setting margins enables you to specify how much whitespace should display for the top, bottom, left, right, and gutter areas on each printed page. You can configure each margin individually by accessing the Margins tab in the Page Setup dialog box, as shown in the figure.

To display the Margin settings, open the Page Setup dialog box, and click the Margins tab.

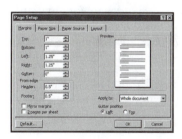

You can specify a variety of margin settings on the Margins tab. The options include the following:

- **Top, Bottom, Left, Right, and Gutter** The *gutter* refers to the amount of extra space you want to add to a margin for binding. By default, Word applies the specified gutter space to the left margin of all pages if the Mirror margins check box is cleared.

Part 1 • Core Level

- **Header and Footer** This setting specifies the distance that the top edge of headers should print from the top edge of the page and the distance that the bottom edge of footers should print from the bottom edge of the page.

- **Mirror margins** This setting adjusts left and right margins so that the inside margins of facing pages are the same width and the outside margins of facing pages are the same width. Commonly, mirrored page settings are used for documents that will be bound like a book. When you select the Mirror margins option, the specified gutter space is added to the inside margin of all pages.

- **2 pages per sheet** You select this option when you want to print two pages on one sheet of paper. This is helpful when a printed page will be folded in half with the two pages on the inside.

- **Apply to** This drop-down list option enables you to specify whether to apply the margin settings to the entire document, selected text, the current section, or following the cursor's current position.

- **Gutter position** This option enables you to specify how much gutter space (if any) to add to a document's margin.

==You can also adjust margins using Word's horizontal and vertical rulers in Print Layout view,== as described in the following steps:

1. In Print Layout view, with the horizontal and vertical rulers open (View, Ruler), point to the edge of the gray margin boundary.

To specify exact margin measurements in Page Layout view, hold down Alt as you drag the margin boundary.

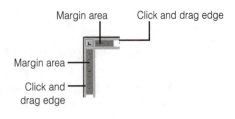

2. Click and drag the edge of the margin area to the desired location.

41 OBJECTIVE

Align Text Vertically

You can align text vertically on a page. In other words, you can specify how you want a document's text to be positioned vertically between the top and bottom margins. Word enables you to vertically align text to the top or bottom margin, to be centered, or to be justified. By default, Word vertically aligns documents along the top margin. The justified setting affects only full pages (partial pages will be aligned along the top margin). The following figure shows how these settings affect text.

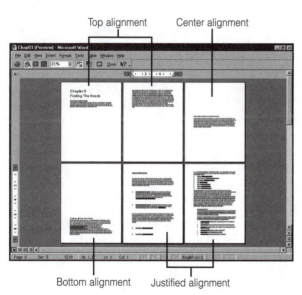

Top alignment Center alignment
Bottom alignment Justified alignment

133

Part 1 • Core Level

To specify a page's vertical alignment, follow these steps:

1. Open the Page Setup dialog box, and click the Layout tab.

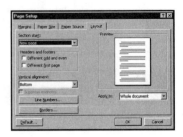

2. Click the Vertical alignment drop-down arrow and select an alignment option.

3. Specify which text should be affected by clicking an option in the Apply to drop-down list.

42 OBJECTIVE

Insert a Page Break

You can insert a page break anywhere within your document. By default, Word inserts page breaks when you reach the bottom of a page. There will be times, however, when you prefer to break text before you fill a page. In those instances, you can manually insert a page break, called a hard page break. A hard page break appears as a light gray line with the nonprinting words *Page Break* in your document in Normal View and Page Layout View when you are displaying nonprinting characters (click ¶ Show/Hide).

To create a hard page break, insert your cursor where you want to create a page break and then use one of these methods:

- Press Ctrl+Enter.

- Open the Insert menu, click Break, click the Page break radio button, and click OK.

- Click within the first paragraph of the text you want to follow a page break, open the Format menu, click Paragraph, click the Line and Page Breaks tab, and select the Page break before checkbox.

To delete a hard page break, double-click the Page Break line and press Back Space or Delete.

135

OBJECTIVE 43

Create Sections

Word gives you the option to break your document into sections. The benefit of using sections is that each section can have its own page formatting, including page orientation, margins, pagination, headers, and so forth. Sections comes in handy, for instance, when you want to partition a document into chapter-like divisions or you want to offset a paragraph or two of text with distinctive margins and other layout specifications, such as columns.

Unlike page breaks, section breaks do not automatically start a new page.

Word identifies section breaks with a double-gray line in Normal View and Page Layout View if nonprinting objects are displayed (click ¶ Show/Hide), as shown in the figure.

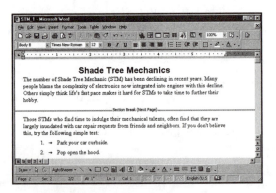

You can create four types of section breaks:

- **Next Page** Inserts a section break and starts the next section at the top of the next page.
- **Continuous** Inserts a section break and starts the new section immediately on the same page.

136

- **Even** Inserts a section break and starts the next section on the next even-numbered page. If the section break falls on an even-numbered page, Word leaves the next odd-numbered page blank.

- **Odd** Inserts a section break and starts the next section on the next odd-numbered page. If the section break falls on an odd-numbered page, Word leaves the next even-numbered page blank.

To create section breaks, follow these steps:

1. Open the Insert menu, and click Break. The Break dialog box opens.

2. Click a section page break radio button and click OK.

After you add a section break, you can format the section independent of other sections within the document.

To format a section, follow these steps:

1. Click in the section you want to format.
2. Open the Page Setup dialog box and specify settings for the section.
3. In the Apply to drop-down list, select This section.

Create a Section

Format a section

To delete a section break, select the section break, then press Delete or Back Space.

If you delete a section break, the preceding text assumes the formatting of the following section.

137

OBJECTIVE 44

Apply a Style

Styles are preset groups of formatting characteristics that you can apply to text in one fell swoop. Styles help to keep document elements consistent. For example, a document can have a chapter title style, heading style, and body text style. To create a sense of cohesion, all chapter titles can be formatted with the chapter title style, headings can be formatted with the heading style, and so forth.

Groups of styles (and their settings) are saved as templates. For the core-level exam, you are not required to create styles and templates, but you must know how to apply styles to your text.

When you create a new blank document in Word, the styles are based on the Normal template. There are a number of styles stored in the Normal template. To view the available styles, click the Style drop-down list in the Formatting toolbar.

To apply a style to text, select the text to format or click within a paragraph to format the entire paragraph and then execute one of the following procedures:

- Click a style on the Style drop-down list.
- Open the Format menu, click Style, click a style in the Styles list box, and click Apply.

Styles are often assigned shortcut key combinations, as well. When a style is associated with a shortcut key, you can select text or click within a paragraph and then press the keyboard combination to apply the desired style. For example, the Normal text style in Word's Normal template is associated with the Ctrl+Shift+N keyboard combination.

To view a style's keyboard shortcut, open the Format menu, click Style, click Modify, and click Shortcut Key. The currently assigned keyboard shortcut appears in the Current keys text box.

TAKE THE TEST

Task 1 Objectives covered: 39, Set Page Orientation; 41, Align Text Vertically; and 43, Create Sections. Open the file named STM_1, which is stored in the Practice folder on the enclosed CD-ROM.

1. Insert a section break below the first paragraph, and start the next section on the next page.
2. Format the first page to align vertically to the bottom of the page.
3. Specify that the second section prints in landscape layout.

Check your work against the solution file, 1147K. To check page layout, click [icon] Print Preview in the Standard toolbar.

Task 2 Objectives covered: 40, Set Margins; 42, Insert a Page Break; and 44, Apply a Style. Open the file named STM_2, which is stored in the Practice folder on the enclosed CD-ROM.

1. Change the left, right, top, and bottom margins to 2 inches.
2. Add a page break directly before the chart.
3. Apply the Num List style to the numbered list.

Check your work against solution file 1147L. To check page layout, click [icon] Print Preview in the Standard toolbar.

Cheat Sheet

Set Page Orientation

1. Open the File menu and click Page Setup.
2. Click the Paper Size tab.
3. Click the Portrait or Landscape radio button.

Set Margins

- Set margin settings on the Margins tab in the Page Setup dialog box.
- Display Page Layout view and drag the margin area edges in the horizontal and vertical rulers.

Align Text Vertically

1. Display the Layout tab in the Page Setup dialog box.
2. Select an option in the Vertical alignment drop-down list.
3. Select an Apply to drop-down option.

Insert a Page Break

- Press Ctrl+Enter.
- Open the Insert menu, click Break, click the Page break radio button, and click OK.
- Select the text you want to follow a page break, click Format, click Paragraph, click the Line and Page Breaks tab, and select the Page break before checkbox.

Create Sections

1. Open the Insert menu, and click Break.
2. Click a section page break radio button, and click OK.

Continued

Format Sections

1. Click within a section.
2. Open the Page Setup dialog box and specify settings.
3. In the Apply to drop-down list, select This Section.

Apply a Style

- Click a style on the Style drop-down list.
- Open the Format menu, click Style, click a style in the Styles list box, and click Apply.

CHAPTER

8

Adding Columns, Tables, and Objects

Frequently, word processing entails formatting text into columns. Because aligning text into columns is a popular formatting technique, Microsoft requires Core Level Office User Specialists to master the basics of creating columns and tables. Therefore, to help fully prepare you for the exam, this chapter reviews formatting text into columns and creating tables. Specifically, you'll review how to:

- Format Text into Columns
- Create a Table
- Revise a Table
- Modify Table Cells
- Rotate Table Text

OBJECTIVE 45

Format Text into Columns

Formatting text into columns is helpful when you are creating newsletter, brochure, and newspaper types of layouts. By default, Word's Columns feature flows text to the bottom of one column and then continues at the top of the next column.

Word has five preset column formats, as shown in the following figure. The column formats follow:

- Single column (Word's default column setting)
- Two equal columns
- Three equal columns
- Two unequal columns with a wider column on the left
- Two unequal columns with a wider column on the right

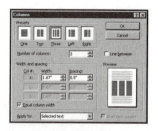

As you can see in the figure's Preview pane, you can apply columnar formatting to selected text. Alternatively, you can apply columns to an entire document. In either case, when you create columns, Word automatically changes to Print Layout. View so you can see how the text will display and print.

To create columns, you can use either of the following tools:

- Columns in the Standard toolbar
- Columns dialog box

To create columns using Columns in the Standard toolbar, perform the following steps:

1. Click within the document to format the entire document into columns, click where you want column formatting to begin, click within the section you want to format, or select text to format into columns.

2. Click Columns in the Standard toolbar. The Columns drop-down list appears, as shown in the following figure.

Create Columns

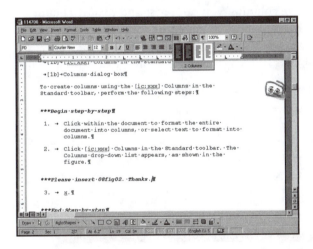

3. Select from one through six columns (click, hold, and drag past the right edge of the drop-down menu to view columns five and six), and click. The text is formatted into equal columns.

You can customize column widths by inserting column settings into the Columns dialog box. To create columns using the Columns dialog box, follow these steps:

1. Click within the document to format the entire document into columns, click where you want column formatting to

145

Part 1 • Core Level

You can create up to 45 equal-width columns by typing a number in the Number of columns text box.

begin, click within the section you want to format, or select text to format into columns.

2. Open the Format menu and click Columns. The Columns dialog box opens.

3. Select a preset column style in the Preset area; or enter a number in the Number of columns text box, and specify each column's width and spacing by typing measurements into the Width and Spacing text boxes.

4. Click the Apply to drop-down list and specify whether to apply columns to Whole document, This point forward (from the cursor's position forward), or Selected text.

5. Click the Line between checkbox to insert rule lines between columns.

Revise Columns

After you create columns, you can revise and remove column formatting. Keep in mind that revising and removing column formatting doesn't affect the actual text—it simply affects how the text displays. To revise existing columns, follow these steps:

1. Click within the column you want to revise.

2. Open the Columns dialog box.

3. Click a new preset column setting, or change column settings by entering measurements into the Width and Spacing text boxes.

You can quickly remove column formatting without deleting your information. Removing column formatting is the same as revising your column settings to single-column format. To remove column formatting, follow these steps:

1. Click within a text column.

2. Click ▤ Columns, and click the single column format; or, open the Columns dialog box, click the One preset option, and click OK.

146

46 OBJECTIVE

Create a Table

Applying Word's basic Columns feature often creates a satisfactory layout effect, but for greater text-manipulation and flexibility, you'll need to use tables. Tables enable you to organize information into rows and columns, similar to spreadsheets. Each area where a row intersects with a table is called a cell.

You can insert tables into your documents in a couple ways. You can use the ▦ Insert Table button on the Standard toolbar, or you can open the Insert dialog box, as shown in the following figure.

Insert A Table

To create a table using the ▦ Insert Table button on the Standard toolbar, perform the following steps:

1. Place the cursor at the position you want to insert a table within a document.

2. Click ▦ Insert Table in the Standard toolbar. The Table drop-down list appears, as shown in the following figure.

147

Part 1 • Core Level

3. Highlight the appropriate number of columns and rows necessary to create your table. (You can drag past the bottom and right edges of the drop-down menu to view additional cell selections.) If you create a 3X4 table, a table will be inserted with three rows and four columns, like this:

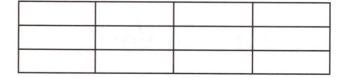

To insert a table based on existing text, highlight the text and click the ▦ Insert Table button on the Standard toolbar or the Tables and Borders toolbar; or open the T<u>a</u>bles menu, click Con<u>v</u>ert, and click Te<u>x</u>t to Table.

To control how a table displays relative to surrounding text, right-click the table, click Table <u>P</u>roperties, click the Table tab, and select alignment and text wrapping styles.

You can also insert tables by using the Insert Table dialog box. To do so, follow these steps:

1. Position your cursor where you want to insert a table, open the T<u>a</u>ble menu, click <u>I</u>nsert, and click <u>T</u>able. The Insert Table dialog box opens.

2. Enter the number of columns and rows you want in the table.

3. Select an AutoFit behavior setting to control the column sizing. You can choose from

   - **Fixed column width**—Column widths are always a specific size in inches or of equal size between the page margins. The default setting is Auto, which means column widths will be equally sized between the document's margins.

   - **AutoFit**—Column widths are automatically adjusted according to the amount of text in each column.

148

Objective 46 • Create a Table

- **AutoFit to window**—Column widths are automatically resized so that the table always fits inside the window of Web browsers.

4. Click OK to insert the table.

Finally, you can create tables based on pre-configured style settings by clicking [icon] Table AutoFormat on the Tables and Borders toolbar, clicking the AutoFormat button in the Insert Table dialog box, or opening the Table menu and clicking Table AutoFormat. When you choose the AutoFormat feature, the Table AutoFormat dialog box displays as shown in the following figure.

You can also access the AutoFit settings on the Table menu.

You can insert a table within the cell of an existing table. These are called nested tables.

Pre-configured table styles — [Table AutoFormat dialog box image] — Preview pane

Click the table formatting options in the Formats list to preview a format's border and shading styles in the Preview pane. When you find a style that suits your requirements, click OK.

For maximum table-creation control, you can opt to draw a table instead of insert a table. By drawing a table, you can create complex tables with different cell sizes, like this:

Draw A Table

[Table illustration with varying cell sizes]

When you draw a table, you must display the Tables and Borders toolbar. To display the toolbar, use any of the following methods:

149

Part 1 • Core Level

- Click Tables and Borders on the Standard toolbar.
- Open the <u>V</u>iew menu, click <u>T</u>oolbars, and click Tables and Borders.
- Open the T<u>a</u>ble menu, and click Dra<u>w</u> Table.

The Tables and Borders toolbar displays as shown in the following figure.

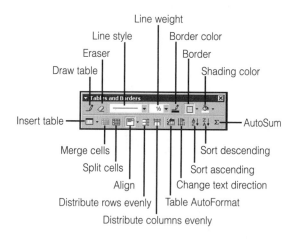

To draw a table, follow these steps:

1. Position your cursor where you want to insert a table, and click Draw Table on the Tables and Borders toolbar; or open the T<u>a</u>ble menu, and click Dra<u>w</u> Table. The cursor changes to a pencil icon.

2. Draw a rectangle to delimit the outer boundaries of the table.

3. Draw the columns and rows within the table rectangle using the pencil icon.

4. If necessary, select columns or rows (as described next) and click the Distribute Rows Evenly or the Distribute Columns Evenly buttons on the Tables and Borders toolbar.

To erase a line (or lines), click Eraser on the Tables and Borders toolbar, and then drag over the line(s).

150

Objective 46 • Create a Table

When you draw and format tables, you will often need to select cells, rows, and columns. To select table components, use the following techniques:

To select this	Perform this action
Cell	Click the cell's left edge or triple-click within the cell
Row	Click in the selection bar (the left margin) next to the row, or click in the row, open the Table menu, click Select, and click Row.
Column	Position the cursor along the top-edge of the column (the cursor changes to a down-pointing arrow), and click; Press Alt, and click in the column; or click within the column, open the Table menu, click Select, and click Column.
Multiple cells, rows, or columns	Drag across cells, rows, and columns; or click in a cell, press and hold down Shift, click where you want the selection to end, and release Shift.
Next cell's text	Press Tab or drag to select text.
Previous cell's text	Press Shift+Tab or drag to select text.
Entire table	Press Alt and double-click the table; click and drag to select all columns and rows; or open the Table menu, click Select, and click Table.

151

Part 1 • Core Level

Add Table Borders

Adding a table border is similar to adding a border to a paragraph or other element in Word. A table with formatted borders can help to offset particular table areas, as shown here:

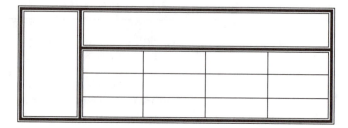

To add table borders, follow these steps:

1. Ensure that the Tables and Borders toolbar is open and the Draw Table button is not selected, and then choose a line style in the Line Style drop-down list.

2. Select the table cells that will have custom borders.

3. To specify which cell borders should be formatted, click ▦ Border on the Tables and Borders toolbar or the Standard toolbar, and then select the appropriate edge setting on the Border drop-down list.

You can also assign border settings by accessing the Borders and Shading dialog box (see Objectives 26 and 27 in Chapter 5, "Formatting Paragraphs," for more information about the Borders and Shading dialog box). To open the Borders and Shading dialog box, select the table, and then use any of the following methods:

- Open the Format menu and click Borders and Shading.

- Open the Table menu, click Table Properties, and click the Borders and Shading button.

- Right-click a table, click Table Properties, and click the Borders and Shading button.

Objective 46 • Create a Table

When using the Borders and Shading dialog box to format tables, remember to select Table (or the table element) in the Apply to drop-down list.

You can shade (or color) tables in a number of ways. You can color the entire background, color complete rows or columns, or color selected cells. In all cases, you follow similar procedures.

Add Table Shading

You can shade tables using the ![icon] Shading button on the Tables and Borders toolbar, or you can use the Shading tab in the Borders and Shading dialog box.

To shade tables with the ![icon] Shading button on the Tables and Borders toolbar, follow these steps:

1. Click a cell you want to shade, or drag and select the cell(s), row(s), and column(s) you want to shade.

2. Click the ![icon] Shading drop-down arrow and click a color on the color palette.

You can also shade tables by applying the Borders and Shading dialog box options. To do so, follow these steps:

1. Click within a table or specific cell, open the Borders and Shading dialog box, and click the Shading tab.

2. Specify shading preferences.

3. In the Apply to drop-down list, specify whether to apply the shade to the table, cell, or selected text.

OBJECTIVE 47

Revise a Table

You can easily revise existing tables by inserting and deleting rows and columns. You will be required to insert and delete rows on the exam. *Although* this sounds like it might be time-consuming, it is a quick task. If you know where to find the proper commands, you should be able to add and delete columns and move on to the next exam task without using more than a minute of exam time.

Insert Rows and Columns

Word provides easy-to-use column and row insert commands. To access the insert commands, open the Table menu and click Insert to display the menu shown in the following figure.

To insert a column, you can use any of the following methods:

- Click within a column near the position you want to insert a new column or columns, open the Table menu, click Insert, and select either the Columns to the Left or Columns to the Right menu option.

- Click within a column near the position where you want to insert a new column or columns, click the arrow next to Insert Table on the Tables and Borders toolbar and click an insert command.

- Highlight a column to the right of where you want to insert a column, right-click, and select Insert Columns on the pop-up menu.

==You can insert multiple columns== by selecting the same number of columns as the number of columns you want to insert. Then, open the Table menu, click Insert, and select the Columns to the Left or Columns to the Right menu option, or click the arrow next to 🔲 Insert Table on the Tables and Borders toolbar and click an insert command.

Another way to insert more than one column or row is to insert a row or column and then execute the Repeat Typing command on the Edit menu or press Ctrl+Y.

To insert a row, use one of the following methods:

- Click within a row near the position where you want to insert a new row or rows, open the Table menu, click Insert, and select either the Rows Above or Rows Below menu option.

- Click within a row near the position you want to insert a new row or rows, click the arrow next to 🔲 Insert Table on the Tables and Borders toolbar and click an insert command.

- Click after the last cell in the row that will display above the row you want to insert, and press Enter.

- Highlight the row that will display below the rows you want to insert, right-click, and select Insert Rows on the pop-up menu.

==You can also add rows to the bottom of a table.== To do so, click after the cell in the last row in the last column (bottom-right corner of the table), and press Enter or Tab.

Delete Rows and Columns

To delete rows and columns, select the row or column and then take one of the following actions:

- Right-click the selected element(s) and click Delete Rows or Delete Columns.

- Press BackSpace.

Part 1 • Core Level

Selecting a row or column and pressing Delete removes the contents of the cells—not the entire row or column.

- Press Shift+Delete.
- Press Ctrl+X.
- Click ✂ Cut in the Standard toolbar.
- Open the T<u>a</u>ble menu, click <u>D</u>elete, click C<u>e</u>lls, and click the Delete entire <u>r</u>ow or the Delete entire <u>c</u>olumn option.

48 OBJECTIVE

Modify Table Cells

In addition to inserting and deleting rows and columns, you need to know how to work with cells to pass the Word certification exam. More precisely, you'll need to know how to merge cells and change cell widths and heights. As with many table-management tasks, displaying the Table and Borders toolbar can help you to easily accomplish cell-management tasks.

Merge Cells

Merging cells means to combine multiple cells into a single cell. When you merge cells, the cells must touch each other either vertically or horizontally. To merge cells, use one of the following methods:

- Select the cells you want to merge, and click 🔲 Merge Cells on the Tables and Borders toolbar.

- Click 🗌 Eraser on the Tables and Borders toolbar, and drag the eraser over cell dividers.

Change Cell Height and Width

You can change the height and width of cells by dragging the row and column lines in Print Layout View. To measure your column and row border movements, ensure the horizontal and vertical rulers are displayed. This is the quickest and easiest way to resize columns and rows during the exam.

Another way to resize a column is to size the column to the widest entry in the column. To do this, select the column, and then double-click the right border of the column you want to

157

To split cells, use Draw Table or click Split Cells on the Tables and Borders toolbar.

resize. If you need to change cell dimensions more precisely, you can access the Table Properties dialog box, as shown in the following figure.

To adjust the row, column, and cell sizes in the Table Properties dialog box, click on the appropriate tab, and enter numbers into the corresponding size text boxes.

49 OBJECTIVE

Rotate Table Text

Last but not least, you need to be prepared to rotate table text to successfully complete the core-level exam. Word's rotate feature is often used when horizontal space is at a premium or when a table contains narrow columns. Most often, the rotate option is applied to header text (therefore, the exam requires you to rotate a table's header text), but you can rotate any table text. Further, in combination with rotating text, you will often need to align text within a cell. To configure table text positioning, follow these steps:

1. Select the text you want to position.

2. Click [icon] Change Text Direction on the Tables and Borders toolbar to cycle through the three text direction choices; or, right-click the selected text, click Text Direction, and click a text direction box in the Text direction box, as shown in the figure.

3. On the Tables and Borders toolbar, click the [icon] Align drop-down arrow, and select an alignment option on the menu; or, right-click the selected text, point to Cell Alignment, and click an alignment option on the menu.

159

TAKE THE TEST

Task 1

Objectives covered: 45, Format Text into Columns; 46, Create a Table; 47, Revise a Table; and 48, Modify Table Cells. Open the file named Sprints1, which is stored in the Practice folder on the enclosed CD-ROM.

1. Insert an 11 row x 5 column table below the existing text.
2. Shade the table's top row with any color.
3. Select and format the text above the table into two columns.
4. Delete a column from the table.
5. Add a rule line between the text columns displaying above the table.
6. Merge the top row of the table with the following row.
7. Open the Table Properties dialog box and center align the table with no text wrapping.

Check your work against solution file 1147M.

Task 2

Objectives covered: 46, Create a Table; 47, Revise a Table; 48, Modify Table Cells; and 49, Rotate Table Text. Open the file named Sprints2, which is stored in the Practice folder on the enclosed CD-ROM.

1. Align the table title in the middle of the shaded box.
2. Insert a row directly below the shaded area, and enter the following headings: Car Driver, Car #, Points, Season Points.

3. Rotate the text you inserted in Step 2 so that the tops of the letters point toward the left.

4. Use the Draw Table tool to divide the bottom right cell into three cells.

5. Add a 1.5 point border to the outer edge of the table.

6. Resize each column so that no text wraps and the extra white space is minimized.

7. Align the rotated text along each cell's left edge and flush with the bottom of the cell.

Check your work against solution file 1147N.

Cheat Sheet

Create Columns

- ▦ Columns.
- Click F_ormat, C_olumns.

Revise Columns

1. Click a column.
2. Click F_ormat, C_olumns.
3. Click a new preset column setting, or change column Wi_dth and S_pacing settings.

Insert a Table

- ▦ Insert Table.
- Click Ta_ble, I_nsert, T_able.

Draw a Table

1. ✏ Draw Table on the Tables and Borders toolbar; or click Ta_ble, Dra_w Table.
2. Draw a rectangle.
3. Draw the columns and rows within the table rectangle.

Add Table Borders

1. Choose a line style in the Line Style drop-down list on the Tables and Borders toolbar.
2. Select the table cells.
3. ▦ Border on the Tables and Borders toolbar or the Standard toolbar.

Add Table Shading

1. Select cell(s), row(s), or column(s).
2. Click Shading drop-down arrow, and click a color square.

Insert Columns

- Click in a column near the position you want to insert a new column or columns; click Table, Insert; and select Columns to the Left or Columns to the Right.
- Click in a column near the position you want to insert a new column or columns, click Insert Table drop-down arrow on the Tables and Borders toolbar, and click an insert command.
- Highlight a column to the right of where you want to insert a column, right-click, and select Insert Columns.

Insert Rows

- Click in a row near the position you want to insert a new row or rows; click Table, Insert; and select Rows Above or Rows Below.
- Click in a row near the position where you want to insert a new row or rows, click Insert Table drop-down arrow on the Tables and Borders toolbar, and click an insert command.
- Click after the last cell in the row that will display above the row you want to insert, and press Enter.
- Highlight the row that will display below the rows you want to insert, right-click, and select Insert Rows on the pop-up menu.

Delete Rows and Columns

- Right-click on the selected element(s) and click Delete Rows or Delete Columns.
- Press BackSpace.
- Press Shift+Delete.

Continued

- Press Ctrl+X.
- Click ✂ Cut in the Standard toolbar.
- Open the Table menu, click Delete, click Cells, and click either the Delete entire row or the Delete entire column option.

Merge Cells

- Select cells, and click ▦ Merge Cells on the Tables and Borders toolbar.
- Click ✐ Eraser on the Tables and Borders toolbar, and erase cell dividers.

Change Cell Height and Width

- Drag table row and column lines in Page Layout view.
- Open the Table Properties dialog box, and change row, column, and cell settings.

Rotate Table Text

- ▦ Change Text Direction on the Tables and Borders toolbar to cycle through the three text direction choices.
- Right-click the selected text, click Text Direction, and click a text direction box.

CHAPTER 9

Working with Art

Gone are the days (at least for the most part) of carefully snipping clip art out of clip art books, gumming them up with a glue machine, and pasting them onto layout boards. Word processing programs make it a snap to insert art and objects in and around text. Further, Word helps you get a jump-start on inserting graphics into your documents by providing a large collection of clip art and objects. As you know, pictures are worth a thousand words; so, Microsoft made pictures worth a few points on the exam too. To become certified, you'll need to know how to:

- Use the Drawing Toolbar
- Insert Objects

OBJECTIVE 50

Use the Drawing Toolbar

In addition to its many other features, the Drawing toolbar enables you to insert lines and shapes. The Drawing toolbar displays as shown in the figure.

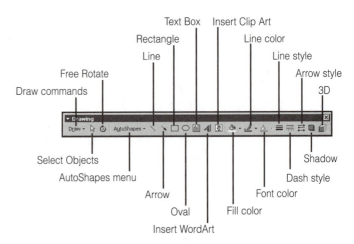

To open the Drawing toolbar, use one of the following methods:

- Click ![icon] Drawing in the Standard toolbar.
- Right-click any toolbar, and click Drawing.
- Open the View menu, click Toolbars, and click Drawing.

You can use the Drawing toolbar to create regular, dashed, and arrow lines. You can also draw basic shapes, 3D shapes, and AutoShapes.

166

Overall, you can add quite a bit of flair to a document using Word's Drawing toolbar, but the core level exam merely requires you to be proficient in performing the basic drawing tasks described in the next few sections.

You can use Word's line feature to create and insert lines and arrows within your documents. Lines are commonly used in documents as rule lines, positioned to offset text or as pointers to emphasize particulars in graphics. ==You can specify line attributes, such as weight (or width), color, and style.== The figure shows a number of regular, dashed, and arrow line styles.

Draw Lines

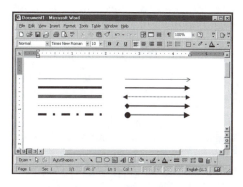

To create lines, follow these steps:

1. Open the Drawing toolbar.

2. Click ⬚ Line or ⬚ Arrow on the Drawing toolbar. Word automatically changes to Print Layout view.

3. Click and drag in the document to create a line.

4. To stylize the line or arrow, ensure that the line is selected and click one of the following:

    - ⬚ Line Color to select a line color.
    - ⬚ Line Style to select a line width (weight) and style.
    - ⬚ Dash Style to select a dashed line style.
    - ⬚ Arrow Style to apply an arrow style.

To keep lines straight, press Shift while drawing the lines.

167

Part 1 • Core Level

To resize, move, or change any line or object attributes, you must first select the item. To select a line or object, click the Select Objects icon on the Drawing toolbar and click the line or object. You can then perform any of the following actions.

To resize a line or object:

- Drag the selected item's selection box (a small square marker).

To move a line or object:

- Click anywhere on a selected line or object (other than on the selection box) and drag the item.

To reformat an item:

- Change the format setting (such as color or line style) using the Drawing toolbar buttons.

Create Shapes and 3D Shapes

Creating shapes is similar to creating lines. You can quickly create squares, circles, rectangles, ovals, and 3D shapes, as shown in the figure.

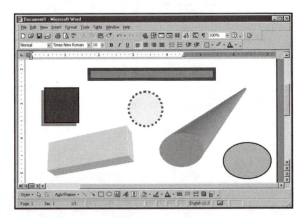

To create a shape, display the Drawing toolbar, and then follow these steps:

1. Click ▢ Rectangle or ◯ Oval on the Drawing toolbar.

2. To create a square or circle, click the document then drag the selection handles to resize the shape, or press Shift and

168

Objective 50 • Use the Drawing Toolbar

then click and drag in the document. To create a rectangle or oval, click and drag in the document.

3. To stylize a shape, select the object (click ![] Select Objects and click the object), and use the following Drawing toolbar options:

   - ![] Fill Color—Shades the entire shape
   - ![] Line Color—Shades the shape's outer edge
   - ![] Line Style—Applies a style to the shape's outer edge
   - ![] Dash Style—Applies a dashed line to the shape's outer edge
   - ![] Shadow—Adds a shadow to the shape
   - ![] 3D—Changes the shape to a 3D shape

As with lines, you can change the appearance of an existing object by clicking ![] Select Objects, clicking the object(s), and then using the various formatting icons on the Drawing toolbar. For example, you can select an existing basic shape and click a setting on the ![] 3D drop-down list to add a three-dimensional appearance to the selected item.

To select multiple lines or objects, click the Select Objects icon, and then click and drag to select the items.

In addition to supplying drawing tools, the Drawing toolbar enables you to insert pre-formatted shapes. In fact, the exam requires you to insert a pre-formatted shape by using the AutoShapes feature. Fortunately, the secret to inserting an AutoShape is knowing that AutoShapes exist! The figure shows a small selection of the many AutoShapes available in Word.

AutoShapes

169

Part 1 • Core Level

To display the AutoShapes menu as a toolbar, open the Insert menu, click Picture, expand the pop-up menu, and click AutoShapes.

As you can see in the figure, some AutoShapes, such as callouts and banners, are pre-formatted to include text boxes, meaning that you can type and format text directly within the AutoShape item.

Inserting an AutoShape is somewhat similar to inserting lines and shapes. To create an AutoShape, follow these steps:

1. Click AutoShapes in the Drawing toolbar. The AutoShapes menu displays, as shown in the figure.

To flip an AutoShape, open the Draw menu, click Rotate or Flip, then select either Flip Horizontally or Flip Vertically.

2. Point to an AutoShapes category and click a shape.

3. Click on the place where you want to insert the AutoShape and then drag to insert the shape.

You can resize, move, and format AutoShapes in the same manner you modify lines and objects.

170

51 OBJECTIVE

Insert Objects

In addition to drawing lines and inserting shapes in your documents, Word enables you to insert art and pictures. Namely, you can create and insert WordArt and insert clip art and image files. If you are a visual person, this part of the exam is fairly fun; if you aren't visually oriented by nature, you can still pass this part of the exam with flying colors simply by knowing the correct procedures.

WordArt is stylized text that is frequently used for headings, logos, and other artistic page elements that incorporate words.

Insert WordArt

Inserting WordArt entails first opening the WordArt Gallery. The WordArt Gallery shows the available WordArt formats.

To insert WordArt, follow these steps:

1. Click [icon] Insert WordArt on the Drawing toolbar or open the Insert menu, click Picture, and click WordArt.

2. Select a WordArt style in the WordArt Gallery, and click OK. The Edit WordArt Text dialog box opens, as shown in the next figure.

171

Part 1 • Core Level

The WordArt toolbar appears automatically when you click an existing WordArt item in Print Layout view.

3. Type the text you want to format, specify any other desired settings, and click OK.

To add or change existing WordArt, select the item and use the buttons on the WordArt and Drawing toolbars.

Insert Clip Art

In addition to drawing art elements in Word, you can also insert clip art and images stored as separate files on a hard disk, CD-ROM, floppy disk, or network. Word comes with a wide selection of Clip Art images, and the exam requires you to insert one of these items and to specify how text flows around the item. Therefore, the following steps show you how to insert a Clip Art image and to specify text-flow options.

To insert clip art, follow these steps:

1. Position the cursor where you want to insert the clip art.

2. Click [icon] Insert Clip Art on the Drawing toolbar, or open the Insert menu, click Picture, and click Clip Art. The Insert ClipArt dialog box displays, as shown in the figure.

To insert audio and video files, click the Sounds or Motion Clips tabs in the Insert ClipArt dialog box.

172

Objective 51 • Insert Objects

3. Click a category.

4. Click a picture. A pop-up menu appears that enables you to insert the clip art, preview the clip art, save the picture to your Favorites or to another category, and find similar clips.

5. Click the Insert Clip icon, which appears at the top of the pop-up menu.

To format an inserted picture, you can open the Format Picture dialog box. The following figure shows the Layout tab in the Format Picture dialog box. The options on this tab enable you to specify how text should flow around the picture.

To find clip art, type a keyword in the Search for clips text box in the Insert ClipArt dialog box and press Enter.

To quickly insert clip art into your document, drag it from the Insert ClipArt dialog box to your document.

To open the Format Picture dialog box, use one of the following methods:

- Double-click the picture
- Right-click the picture and select Format P<u>i</u>cture
- Click the picture, open the F<u>o</u>rmat menu, and click P<u>i</u>cture

You can insert images stored in files in a manner similar to inserting clip art images. The main difference is that to insert an image from a file you must specify where the file is stored.

Insert Images

To insert an image from a file, follow these steps:

1. Position the cursor where you want to insert the picture.

2. Open the <u>I</u>nsert menu, click <u>P</u>icture, and click <u>F</u>rom File; or display the Picture toolbar and click [icon] Insert Picture

Part 1 • Core Level

To resize a picture, click the picture and drag its selection handles. To move a picture, click the picture and drag it.

(notice that the Picture toolbar also contains the [icon] Text Wrapping icon). The Insert Picture dialog box opens, as shown in the figure.

3. Navigate to the location of the picture you want to insert.

4. Double-click the picture filename's icon, or select the filename and click Insert.

You can manipulate pictures in the same way that you manipulate lines, objects, and clip art items.

TAKE THE TEST

Objectives covered: 50, Use the Drawing Toolbar; and 51, Insert Objects. Open the filenamed `Hiking`, which is stored in the `Practice` folder on the enclosed CD-ROM.

Task 1

1. Insert a WordArt title using the text *Arizona Trails*.

2. Insert a hiking-related clip art item into the document. Ensure the clip art item appears within the lower-right area of the text, and the text wraps tightly around the picture.

   Draw an orange 2 1/4-point, dashed line below the last paragraph of text.

4. Draw a 3D rectangle below the dotted line.

5. Insert a callout to the right of the 3D rectangle. Include Arial 28-point, centered text that states *Let's go hiking!* within the callout.

Check your work against solution file `11470`.

Cheat Sheet

Draw Lines

1. Line or Arrow on the Drawing toolbar.
2. Click and drag.
3. Select Line Color, Line Style, Dash Style, and Arrow Style settings.

Create Shapes and 3D Shapes

1. Rectangle or Oval on the Drawing toolbar.
2. Draw the shape.
3. Use Drawing toolbar icons to stylize the shape.

AutoShapes

1. Click AutoShapes in the Drawing toolbar.
2. Point to an AutoShapes category and click a shape.
3. Click and drag where you want to insert the AutoShape.

Insert WordArt

1. Insert WordArt on the Drawing toolbar or click Insert, Picture, WordArt.
2. Select a WordArt style and click OK.
3. Type text, specify settings, and click OK.

Insert ClipArt

1. Insert Clip Art on the Drawing toolbar or click Insert, Picture, Clip Art.
2. Click a category.
3. Click a picture.
4. Click the Insert Clip icon

Insert Images

1. Click <u>I</u>nsert, <u>P</u>icture, <u>F</u>rom File; or ![icon] Insert Picture on the Picture toolbar.
2. Navigate to the location of the picture file.
3. Double-click the picture filename's icon, or select the filename and click Insert.

CHAPTER 10

Printing

Last but not least, the core-level exam tests your ability to preview and print documents, envelopes, and labels. While the world of communication increasingly relies on electronic exchange, hard copy documentation continues to serve as the overwhelming means of written communication. Therefore, logically enough, to become a certified Microsoft Office User Specialist, you need to know how to:

- Use Print Preview
- Use Web Page Preview
- Print a Document
- Print Envelopes
- Print Labels

OBJECTIVE 52

Use Print Preview

Print preview enables you to view how your documents will print before you print them. Having this ability can be especially helpful when you are adjusting margins, wrapping text around pictures and objects, using columns and tables, and applying other formatting techniques.

Word's Print Preview feature enables you to view from 1 to 32 pages at a time. Of course, the more pages you view at once the smaller the preview page appears on your screen. This figure shows six pages being viewed in Print Preview mode.

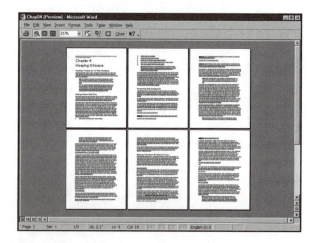

To preview a document, open the document and then perform one of the following commands:

- Click [icon] Print Preview on the Standard toolbar.

180

- Press Ctrl+F2.
- Open the File menu and click Print Preview.

When you display a document in Print Preview mode, the Print Preview toolbar automatically opens, as shown in the following figure.

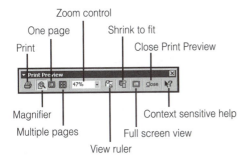

Although most of the Print Preview toolbar buttons are self-explanatory, there are a couple notes about Print Preview's capabilities that you should be aware of, including the following:

- When you click ![] Print in Print Preview mode, Word sends the document to the printer immediately—without opening the Print dialog box.

- You can click ![] Magnifier and then click a page to magnify the page. Then, click the ![] Magnifier button again and click on the document to edit the document's text while in Print Preview mode.

- To preview a single page, click ![] One Page. To preview multiple pages, click ![] Multiple Pages and then drag across the page icons to select the number and position of the pages you want to preview.

- You can select a percentage in the Zoom drop-down list box to increase or decrease the size of the document view.

- To toggle the horizontal rulers on and off, click ![] View Ruler.

- Click ![] Shrink to Fit to prevent a small amount of text from flowing on to the document's last page. This feature

181

Part 1 • Core Level

adjusts formatting, such as font and margin settings, to reduce a document's page count.

- To maximize Print Preview mode's viewing space, click ▣ Full Screen View.

- Click Close or press Esc to close the Print Preview window and return to the document. If you click the Close icon in the upper-right corner of the window, you will close the document.

53 OBJECTIVE

Use Web Page Preview

You can use Word's Web Page Preview option to view a document or Web page in your default Web browser. When you select this option, Word automatically opens your default browser and displays the current document in the browser.

To preview a document in Web Page Preview, perform the following action:

- Open the File menu and click Web Page Preview.

Keep in mind that Web Page Preview differs from Web Layout view. Web Page Preview opens your document in your default browser, whereas Web Layout view displays your document in Word as it would appear as a Web page. To use Web Layout View, click ⬚ Web Layout View on the horizontal scroll bar or open the View menu and select Web Layout.

OBJECTIVE 54

Print a Document

After you have previewed your document or you feel secure that your document is ready to be set on paper, you can print your document. You can print a Word document in several ways. If you want to send the document directly to the printer, you can use the following quick-print commands:

- Click [icon] Print on the Standard toolbar.

- Display the document in Print Preview mode and click [icon] Print on the Print Preview toolbar.

If you prefer, you can opt to open the Print dialog box before you print. As you can see in the following figure, the Print dialog box offers a variety of print choices, including the option to specify page ranges or the number of copies.

Before printing, modify your page setup parameters using the Page Setup dialog box, as discussed in Chapter 8, "Adding Columns, Tables, and Objects."

To open the Print dialog box before printing a document, follow either of these procedures:

- Open the File menu, click Print, configure the Print dialog box options, and click OK.

- Press Ctrl+P, configure the Print dialog box options, and click OK.

184

55 OBJECTIVE

Print Envelopes

Although you might not use Word's envelope-printing capabilities, the MOUS Word core-level exam expects you to know how to perform this task. Pay close attention to the printing-envelopes exam question. You must configure Word to print a specific size envelope and place the to and from text appropriately. That's your "keep alert" warning. Now, you're ready to review the basics.

Because you are probably familiar with addressing envelopes on a theoretical level, this review focuses on the steps required within Word to print envelopes.

Prepare and Print Envelopes

To print envelops:

1. If you are creating an envelope for an existing letter, click in the recipient's address or highlight the recipient's address if it is longer than five lines. When you perform this action, Word automatically displays the address in the Delivery Address field of the Envelope tab.

2. Open the Tools menu, click Envelopes and Labels, and click the Envelopes tab, as shown in the figure.

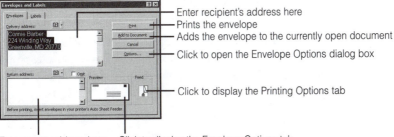

185

Part 1 • Core Level

Use the Omit return address option to print on stationery envelopes that have a preprinted return address.

3. In the <u>D</u>elivery address box, edit existing address text, enter new text, or click [📖] Address Book to insert an address from an electronic address book.

4. In the <u>R</u>eturn address window, edit or enter the return address information, click [📖] Address Book to insert an address from an electronic address book, or click the O<u>m</u>it checkbox to specify not to show a return address on the envelope.

5. Click the envelope in the Preview pane or click the Options button. The Envelope Options dialog box opens, as shown in the figure.

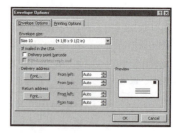

6. In the Envelope Options dialog box, perform the following tasks:

   - <mark>Select an envelope size</mark> with the Envelope <u>s</u>ize drop-down list.

Word cannot print a POST-NET bar code if you use a daisy-wheel printer.

   - <mark>Specify whether to include a delivery point <u>b</u>arcode.</mark> This option adds a POSTNET (POSTal Numeric Encoding Technique) bar code to your envelope. A POSTNET bar code is a machine-readable representation of the recipient's U.S. Zip code and delivery address.

   - Format the delivery and return address fonts by clicking the <u>F</u>ont button to open the Font dialog box. You can also select address text on the <u>E</u>nvelopes tab, right-click, and click <u>F</u>ont to format envelope text with the Font dialog box.

186

Objective 55 • Print Envelopes

- Click the Printing Options tab to specify how the envelope will feed into the printer. Click on any page feed icon to select a feed method.

7. After setting the printing options for the envelope, click OK to return to the Envelopes and Labels dialog box.

8. After returning to the Envelopes and Labels dialog box, you can do either of the following:

    - Insert an envelope into the printer as shown in the Feed box and click Print.

    - Click Add to Document to attach the envelope to the current document for later editing or printing.

You can click the Feed icon in the Envelopes and Labels dialog box to go directly to the Printing Options tab.

You can modify and print envelopes that are attached to documents. Attached envelopes are offset from the main letter's text by section breaks, as shown in the following figure.

Work with Attached Envelopes

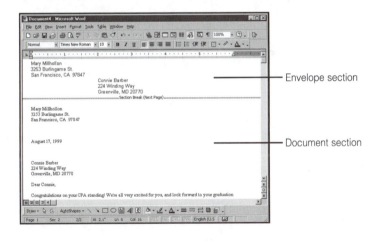

To modify an envelope that's attached to a document, follow these steps:

1. Open the document and open the Envelopes and Labels dialog box.

2. Make changes to the envelope text.

3. Specify the size of the envelope, and specify the printer feed options.

187

4. Click Change Document (which displays in place of the Add to Document button).

To print an attached envelope, follow these steps:

1. Open a document that has an attached envelope and click in the envelope section.
2. Insert an envelope into the printer according to the feed specification.
3. Open the File menu and click Print or press Ctrl+P to open the Print dialog box. Be careful—clicking Print in the Standard toolbar prints the envelope and the entire document without opening the Print dialog box.
4. In the Pages text box, enter 0 (zero).

56 OBJECTIVE

Prepare and Print labels

Similar to printing envelopes, is the way you configure Word to print labels. For the core-level exam, you need to know how to print return address labels or individual shipping labels (more complex label-printing tasks are reserved for the expert-level exam). To prepare and print labels, follow these steps:

1. If available, click in a document's address area or envelope section.

2. Open the Tools menu, click Envelopes and Labels, and click the Labels tab, as shown in the figure.

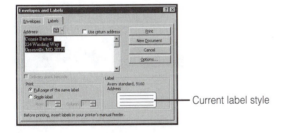
Current label style

If you opened the Labels dialog box after clicking in a document's attached envelope section, the recipient's address appears in the Address text box by default. You can click the Use return address checkbox to display the return address text instead.

3. Ensure the label text appears correctly by adding, editing, or inserting text as needed.

4. In the Print area, specify whether you want to print a single label or a sheet of labels for the same address.

5. Click the icon in the Label area or click the Options button to open the Label Options dialog box, as shown in the figure. Select the desired label product.

6. Insert a sheet of labels into the printer and click Print; or click New Document to save the label settings in a document for later printing, as shown in the figure.

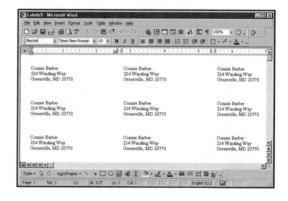

TAKE THE TEST

Task 1

Objectives covered: 52, Use Print Preview; 54, Print a Document; and 56, Print Labels. Open the file named Connie_1, which is stored in the Practice folder on the enclosed CD-ROM.

1. Display the file in Print Preview mode.

2. Zoom in to view the envelope address, and then close the Print Preview window without closing the document.

3. Use the Print dialog box to print only the letter.

4. Add your return address to the existing attached envelope. Format the return address font to match the address text font.

5. Create a new document containing a sheet of 3112 Sticker style return address labels based on the Connie_1 envelope.

Check your work against solution files 1147P and 1147Q.

Task 2

Objectives covered: 53, Use Web Page Preview; and 55, Print Envelopes. Open the file named Connie_2, which is stored in the Practice folder on the enclosed CD-ROM.

1. Preview the document as a Web page in your browser.

2. Attach an envelope to the letter using your return address and the following recipient address: *Connie Barber, 224 Winding Way, Greenville, MD 20770.*

3. Print the attached envelope without printing the letter.

Check your work against solution file 1147R.

Cheat Sheet

Use Print Preview

- ![icon] Print Preview on the Standard toolbar.
- Press Ctrl+F2.
- Click File, Print Preview.

Use Web Page Preview

- Click File, Web Page Preview.

Print a Document

- ![icon] Print on the Standard toolbar.
- ![icon] Print Preview, ![icon] Print on the Print Preview toolbar.
- Press Ctrl+P.
- Click File, Print.

Prepare and Print Envelopes

1. If available, click in the recipient's address or highlight the recipient's address.
2. Click Tools, Envelopes and Labels, and click the Envelopes tab.
3. Specify the recipient's address.
4. Specify the return address, if any.
5. Set the envelope options.
6. Attach or print the envelope.

Work with Attached Envelopes

- Make changes in the Envelopes and Labels dialog box, and click Change Document.
- To Print attached envelopes, follow these steps:
    1. Open the document, and click in the envelope section.
    2. Insert an envelope into the printer.
    3. Click File, Print, or press Ctrl+P.
    4. In the Pages text box, enter 0 (zero).

Prepare and Print Labels

1. If available, click a document's address area or envelope section.
2. Click Tools, Envelopes and Labels, and click the Labels tab.
3. Ensure the label text appears correctly.
4. Specify whether to print a single label or sheet of labels.
5. Set label options.
6. Print the labels or save the labels in a new document.

PART II

Expert Level

- Applying Advanced Paragraph Formatting
- Applying Advanced Page Formatting
- Using Document Reference Features
- Collaborating with Workgroups
- Adding Spreadsheet Capabilities to Tables
- Working with Advanced Graphics and Charts Features
- Designing Forms
- Using Mail Merge
- Activating Macros and Customizing Toolbars

CHAPTER 11

Applying Advanced Paragraph Formatting

Beginning with this chapter, the remainder of the book presents expert-level topics and builds on the core-level skills presented in Chapters 1 through 10. Keep in mind that to pass the expert exam, you'll need to be proficient in core-level topics as well as the topics presented in the expert chapters. As a starting point for your expert-level exam preparation, this chapter reviews advanced paragraph-formatting topics. Therefore, to pass the expert exam, in addition to being proficient with the paragraph formatting topics presenting in Chapter 5, "Formatting Paragraphs," you will also know how to:

- Implement text flow options
- Insert nonbreaking spaces
- Insert fields
- Sort information
- Perform advanced Find and Replace tasks

OBJECTIVE 57

Implement Text Flow Options

Often, text needs to be controlled in detail to properly lay out a document. For example, if you are creating a newsletter, you might want to avoid having the last line at the end of a story carry over to the next page or column. Or, in another instance, you might want to prevent Word from inserting a page break between a heading and the following paragraph.

Using Word's Paragraph dialog box, you can control text flow within paragraphs to an extent. Namely, you can control widows and orphans (more about those in a moment) and ensure that specified lines or paragraphs are kept together.

Use the Widows/ Orphans Feature

Widows and *orphans* are single lines of text at the beginning or end of a paragraph that display at the top or bottom of a page without the rest of the paragraph. A widow occurs when the last line of a paragraph prints by itself at the top of a page, and an orphan occurs when the first line of a paragraph prints by itself at the bottom of a page.

By default, Word prevents widows and orphans. To correct a widow, Word takes the second-to-the last sentence on the preceding page and inserts it at the top of the next page to accompany the lone line of text. To correct an orphan, Word forces the single sentence at the bottom of the page to the top of the next page.

The exam expects you to know how to activate and deactivate Word's widows and orphans features. You can change the default setting by clearing the Widow/Orphan Control checkbox in the Paragraph dialog box.

To display the Widow/Orphan Control, choose either of the following methods:

- Open the Format menu, click Paragraph, and click the Line and Page Breaks tab.

- Right-click within a paragraph, click Paragraph, and click the Line and Page Breaks tab.

To turn off the Widow/Orphan Control feature, clear the check box. To turn the feature back on, select the empty check box.

Keep Text Lines Together

In addition to controlling the first and last lines of paragraphs, you can also use commands in the Line and Page Breaks tab to prevent page breaks within or between specified paragraphs.

As you know, Word automatically adds page breaks when your text reaches the bottom margin of a page. For the most part, the automatic page break feature is convenient; occasionally, however, it might not work to your advantage. For example, when you are working with headings, you probably wouldn't want an automatic page break between a heading and the following text. Therefore, Word enables you to indicate specific paragraphs or lines that you want to keep together.

To prevent a break within a paragraph:

- Select the Keep lines together check box on the Lines and Page Breaks tab in the Paragraph dialog box.

Part 2 • Expert Level

To prevent a break between paragraphs:

- Select the Keep with ne$\underline{x}$t check box on the Lines and $\underline{P}$age Breaks tab in the Paragraph dialog box.

If you display nonprinting objects on your screen, lines and paragraphs that you have indicated you want kept together display with small black squares in the left margin's selection bar.

58 OBJECTIVE

Insert Nonbreaking Spaces

Similar to the way you can request Word to keep certain lines and paragraphs together, Word also enables you to keep words together within paragraphs when Word automatically wraps text. For example, you might want to keep a person's first and last names together or to avoid breaking a number containing spaces, such as a phone number or a serial number.

The secret to keeping words committed to each other is to insert a nonbreaking space between the two words. The procedure for inserting a nonbreaking space is the same as for inserting a special character. If you insert a nonbreaking space and your document is displaying nonprinting characters (paragraph marks, spaces, and so forth), Word displays a small, superscript circle in place of the dot that represents a regular space.

To insert a nonbreaking space between words, select the space you want to change to a nonbreaking space and then use either of the following procedures:

- Press Ctrl+Shift+Space.
- Open the Insert menu, click Symbol, click the Special Characters tab, click the Nonbreaking Space entry (as shown in the following figure), click Insert, and then click OK.

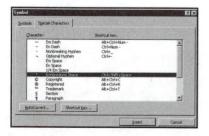

Instead of replacing an existing space with a non-breaking space, you can create non-breaking spaces as you enter text.

201

OBJECTIVE 59

Insert Fields

Up to this point in the chapter, you've reviewed ways to restrict the text flow within a document. In this section, you'll review how to expand the information included within a document by inserting *fields*.

Fields are often used in headers and footers to insert page numbers, dates, chapter names, and so on.

Fields are placeholders for special instructions or codes that specify to Word what you want to insert. You can use fields to insert and update information that Word obtains from documents or system data. For example, you can use fields to automatically insert a document's name, the current date, the contents of another document, and so forth.

To insert a field into your document, follow these steps:

1. Click where you want to insert the field information.

2. Open the Insert menu and click Field. The Field dialog box opens, as shown in the following figure.

3. Select a category in the Categories list, select an option in the Field names list, and insert information in the Field codes text box if necessary (enter text as shown in the

sample field entry displayed above the text box). You can add additional field options by clicking the Options button, and adding options from the Field Options dialog box.

For specific information about a field or option, click the question mark Help icon in the upper-right corner of the Field dialog box, and then click the option.

4. Click OK. Word automatically inserts the specified contents into the field.

To view a field's underlying code, use either of the following methods:

- Click in the field and press Shift+F9.
- Right-click the field and select Toggle Field Codes.

The following figure shows the AUTHOR, DATE, and INCLUDETEXT fields with the text automatically inserted as well as with the actual field codes inserted by Word.

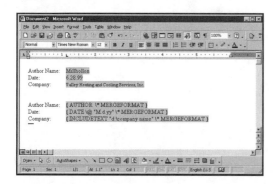

203

Part 2 • Expert Level

In the figure, the AUTHOR field inserts the name of the author who created the document, the DATE field inserts the date, and the INCLUDETEXT field inserts the text from the d:\company name file. If the text is changed in the company name file, you can update the field information by right-clicking the field and clicking Update Field.

You can also insert common fields by entering the following keyboard commands:

Press	To Insert
Alt+Shift+D	DATE field
Alt+Ctrl+L	LISTNUM field
Alt+Shift+P	PAGE field
Alt+Shift+T	TIME field
Ctrl+F9	Empty field

60

OBJECTIVE

Sort Information

Often, it is desirable to show text in a particular order. You can use Word's Sort feature to arrange paragraph and table text, numbers, or dates in ascending order (A to Z, zero to 9, or earliest to latest date) or descending order (Z to A, 9 to zero, or latest to earliest date). Further, you can sort tables using the Sort Text dialog box shown in the following figure.

Sort Paragraphs

As mentioned, you can sort paragraphs using Word's Sort feature. Remember that Word considers text separated by a paragraph mark to be a paragraph. Therefore, if you create a list of items by typing an item name, pressing Enter, typing another item name, pressing Enter, and so forth, you create a list of paragraphs. You can then sort the paragraphs in ascending or descending order.

Furthermore, if your list contains tab-separated items, you can sort by a particular field. For example, let's say you have the following items:

Towels	green
Wash clothes	blue
Hand towels	purple

205

In the preceding list, a tab separates each towel type from the color name. You can choose to sort the preceding list by paragraphs, field 1 (the towel type), or field 2 (the colors). Sorting in ascending order by paragraphs or field 1 results in the following:

Hand towels	purple
Towels	green
Wash clothes	blue

In contrast, sorting in ascending order by field 2 results in the following:

Wash clothes	blue
Towels	green
Hand towels	purple

In addition to sorting by specified fields, you can perform multi-tiered sorting tasks. This means you can sort your list by one criteria, and then sort that set by a second and third criteria. For example, let's say you have the following list:

Wash clothes	blue
Towels	green
Hand towels	purple
Wash clothes	red
Towels	purple
Hand towels	white

You could sort the preceding list in ascending order, first by towel type (field 1) and then by color (field 2). The figure shows how you would specify this sort order in the Sort Text dialog box.

Objective 4 • Selecting Menu Commands

The resulting list displays like this:

Hand towels	purple
Hand towels	white
Towels	green
Towels	purple
Wash clothes	blue
Wash clothes	red

As you can see, the towel types appear in ascending order, and the color listings for each towel type are listed in ascending order within the particular towel category.

To sort paragraphs, follow these steps:

1. Select the text you want to sort.

2. Open the Table menu, and click Sort. The Sort Text dialog box opens.

3. Select Paragraphs or a Field in the Sort by list box.

4. Specify whether to sort by text, number, or date in the Type text box.

5. Select either the Ascending or Descending radio button.

6. If desired, specify further sort criteria by completing the Then by text boxes and radio buttons.

7. Click OK to sort the selected text.

Sorting tables is similar to sorting paragraphs. The main difference is that you can also sort table information by using the Tables and Borders toolbar. To sort table information, perform the following actions:

- Place the insertion point anywhere within the table you want to sort, open the Sort dialog box, and specify sort criteria, as described in the previous section.

- Open the Tables and Borders toolbar, select the table column you want to sort, and then click ▲ Sort Ascending or ▼ Sort Descending.

Sort Tables

In the Sort dialog box, field names in the Sort by and Then by boxes display as the table's column names.

207

The Sort Text dialog box enables you to specify whether your table has a header row. If you specify that your table has a header row, the sort operation will not sort the first row of text. If you use the Tables and Borders toolbar icons, Word automatically assumes header information based on the previous option selected in the Sort Text dialog box.

61 OBJECTIVE

Perform Advanced Find and Replace Tasks

Word provides the capability to find and replace items other than letters and words, using the Find and Replace dialog box. To become a certified expert user, you need to be fully versed in Word's advance finding and replacing capabilities as well as those discussed in Chapter 3, "Working with Text."

Advanced finding and replacing is usually implemented when you are editing and fine-tuning documents or making repetitive changes throughout. For example, you can find and replace all bold items and reformat them in italics, replace en dashes with em dashes (em dashes are twice as long as en dashes), or replace double-spaces with single spaces.

To find and replace formats, special characters, and nonprinting elements, you must first open the Find and Replace dialog box (press Ctrl+H) and click the More button. The expanded dialog box is shown in the following figure. Notice that the More button now displays as Less.

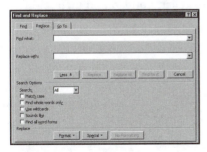

209

After you expand the Find and Replace dialog box, ==you can use the Format and Special buttons to specify formats, special characters, and nonprinting elements== to find and replace.

To specify a format or a special character to find, follow these steps:

1. Click in the Find what text box.

2. Click the Format or Special button.

3. Select a Format or Special menu item to specify what you want to find.

Similarly, to specify a replacement format or character, follow these steps:

1. Click in the Replace with text box.

2. Click the Format or the Special button.

3. Select a Format or Special menu item to specify what you want to find.

To incorporate formatting in the Find what or Replace with text boxes, you can use keyboard commands, as follows:

- Click in the text box, and press keyboard formatting commands, such as Ctrl+B (bolding), Ctrl+I (italics), or Ctrl+U (underlines).

When you click either the Format or Special button, you receive a pop-up menu. Clicking an item on the Format button's menu results in opening a find or replace dialog box that you can use to specify formatting criteria. For example, the figure shows the Find Font dialog box that displays when you click in the Find what text box, click Format, and then select Font.

To clear formatting associated with the Find what, click the Clear Formatting button in the text box.

Clicking an item on the Special button's menu results in a special character, such as ^t for a tab space, displaying in the Find what or Replace with text box. For example, the following figure shows the Find and Replace dialog box formatted to replace all tabs with nonbreaking spaces.

After you fill the Find what and Replace with text boxes, the procedure to find and replace elements is the same as finding and replacing text, and it is described in Objective 10 of this book.

PRACTICE

TAKE THE TEST

Task 1 Objectives covered: 57, Implement Text Flow Options; 58, Insert Nonbreaking Spaces; and 59, Insert Fields. Open the file named Fruitstand_1, which is stored in the Practice folder on this book's CD-ROM.

1. Add a date field after the Weekly Update heading.
2. Insert a nonbreaking space between the words Cale and Sunday below the Days off this week heading.
3. Ensure that the Other News heading isn't separated from the following bulleted list text.

Check your work against solution file 1147XA.

Task 2 Objectives covered: 60, Sort Information; 61, Perform Advanced Find and Replace Tasks. Open the file named Fruitstand_2, which is stored in the Practice folder on this book's CD-ROM.

1. Replace all nonbreaking spaces with tabs.
2. Display the Fruit column items in the table in ascending alphabetical order.
3. Sort the Days off this week list in ascending order by code number (field 2) and then by names.

Check your work against solution file 1147XB.

Cheat Sheet

Use The Widows/Orphans Feature

- Click Format, Paragraph, Line and Page Breaks tab, and select the Widow/Orphan Control check box.

- Right-click a paragraph, click Paragraph, click the Line and Page Breaks tab, and select the Widow/Orphan Control check box.

Keep Text Lines Together

- Select the Keep lines together check box on the Lines and Page Breaks tab in the Paragraph dialog box.

- Select the Keep with next check box on the Lines and Page Breaks tab in the Paragraph dialog box.

Insert Nonbreaking Spaces

- Press Ctrl+Shift+Space.

- Click Insert, Symbol, display the Special Characters tab, click the Nonbreaking Space entry, click Insert, and click OK.

Insert Fields

1. Click where you want to insert a field.
2. Click Insert, Field.
3. Select a category in the Categories list.
4. Select an option in the Field names list.
5. Insert information in the Field Codes text box if necessary, and click OK.

Sort Paragraphs

1. Select text.
2. Click Table, Sort.
3. Select a Sort by parameter.

Continued

4. Specify whether to sort by text, number, or date.
5. Select <u>A</u>scending or <u>D</u>escending.
6. Specify Then by sort criteria, if desired.

Sort Tables

- Click the table, open the Sort dialog box, and specify sort criteria.
- Open the Tables and Borders toolbar, select the table column you want to sort, and click [A↓] Sort Ascending or [Z↓] Sort Descending.

Find and Replace Formats, Special Characters, and Nonprinting Elements

1. Open the Find and Replace dialog box.
2. Click <u>M</u>ore.
3. Click the Fi<u>n</u>d what text box.
4. Click the F<u>o</u>rmats or Sp<u>e</u>cial button, and insert format or special character to find.
5. Click the Replace w<u>i</u>th text box.
6. Click the F<u>o</u>rmats or Sp<u>e</u>cial button, and insert the replacement format setting or special character.
7. Follow regular find and replace procedures.

CHAPTER 12

Applying Advanced Page Formatting

Not to sound flip, but advanced page-formatting techniques aren't particularly advanced in terms of complexity. In general, the page formatting topics labeled as "advanced" by Microsoft seem to address features that are less frequently used. So, don't glaze over at the thought of completing advanced page formatting techniques—the procedures are straightforward. According to Microsoft, expert users of Word 2000 need to know how to:

- Format the First Page Differently
- Create Watermarks
- Add Page Borders
- Insert Footnotes
- Insert Endnotes
- Create and Edit Styles
- Balance Column Lengths

OBJECTIVE 62

Format the First Page Differently

Often, you will want to format the first page of a document differently than the subsequent pages. For example, if the first page is a chapter opening, you might want to hide the page number or customize the header or footer. On the exam, you will need to format the first page of a document differently. For instance, you might be asked to format the header for first page differently than subsequent headers.

To format the first page of a document differently, follow these steps:

1. Open the File menu, and click Page Setup.
2. Click the Layout tab.
3. In the Headers and Footers area, select the Different first page check box, and click OK.

If the document does not have headers and footers, you can customize the first page by hiding the page number of the first page by using the Page Numbers dialog box. To do this, open the Insert menu, click Page Numbers, and ensure that the Show number on first page check box is cleared.

63 OBJECTIVE

Create Watermarks

Another header-and-footer-related task that you'll be required to perform on the exam involves creating watermarks. Watermarks are background text or images printed on top of or behind document text. For example, you might want to add words, such as "Sample Copy" or "First Draft" below document text, "SOLD OUT" on top of text, or you might want to print a company logo lightly in the background. The figure shows a watermark created with a text box containing the words "Rough Draft."

You can only see watermarks in Page Layout View and Print Preview mode.

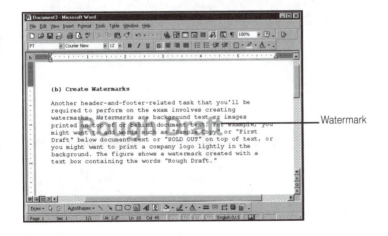

217

Part 2 • Expert Level

To remove a watermark, open the header or footer that contains it, and then select it and press Delete.

Creating a watermark entails anchoring a picture or text box in a header or footer. Then, you set the properties of the picture or text box to specify how the watermark should display. The detailed steps for creating a watermark are as follows:

1. Open the <u>V</u>iew menu and click <u>H</u>eader and Footer, or display Print Layout View and double-click an existing header or footer.

2. On the Header and Footer toolbar, click 🔲 Show/Hide Document Text to hide the document's body text. This makes placing and sizing the watermark object easier. After you create and place the watermark, you can redisplay the document body text to verify the watermark's display.

3. Position the cursor anywhere within the header or footer, open the <u>I</u>nsert menu, and click either of the following:

    - Te<u>x</u>t Box to create a text-based watermark. On the exam, you will be asked to create a text box watermark. When you create the text box watermark, you will need to enter, select, and properly format the watermark's text to earn a correct score on the task.

    - <u>P</u>icture and select <u>C</u>lip Art, <u>F</u>rom File, or AutoShapes.

4. Draw the text box where you want it to appear on the page and type the desired text, or insert the picture and drag it to the desired position. You can resize, drag-and-drop, set properties, and format watermark objects just as you manipulate other objects. For example, you can right-click a watermark object and specify whether the object should be placed in front of or behind other page items, and you can drag selection handles to resize watermark objects.

5. Click <u>C</u>lose on the Header and Footer toolbar to return to the document.

64 OBJECTIVE

Add Page Borders

You can spruce up any page by adding page borders. Adding borders to a page is similar to adding borders to a paragraph (as discussed in Objective 26, in Chapter 5, "Formatting Paragraphs"). When you work with page borders, you must display the Page Border tab in the Borders and Shading dialog box, as shown in the following figure.

The Art drop-down list on the Page Border tab enables you to insert clip-art type imagery into page borders.

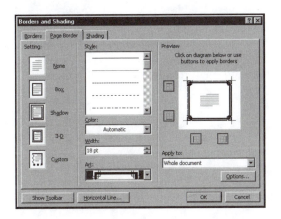

To add a page border, follow these steps:

1. Click in the document or if you only want to format the current section, within a specific section.
2. Open the Format menu, and click Borders and Shading.
3. Click the Page Border tab.
4. Select a preformatted page border, such as Shadow, or specify other settings, including line style, color, width, art, and border placement. The Preview pane displays the current settings.

219

Part 2 • Expert Level

5. Click the Apply to drop-down list arrow, and specify whether to apply the border to the whole document, the current section only, the current section's first page only, or all pages in the current section other than the first page.

6. Click Options to open the Border and Shading Options dialog box and specify border margin settings, as shown in the following figure.

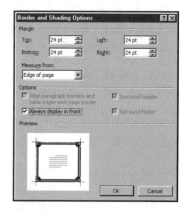

7. Close the Border and Shading Options dialog box, and click OK.

65 OBJECTIVE

Using Footnotes

Footnotes provide references to source documents and other notes relevant to a document's text. Footnotes appear as small numbers or letters within the document's body text that correspond to notes displaying at the bottom of the same page.

The exam requires you to insert and work with footnotes on a several occasions. Therefore, if you master the art of creating and modifying footnotes (which is easy), you'll be able to speed up more than a few exam questions.

Inserting footnotes entails clicking where you want to insert the footnote number or letter and then opening the Footnote and Endnote dialog box, as shown in the following figure.

Create Footnotes

To insert a footnote, follow these steps:

1. Click where you want to insert the footnote's number or letter (the exam will tell you exactly where to place a footnote).

2. Open the Insert menu and click Footnote. The Footnote and Endnote dialog box appears.

221

Part 2 • Expert Level

3. Select Footnote, and specify AutoNumber or Custom mark. If you select Custom mark, click Symbol to open the Symbol dialog box and select which mark you want to use.

4. Click the Options button to open the Note Options dialog box, as shown in the figure. ==You can use the Note Options dialog box to specify footnote settings, such as the number format.==

To quickly insert a footnote and open the footnote pane, press Ctrl+Alt+F.

5. Close the Note Options dialog box and click OK to insert the footnote. A footnote number is inserted into the text, and, if you are working in Normal View, the footnote pane appears, as shown in the following figure. If you are working in Print Layout View, your cursor displays at the bottom of the page in the footnote area.

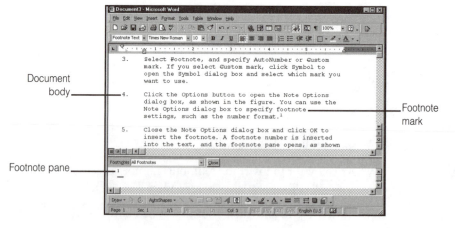

222

Objective 65 • Using Footnotes

6. Enter text into the footnote pane or footnote area.

7. Click Close to close the footnote pane, or continue to work in the document with the footnote pane open.

After you create footnotes, you can revise them at any time. In fact, the exam requires you to revise footnotes to show your footnote proficiency. You can revise footnotes in a variety of ways, including changing footnote text, moving footnote marks, and changing the number style of footnote marks:

- To revise footnote text, double-click a footnote mark to open the footnote pane. Edit the text in the footnote pane.

- To move a footnote mark, drag-and-drop or cut-and-paste the footnote mark to change its position within the text.

- To revise a footnote numbering style, select a footnote mark, open the Footnote and Endnote dialog box, and click Options. In the Note Options dialog box, change the Number format setting.

Modify Footnotes

To delete a footnote or endnote, select the note mark in the text and press Delete.

223

OBJECTIVE 66

Insert Endnotes

To find foot-note/endnote marks, open the Find dialog box, click Special, and select Endnote Mark or Footnote Mark.

Click the Convert button in the Note Options dialog box to change all footnotes to endnotes or vice versa.

To quickly insert an endnote and open the endnote pane, press Ctrl+Alt+D.

Working with endnotes is essentially the same as working with footnotes. The main difference between endnotes and footnotes is that, instead of listing marked notes at the bottom of each page, endnotes are listed en masse at the end of the document.

To insert an endnote, follow these steps:

1. Click where you want to insert an endnote's number or letter mark, open the Insert menu, and click Footnote.
2. Select Endnote, and specify AutoNumber or Custom mark.
3. Click the Options button if you want to configure the endnote's options.
4. Close the Note Options dialog box and click OK. An endnote number is inserted into the text, and the endnote pane appears (which is similar to the footnote pane shown in Objective 64) or your cursor displays in the endnote area (if you are working in Print Layout View).
5. Enter text in the endnote pane or endnote area, and click Close to close the endnote pane or continue to work in the document with the endnote pane open. You can modify endnotes in the same manner you modify footnotes.

OBJECTIVE 67

Create and Edit Styles

As reviewed in Chapter 7, "Formatting A Document," you can quickly and consistently format document text by applying styles. For the core-level exam, knowing how to apply styles is sufficient to pass the styles portion of the exam. However, to pass the expert-level exam, you need to know how to create and edit styles.

To create and modify styles, you can access the Style dialog box, as shown in the following figure. Alternatively, you can format text and use the Style text box on the Formatting toolbar.

Styles can be divided into two main types: paragraph and character. Paragraph styles are styles that consist of formatting specifications for text, tabs, indents, margins, and other paragraph setup specifications. In contrast, character styles apply only text format settings.

225

Part 2 • Expert Level

Create a Style

You can use a number of methods to create styles. In this section, you'll review the two main methods used to create a style. The exam simply requires you to create a style—the method you use is irrelevant.

To quickly create a paragraph (or non-specified) style, follow these steps:

1. Format a paragraph or text that you want to use as the basis of your style.
2. Select the formatted text or paragraph.
3. On the Formatting toolbar, click in the Style text box, type the name of the new style, and press Enter.

When the exam does not specify whether to create a paragraph or character style, you should create the style using the quick Formatting toolbar method just described. In other instances, you can create a new style using the Style text box. To create a paragraph or character style, follow these steps:

1. Open the F_ormat menu, and click S_tyle. The Style dialog box appears.
2. Click N_ew. The New Style dialog box appears, as shown in the figure.

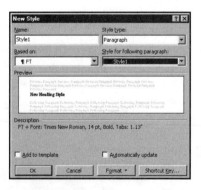

3. In the N_ame text box, enter a style name.
4. In the Style t_ype text box, select Character or Paragraph.
5. Specify whether the style is based on an existing style. (If not, select (no style) in the B_ased on drop-down list.)

226

Edit a Style

6. Click the Format button to set the style's options. Clicking Format results in a pop-up menu that you can use to apply format settings.

As you know, styles change, and document styles are no different. You can easily edit a style using the Formatting toolbar and the Styles dialog box.

To quickly edit a style, follow these steps:

1. Reformat an existing paragraph or text that was previously used the style you want to edit.
2. Select the reformatted paragraph or text.
3. Click in the Style text box on the Formatting toolbar and press Enter, or type the style's name in the Style text box and press Enter. The Modify Style dialog box appears.
4. Click the Update the style to reflect recent changes? radio button, and click OK.

You can maintain a higher degree of control over your editing changes by making style changes in the Style dialog box, as described here:

1. If possible, click text formatted with the style you want to edit, and then open the Style dialog box. If your window displays the styles area (Tools, Options, View tab, Style area width), you can double-click a style name in the style area to open the Style dialog box.
2. If necessary, select the style you want to edit in the Styles list. By opening the List drop-down list and selecting Styles in use, All styles, or User-defined styles, you can specify which styles appear in the Styles list.
3. Click Modify. The Modify Style dialog box appears, as shown in the figure. Notice the Modify Style dialog box offers options similar to those in the New Style dialog box.

When you create a character style, only selected Format pop-up menu items are available in the Style dialog box.

When the Style dialog box appears, the cursor's current position dictates which style parameters display by default.

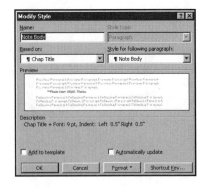

4. Edit the style's settings, click OK, and close the Style dialog box.

68 OBJECTIVE

Balance Column Lengths

The final objective in this chapter concerns creating and balancing column breaks. As you know, you can format text to display in columns. To manually insert column breaks:

- Position your cursor where you want to insert a break, open the Insert menu, click Break, click Column break, and click OK.

Manually inserting column breaks is similar to adding page breaks and section breaks.

For the exam, you'll also need to know how to balance column lengths. You could balance columns by manually inserting column breaks, but that approach can be tedious and time-consuming. Instead, you can automatically balance columns, as shown in the following figure.

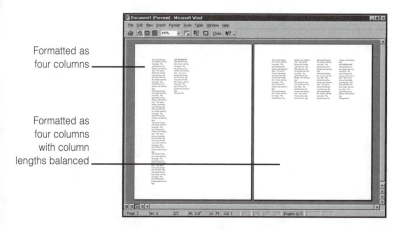

Formatted as four columns

Formatted as four columns with column lengths balanced

229

To balance columns, follow these steps:

1. Display the columns in Print Layout View and click at the end of the text in the rightmost column.

2. Open the Insert menu, click Break, and click Continuous. Word inserts a continuous section break and balances the text equally across the columns.

TAKE THE TEST

Task 1

Objectives covered: 62, Format the First Page Differently; 64, Add Page Borders; 65, Insert Footnotes; and 67, Create and Edit Styles. Open the file named `Classifieds_1`, which is stored in the `Practice` folder on the enclosed CD-ROM.

1. Create a style named *Category* based on the *Radios* heading, and apply the style to the other category headings in the document.

2. Format the first page differently by inserting center-aligned text in the header that states *This Week's Featured Ads!*

3. Add a shadow page border to the document.

4. Insert a footnote after the green *Phoenix metro area* text. Type the following text in the footnote: Free Trader is not liable for fraud or misrepresentation.

Check your work against solution file `1147XC`.

Task 2

Objectives covered: 63, Create Watermarks; 66, Insert Endnotes; and 68, Balance Column Lengths. Open the file named `Classifieds_2`, which is stored in the `Practice` folder on the enclosed CD-ROM.

1. Change the endnote format from i, ii, iii to 1, 2, 3.

2. Create a watermark by inserting a text box without a border containing the following 48-point text: Free Free Free!

3. Format the category headings and text into three balanced columns.

Check your work against solution file `1147XD`.

Cheat Sheet

Format the First Page Differently

1. Click File, Page Setup.
2. Click Layout tab.
3. Select Different first page check box.

Create Watermarks

1. Click View, Header and Footer, or double-click a header or footer in Print Layout View.
2. ⬚ Show/Hide Document Text on the Header and Footer toolbar.
3. Click the header or footer, and insert a text box, picture, or other object.
4. Close the Header and Footer toolbar.

Add Page Borders

1. Click in a document or specific section.
2. Click Format, Borders and Shading.
3. Click the Page Border tab.
4. Click the Apply to drop-down list arrow, and specify where to apply borders.

Create Footnotes

1. Click where you want to insert the footnote mark, and click Insert, Footnote.
2. Select Footnote, and specify AutoNumber or Custom mark.
3. Click the Options button if necessary.
4. Close the Note Options dialog box and click OK.
5. Enter text in the footnote pane.

Modify Footnotes and Endnotes

- Double-click a footnote mark, and edit the text in the footnote pane.
- Drag-and-drop or cut-and-paste footnote marks.
- Select a footnote mark, open the Footnote and Endnote dialog box, and click Options.

Insert Endnotes

1. Click where you want to insert an endnote's mark, and click Insert, Footnote.
2. Select Endnote, and specify AutoNumber or Custom mark.
3. Click the Options button, if necessary.
4. Close the Note Options dialog box and click OK.
5. Enter text in the endnote pane.

Create a Style

- Select the formatted text or paragraph, type a style name in the Style text box on the Formatting toolbar, and press Enter.
- Open the Style dialog box, enter a style name, specify formatting preferences, and click OK.

Edit a Style

- Reformat and select an existing paragraph or text, type the style's name in the Style text box, press Enter, click the Update the style to reflect recent changes? radio button, and click OK.
- Open the Style dialog box, select a style to edit in the Styles list, click Modify, edit the style's settings, click OK, and close the Style dialog box.

Continued

Balance Columns Lengths

1. Display the columns in Print Layout View, and click at the end of the text in the last column.

2. Open the Insert menu, click Break, and click Continuous. Word inserts a continuous section break and balances the text equally across the columns.

CHAPTER 13

Using Document Reference Features

A benefit of being an expert-level Word specialist is that you know how to take advantage of Word's automated document reference features. For example, instead of tediously typing and manually updating tables of contents and indexes, an expert can have Word automatically generate these elements. Furthermore, after the elements are generated, they can be instantly updated whenever your document changes. To prepare you for completing these types of tasks on the exam, this chapter reviews how to:

- Add a Bookmark
- Insert a Cross-Reference
- Generate a Table of Contents
- Create an Index

OBJECTIVE 69

Add a Bookmark

A bookmark is a nonprinting mark that identifies any specified portion of a document, including words, phrases, headings, paragraphs, sections, and so forth.

A bookmark on its own doesn't do much—it just sits quietly as a hidden, or nonprinting character, in your document and points to text. However, having bookmarks in your document enables you to do any of the following:

- Use the Go To feature to move quickly to bookmarked areas. (Press Ctrl+G or F5, select Bookmark in the Go to what list, enter the bookmark name, and click Go To).
- Identify text blocks that span more than one page for use in indexes.
- Mark reference points for cross-references and macros.

When you create a bookmark, Word inserts hidden square brackets ([]) around the text in your document. To display bookmarks' nonprinting characters

- Open the Tools menu, click Options, display the View tab, and click the Bookmarks check box.

On the exam, you will be required to create a bookmark. To do so, follow these steps:

1. Select the text that you want to bookmark (such as a heading or series of paragraphs), or position your cursor where you want to insert a bookmark.

236

2. Open the Insert menu and click Bookmark, or press Ctrl+Shift+F5. The Bookmark dialog box opens, as shown in the following figure.

3. In the Bookmark name text box, enter the name of the bookmark. Bookmark names can contain numbers, but they must begin with a letter. Further, you can't include spaces in bookmark names. If you need to specify a space, consider using an underscore (_) to mark the space, such as Table_Tennis.

4. Click Add.

After you create a bookmark, you can easily delete it by opening the Bookmark dialog box, clicking the bookmark name, and then clicking Delete.

To delete both a bookmark and the bookmarked text, select the text and press Delete.

237

OBJECTIVE 70

Insert a Cross-Reference

If you've ever used a hard copy of a yellow-pages directory, you're familiar with cross-references. A cross reference is a small blurb within a document that points (or refers) to another section within the same document, such as, "See Table 4 on page 8."

In Word, you can create cross-references that point to headings, footnotes, bookmarks, captions, numbered paragraphs, and so forth. Furthermore, if you're creating a document that will be viewed on a computer, you can format cross-reference text as hyperlinks. Cross-reference hyperlinks enable readers to jump directly to a referenced item when the document is viewed on a computer. You need to know how to create cross-reference hyperlinks, because, in addition to being a cool feature, they are also worth a few points on the exam.

The main benefit of creating a cross-reference instead of simply entering standard text is that you can easily update cross-references if text is added, deleted, or moved.

To create a cross-reference, follow these steps:

1. Enter the beginning portion of the cross-reference text, such as "For detailed information, see…".

2. Open the Insert menu and click Cross-reference. The Cross-Reference dialog box displays, as shown in the following figure.

3. In the Reference type drop-down list, select the type of item you want to reference. You can refer to numbered items, headings, bookmarks, footnotes, endnotes, equations, figures, listings, and tables.

4. In the Insert reference to list box, select the type of reference you want to insert into the text, such as heading text or page number. The choices in the Insert reference to text box will vary depending upon the reference type selected.

5. Select the Insert as hyperlink check box, if desired.

6. In the For which text box, click the item you want to reference.

7. Click Insert, and complete the cross-reference text, if necessary.

To update cross-references, perform one of the following actions:

- Select a particular cross-reference, right-click, and click Update Field.

- Select the entire document (Ctrl+A), right-click, and click Update Field.

To delete a cross-reference, simply select a cross-reference and its surrounding text, and press Delete.

To cross-reference items in other documents, create a master document, as described in Chapter 14, "Collaborating with Workgroups."

239

OBJECTIVE 71

Generate a Table of Contents

==A table of contents lists a document's headings along with page number references.== Tables of contents display in documents that are divided into sections—such as multi-page newsletters and documents with multiple headings.

Creating tables of contents can be honed to an art form, but, for once, the exam's time limitation works to your advantage. You won't have time to create an entire table of contents during the exam. Therefore, the test only quizzes you on generating and modifying a table of contents.

Generate a Table of Contents

To assign TOC fields, click Insert, Field, select the Index and Tables category, and use the TC field name.

Tables of contents can be generated based on Word's built-in headings, custom template styles that have been assigned to table of content levels or to field marks inserted next to each heading. On the exam, the table of contents heading associations are taken care of for you. You simply need to know how to generate a table of contents from existing identifiers and then modify the table to show a different number of levels.

To generate a table of contents, follow these steps:

1. Place the insertion point where you want the table of contents to display.
2. Open the Insert menu, click Index and Tables, and click the Table of Contents tab, if necessary. The Index and Tables dialog box opens, as shown in the following figure.

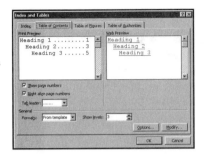

Notice the Table of Contents tab shows how the entries will appear in Print Preview, as well as in Web page view. When you automatically generate a table of contents in Word, the entries are formatted as hyperlinks. When you view the document on a computer, you can click a table of contents entry to jump to that heading's section.

3. On the Formats drop-down list, select the format you want to apply to the table of contents. The preview windows display a sample of the selected format.

4. Select the Show page numbers and Right-align page numbers check boxes if you want to activate those options. Either option might be unavailable (grayed out) if you've selected a format that dictates the option's setting.

5. Specify how you want to format the space between heading titles and page numbers by selecting an option in the Tab leader drop-down list box. This option might be grayed out if you've selected a format that doesn't enable you to specify tab leaders.

6. In the Show levels text box, specify how many heading levels to include in the table of contents. You can use the text box arrows or simply type a number into the text box.

7. Click OK.

To assign custom template styles to table of contents levels, click the Options button in the Index and Tables dialog box.

To create a TOC from fields, click Options, clear Styles, and click Table entry fields.

Modify a Table of Contents

To select a TOC or index, click in the left-margin next to the first TOC or index entry.

To move a TOC, right-click and select Toggle Field Codes.

You can modify a table of contents in a number of ways. For example, you can change a table of contents' format settings in the Index and Tables dialog box. To access an existing table of content's settings:

- Select the table of contents, open the Insert menu, and click Index and Tables.

You can also modify a table by updating the table of contents' information. Essentially, a table of contents is a single field; so, updating a TOC is similar to updating any other field. To update a table of contents, use either of the following options:

- Right-click the table of contents, click Update Field, specify whether to update page numbers only or the entire table, and click OK.

- Select the table of contents, press F9, specify whether to update page numbers only or the entire table, and click OK.

To delete a table of contents:

- Select the table of contents (you can select the entire text or display the TOC as a field and select the field), and press Delete.

72 OBJECTIVE

Create an Index

Similar to automatically generating tables of contents, Word also provides features for generating indexes. An index is a detailed list included at the end of a document that references document terms and topics by page number.

Creating an index is a two-part process. First, you use fields to mark which words, phrases, and symbols in the document you want to include in the index. Then, you generate the index.

Like creating tables of contents, creating indexes can be honed to a refined skill (in fact, some people make a living by creating indexes). The exam doesn't expect you to be an all-star indexer, but you will be required to demonstrate that you know how to mark an index entry as well as generate an index.

The key to marking index entries lies in the Mark Index Entry dialog box, as shown in the following figure.

Mark Index Entries

To open the Mark Index Entry dialog box, use any of the following methods:

- Press Alt+Shift+X.

- Open the Insert menu, click Index and Tables, choose the Index tab, and click Mark Entry.

243

Part 2 • Expert Level

When you mark an index entry, Word inserts a nonprinting index entry (XE) field, formatted as

{ XE "main index heading" }

An index entry that has been expanded to show sub-levels and cross-references, displays as follows:

{ XE "main index heading:second level" \t "See cross reference index heading" }

To display index markers in your document, click ¶ Show/Hide in the Standard toolbar. You can edit index entries by changing text inside the quotation marks. You can delete an index entry by selecting the entire index entry field (including the braces) and pressing Delete.

To create an index entry, follow these steps:

1. Select the text you want to serve as an index entry or click where you want to insert an index entry, and open the Mark Index Entry dialog box. If you select text before opening the Mark Index Entry dialog box, the selected text displays in the Main entry box.

2. If necessary, enter text in the Main entry and Subentry text boxes. To insert a third-level topic, type a colon after the Subentry text, and type the third-level text in the Subentry text box.

3. Specify whether you want to create a cross-reference, mark the current page, or mark a page range. If you want to associate the index entry with a range, you select the Page range bookmark radio button, and select the name of the bookmark's in the drop-down list box.

4. In the Page number format area, specify whether you want to format the index with Bold or Italic page numbers.

5. Click Mark to mark the entry, or click Mark All to mark the first occurrence in each paragraph in the document that exactly matches the text and case of the index entry. The Mark Index Entry dialog box remains open so you can continue to create index entries.

Objective 4 • Selecting Menu Commands

6. To continue to mark index entries, select text in the document (double-click a word), click on the Mark Index Entry dialog box to automatically display the newly selected text in the Main <u>e</u>ntry text box, and click <u>M</u>ark or Mark <u>A</u>ll.

7. Click Cancel to close the Mark Index Entry dialog box.

After you've worked through your document and carefully inserted index entries, you are rewarded with the much-less-time-consuming task of generating an index.

Generate an Index

To generate an index, follow these steps:

1. Click where you want to insert the index.

2. To ensure proper index pagination, hide nonprinting characters by clicking ¶ Show/Hide on the Standard toolbar.

3. Open the <u>I</u>nsert menu, click In<u>d</u>ex and Tables, and click the Inde<u>x</u> tab.

4. Select one of the pre-formatted index designs in the Forma<u>t</u>s list box or specify custom layout settings by clicking the desired Index tab options.

5. Click OK.

Like an automatically generated table of contents, an automatically generated index is a field. Therefore, managing an index is similar to managing a table of contents. To update an index, select the index and press F9. To delete an index, select the index and press Delete.

Finally, keep in mind that when you update an index, you lose any changes made directly to the index. Therefore, whenever possible, change index field entries—not the generated index.

245

PRACTICE

TAKE THE TEST

Task 1

Objectives covered: 69, Add a Bookmark; 70, Insert a Cross-Reference; 71, Generate a Table of Contents; and 72, Create an Index. Open the file named `pingpong`, which is stored in the `Practice` folder on the enclosed CD-ROM.

1. Insert a table of contents in the first column of the document, directly above the first rule. Use the `Formal` style for the table of contents, and show 3 levels.

2. Create a bookmark named `Rule1` that refers to the entire Rule 1 section.

3. Modify the table of contents to show only 2 heading levels.

4. Create an index entry using the text `Rule 1` that refers to the `Rule1` bookmark.

5. Insert a cross-reference hyperlink at the end of rule 1.2 that states: `See Rule 3: The Ball`.

6. Insert a two-column `Modern` style index after the green line displaying at the end of the document.

Check your work against solution file `1147XE`.

Cheat Sheet

Add a Bookmark

1. Select text or click where you want to insert a bookmark.
2. Click Insert, Bookmark, or press Ctrl+Shift+F5.
3. Enter the name of the bookmark.
4. Click Add.

Insert a Cross-Reference

1. Enter the beginning portion of the cross-reference text.
2. Click Insert, Cross-reference.
3. Select an item type.
4. Select a reference type.
5. Click Insert as hyperlink, if desired.
6. Click an item to refer to.
7. Click Insert, and complete the cross-reference text, if necessary.

Generate a Table of Contents

1. Click where you want to insert the table of contents.
2. Click Insert, Index and Tables, and click the Table of Contents tab.
3. Select a format.
4. Select page number, tab, and level settings.
5. Click OK.

Modify a Table of Contents

- Select the TOC, and click Insert, Index and Tables.
- Right-click the TOC, click Update Field, specify whether to update page numbers only or the entire table, and click OK.
- Select the TOC, press F9, and specify whether to update page numbers only or the entire table, and click OK.

Continued

- Select the TOC and press Shift+F9, then drag-and-drop the field code.
- Select the TOC and press Delete.

Mark Index Entries

1. Select text or click where you want to place an index entry.
2. Enter text in the Main entry and Subentry text boxes.
3. Specify whether you want to create a cross-reference, mark the current page, or mark a range.
4. Specify bold or italic page number settings, if desired.
5. Click Mark or Mark All.
6. Continue to mark index entries or click Cancel.

Generate an Index

1. Click where you want to insert the index.
2. ¶ Show/Hide to hide nonprinting characters.
3. Click Insert, Index and Tables, Index tab.
4. Specify format settings.
5. Click OK.

CHAPTER 14

Collaborating with Workgroups

Frequently, a document passes through a number of hands (or, in this case, across a number of computer desktops) before it reaches its final form. Word comes equipped with a selection of features designed to help streamline the collaboration process, and you'll need to know how to implement these features to pass the exam. To correctly answer the test's collaboration questions, you need to know how to:

- Track Changes to a Document
- Insert Comments
- Work with Master Documents
- Apply Document Protection
- Create Multiple Versions of a Document
- Set the Default Location for Workgroup Templates
- Use Round Trip Documents

OBJECTIVE 73

Track Changes to a Document

You can track the changes you make to your document in addition to tracking changes made by others.

Having a second set of eyes look over a document is a common practice (often there's a third and fourth set of eyes, as well). You can track the changes each person makes to a document by using Word's revisions feature. The revisions feature color codes changes made by each reviewer. In this way, you can quickly see what changes have been made to the original document and who made the changes.

The following figure shows a document that has been revised with Word's revisions feature turned on. As you can see, the revisions feature enables you to see added text in addition to struck, or deleted, text.

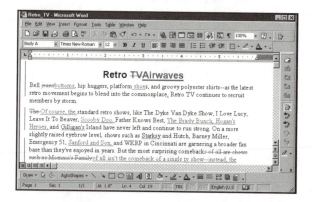

To be an expert-level specialist, you need to know how to work with Word's revisions feature. The next few sections review everything you need to know about revisions for the exam. For added practice before the exam, consider turning the revisions feature on as you work in Word before you take the exam.

250

Turn On the Revisions Feature

Before you can track a document's changes, you must turn on the revisions feature. By default, Word's revisions feature is turned off, which means changes are not color-coded and deleted text does not display with a line drawn through it. ==To turn the revisions feature on and manage the feature's options, you can open the Reviewing toolbar or the Highlight Changes dialog box.== The following figure shows the Reviewing toolbar. To display the Reviewing toolbar, open the View menu, click Toolbars, and select Reviewing; or right-click a toolbar and click Reviewing.

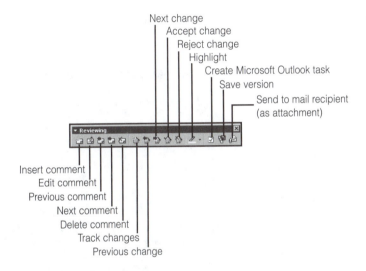

As mentioned, you can also use the Highlight Changes dialog box to manage your tracking options, as shown in the following figure.

To turn on the tracking feature, follow one of these procedures:

- Open the Reviewing toolbar and click ![icon] Track Changes.

Part 2 • Expert Level

- Open the Tools menu, click Track Changes, click the Track changes while editing check box, and click OK.
- Press Ctrl+Shift+E

After the revisions feature is activated, Word color codes changes according to each user's name. Word assigns a distinct tracking color for up to eight users, and recycles the colors for additional reviewers. To specify a tracking color, click Options in the Highlight Changes dialog box or click Tools, Options, Track Changes tab.

Word identifies users based on the information in the User Information tab in the Options dialog box (click Tools, Options, User Information tab), as shown in the following figure.

View Revisions

After you turn on the revisions feature, you might not want to view the revisions while you work. Frequently, working with revisions visible can diminish the readability of the text. In those instances, you can hide the revision marks and then later redisplay them. To control the display of revision marks, perform the following steps:

1. Open the Tools menu, and click Track Changes. The Highlight Changes dialog box opens.
2. Select the Highlight changes on screen check box to view changes and clear the Highlight changes on screen check box to hide changes.

Objective 73 • Track Changes to a Document

After changes have been marked in a document (by now, it is most-likely rather colorful), you can opt to accept and reject changes. You can accept and reject changes globally (all at once), or you can accept and reject changes one change at a time. When you accept or reject a change, the text changes to the default text color and no longer identifies which user is associated with the change.

Accept and Reject Revisions

To accept and reject all changes in a document, You can select the entire document (Ctrl+A) and click 🖉 Accept Change or 🖉 Reject Change on the Reviewing toolbar, or you can use the Accept or Reject Changes dialog box as described in the following steps:

1. Open the <u>T</u>ools menu, click <u>T</u>rack changes, and click <u>A</u>ccept or Reject Changes; or right-click a revision mark and click Ac<u>c</u>ept or <u>R</u>eject Changes. The Accept or Reject Changes dialog box opens, as shown in the figure.

2. Click <u>A</u>ccept All or Reject All, and then click <u>C</u>lose.

To accept and reject changes one at a time, ensure revisions marks display and select the change you want to accept or reject. Then, accept or reject the change using one of the following methods:

- Click <u>A</u>ccept or <u>R</u>eject Change in the Accept or Reject Changes dialog box.
- Click 🖉 Accept Change or 🖉 Reject Change on the Reviewing toolbar.
- Right-click a change and select Ac<u>c</u>ept Change or <u>R</u>eject Change.

Part 2 • Expert Level

To quickly move between revision marks, you can use the Find buttons in the Accept or Reject Changes dialog box. In addition, you can click 🖻 Previous Change and 🖻 Next change in the Reviewing toolbar to jump from change to change.

74 OBJECTIVE

Insert Comments

The comments feature provides another way in which people can collaborate on Word documents. Comments enable you and other reviewers to insert annotations regarding the text without changing the document text. When you add comments to a document, Word inserts chronologically numbered reference marks in the text and shades the text with light yellow. Furthermore, whenever you add a comment, your cursor automatically moves to the Comments pane and enables you to record your comment, as shown in the figure.

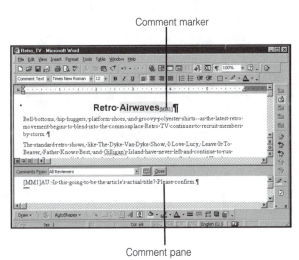

As with revision marks, Word tracks up to the first eight reviewers' comment reference marks in distinct colors.

255

Part 2 • Expert Level

On the exam, you will be asked to insert a comment into a document. To do so, follow these steps:

1. Click near the text or item you want to comment on or select the text or item.

2. Click ☐ Insert Comment on the Reviewing toolbar, open the Insert menu and click Comment, or press Alt+Ctrl+M. The comment pane opens.

3. Type the comment in the comment pane, and click Close to close the comment pane.

To view the contents of an existing comment, first, ensure non-printing characters display in your document (click ¶ Show/Hide). Then, perform any of the following actions:

- Point to a comment marker. A ScreenTip opens and displays the comment's text.

- Double-click a comment marker. The comment pane opens.

- Click ☐ Edit Comment on the Reviewing toolbar. The comment pane opens.

You can delete and edit text in the comment pane, but you cannot delete comments from within the pane. To completely remove a comment, you must select the comment marker in the text and press Delete or click ☐ Delete Comment on the Reviewing toolbar. If another user created the comment, you will need to delete the comment and then select the deleted comment and click ☐ Accept Change on the Reviewing toolbar.

OBJECTIVE 75

Work with Master Documents

A master document can be likened to a filing cabinet that helps you organize sections of a long document. All the sections, or *subdocuments*, are contained in the cabinet (the master document), yet users can opt to work on selected sections without pulling all the paperwork out of the drawer.

At some point, you might need to work with a long document. Managing a large document can become cumbersome, but simply dividing the document into smaller separate documents might complicate matters further down the road. For example, you might run into problems when you want to implement some of Word's other features, such as adding continuous page numbers, printing, formatting headers and footers, and generating a table of contents and index.

Instead of complicating matters by creating a number of smaller documents, you can use a master document to associate the components of your long document. ==When you take advantage of the master document feature, you ensure that you can use Word's other document features throughout the document-creation process.==

In sum, the master document enables you to create, associate, and manage subdocuments. For example, if you are creating a book, you could create a master document named *book*, and each subdocument could be named Chapter 1, Chapter 2, and so forth. You and others could then work on each chapter separately, yet, behind the scenes, each chapter is a master document component.

Part 2 • Expert Level

You can create a master document from an existing document (in which case, you configure headings to identify subdocuments), or you can create a new master document and add new headings or insert existing documents as subdocuments. In either scenario, ==when you create a master document, you work with subdocument names and text within Word's Outline View.==

Create a Master Document

To create a master document, follow these steps:

1. Open a new or existing document, and then click 📄 Outline View, or open the <u>V</u>iew menu and click <u>O</u>utline.

2. If you are creating a master document from a new document, you can enter an outline to serve as the master document's hierarchy (or you can insert documents as described in the next section). You can create the outline text using Word's heading styles or use the ⬅ Promote and ➡ Demote buttons in the Outlining toolbar. The following figure shows a simple master document outline.

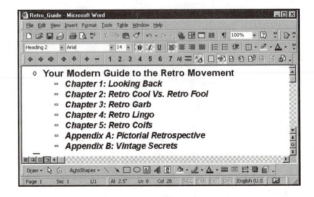

If you are creating a master document from an existing document, the headings will automatically display in Outline View. You might want to collapse any expanded sections to keep the outline's view clean and simple.

Objective 75 • Work with Master Documents

3. Select a heading that you want to format as a subdocument, and click ![icon] Create Subdocument on the Outlining toolbar. The section is marked as a subdocument, as shown in the following figure.

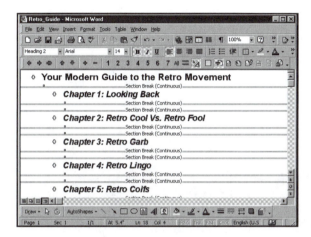

4. Continue to mark subdocuments, until all subdocuments are marked. To simplify working within the master document framework, subdocument divisions should be as logical and intuitive as possible.

5. Click ![icon] Save to save the master document. When you save a master document, the subdocuments are automatically saved as individual documents in the same directory as the master document.

Add an Existing Document to a Master Document

Instead of separating existing documents into subdocuments or creating subdocuments from scratch, you might want to add existing documents to a master document. To add an existing document to a master document, follow these steps:

1. Open the master document you want to configure.

2. Click ![icon] Master Document View on the Outlining toolbar.

3. Click a blank line above, below, or between existing subdocuments where you want to add a subdocument.

259

Part 2 • Expert Level

4. Click ▦ Insert Subdocument on the Outlining toolbar. The Insert Subdocument dialog box opens.

5. In the Insert Subdocument dialog box, locate the document you want to insert, and double-click the filename's icon.

You can open subdocuments from within the master document. To do so, you can use the following methods:

- In Master Document View, double-click the subdocument icon.

- Click ▦ Collapse Subdocuments on the Outlining toolbar, and click the subdocument's hyperlink.

==If you open a subdocument that someone else is currently working on, the document is locked.== This means that you have read-only permission—you can view the subdocument, but you can't modify it until the person closes the subdocument. After the other person closes the document, you can open the document and make changes just as would you make changes to any other document.

76 OBJECTIVE

Apply Document Protection

Word offers a few document-protection features that you can use to control who can access and change documents. You can protect a document by specifying it as read-only, or you can grant password protection to the document. The main interface used to apply document protection settings is the Save dialog box, as shown in the following figure.

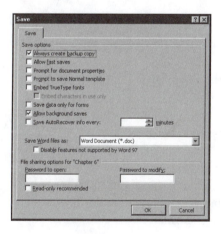

Notice in the figure that the File sharing options portion of the Save dialog box offers password protection text boxes and a read-only check box. You can use these options to apply document protect, as described in the following steps:

1. Open the File menu and click Save As. The Save As dialog box opens.

2. In the Save As dialog box, click the Tools button, and click General Options. The Save dialog box opens.

261

Part 2 • Expert Level

3. To require users to enter a password to open a document, type a password in the Password to open text box.

4. To require users to enter a password before they can make changes to a document, type a password in the Password to modify text box.

5. To configure the document to automatically recommend users to open the document as read-only, click the Read-only recommended check box.

6. Click OK. A Confirm Password dialog box displays for each password you've created, as shown in the following figure. If you assigned a password to open the document and a password to modify the document, you will need to complete the Confirm Password dialog box twice.

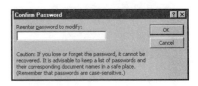

7. Type the password, and press Enter.

8. Click Save.

When a document has password protection applied, users need to provide the password in a password text box before they can open or modify the document. Similarly, when the read-only recommendation option is set for a document, users are presented with a dialog box that asks whether the document should be opened in read-only format.

77 OBJECTIVE

Create Multiple Versions of a Document

At times, you might want to keep track of various versions of a document while you or others work on it. You can easily save and view versions of a document in Word. On the exam, you'll need to show that you know how to save a version of a document.

When you save versions of a document, Word stores all the versions within the same file. By default, you only see the most current version. You can choose to view an earlier version by specifically opening an earlier version using the Versions dialog box.

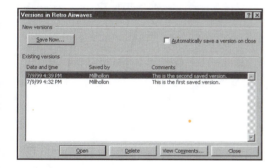

As you can see in the figure, Word records the date and time of each saved version along with the name of the person making the changes. You can view any version in a separate window by selecting a version in the Versions dialog box and clicking Open.

Part 2 • Expert Level

Saving versions conserves more space than saving multiple copies—only the differences between versions are saved.

To save a version of a document, follow these steps:

1. Open the File Menu and click Versions. The Versions dialog box opens. Notice the Automatically save a version on close check box. You can select this option to save a version each time the document is closed.

2. Click Save Now. The Save Version dialog box opens, as shown in the figure.

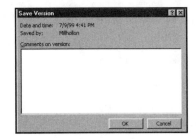

3. In the Save Versions dialog box, enter comments if desired and click OK.

You can also quickly access the Save Versions dialog box by using either of the following methods:

- Click ![icon] Save Version on the Reviewing toolbar.
- Open the File menu, click Save As, click Tools, and click Save Version.

78 OBJECTIVE

Set the Default Location for Workgroup Templates

When you work with others on a document, you'll often need to share templates to keep styles consistent. You can specify where templates are stored on your computer or network. To do so, open the File Locations tab in the Options dialog box, as shown in the following figure.

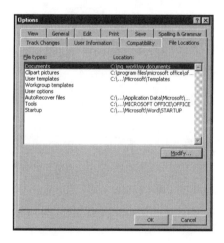

Basically, this task entails specifying the storage location for workgroup templates. Completing this exam task should be quick and easy. The exam tells you where the workgroup templates are stored, and then you configure the File Locations tab to reflect the location. To do this, follow these steps:

1. Open the Tools menu, click Options, and click the File Locations tab.

265

2. In the File types list, select the Workgroup templates option, and click Modify. The Modify Location dialog box opens.

3. Navigate to the location in which the templates are stored, and click OK.

79 OBJECTIVE

Use Round Trip Documents

Round trip documents enable you to share Word documents with others over an intranet, the Internet, or other network setup. Basically, you can save a Word document as a Web page, and then anyone can view the document in a Web browser. Furthermore, after you've saved a Word document as a Web page, you can later resave the Web page as a Word document without losing the formatting. The document will look relatively the same whether it's saved as a Word document or a Web page.

In the following figures, the first figure is a Word document, the second figure shows the document saved as a Web page and displayed in Internet Explorer, and the third document shows the Web page document saved as a Word document.

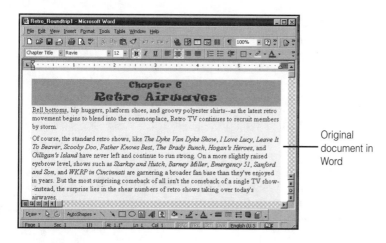

Original document in Word

267

Part 2 • Expert Level

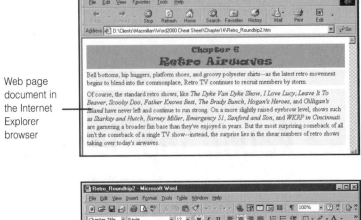

Web page document in the Internet Explorer browser

Web page document in Word's Normal view

Notice in the preceding figures that none of the formatting was lost in transition. To take advantage of round tripping, follow these steps

1. Open the File menu and click Save As. The Save As dialog box opens.

2. In the Save as type drop-down list box, select Web Page, and click Save. Others can now view the saved document page in a Web browser.

3. To reopen the Web page in Word, click [icon] Open on the Standard toolbar, and double-click the file name's icon in the Open dialog box. After you open a Web page in Word, you might want to click the Normal View or Print Layout View icon on the horizontal scrollbar. If you want

268

Objective 79 • Use Round Trip Documents

to save the Web page as a Word document, open the Save As dialog box, and click Word Document in the Save as type drop-down list box.

Because of browser limitations, you might lose some format settings (such as embossed, shadowed, or outlined text attributes) when you round-trip documents between Word and Web page formats. When a document uses a format that will be lost, Word presents a dialog box informing you of the impending change. For example, if the document contains shadowed text, Word displays a dialog box that states the shadowed text will display as bold text. You can click Continue or Cancel. To see a review of common format alterations, open the Office Assistant and type, "What happens when I save a Word 2000 document as a Web page?" and follow the links.

PRACTICE

TAKE THE TEST

Task 1
Objectives covered: 73, Track Changes to a Document; 74, Insert Comments; and 76, Apply Document Protection. Open the file named Retro_TV, which is stored in the Practice folder on the enclosed CD-ROM.

1. Accept the changes in the document's heading, and, at the beginning of the first paragraph, change *Bell jeans* to *Bell bottoms*.

2. Hide the revision marks.

3. Insert a comment next to the chapter title using the text: *Please verify this chapter title.*

4. Password protect the Retro_TV document using the word *super*.

Check your work against solution file 1147XF.

Task 2
Objectives covered: 75, Work with Master Documents; 77, Create Multiple Versions of a Document; 78, Set the Default Location for Workgroup Templates; and 79, Use Round Trip Documents. Open the file named Retro_Guide, which is stored in the Practice folder on the enclosed CD-ROM.

1. In the Retro_Guide master document, insert the file named Chapter 6 from the Practice Folder on the CD-ROM as a subdocument directly following the Chapter 5 subdocument.

2. Make Appendix B a subdocument.

3. Open the Chapter 6 subdocument.

4. Save a version of the `Chapter 6` subdocument.

5. Set the default location for Workgroup templates to `C:\My Documents`.

6. Open the `Retro_Roundtrip` Web page document, stored in the `Practice` folder on the enclosed CD-ROM, in Word, and then open the document in your browser.

Check your work against solution file `1147XG`.

Cheat Sheet

Turn On The Revisions Feature

- Click ![icon] Track Changes on the Reviewing toolbar.
- Click Tools, Track Changes, Track changes while editing, and click OK.
- Press Ctrl+Shift+E.

View Revisions

1. Click Tools, Track Changes.
2. Select Highlight changes on screen.

Accept and Reject Revisions

- Click Accept All, Reject All, Accept, or Reject Change in the Accept or Reject Changes dialog box.
- Click ![icon] Accept Change or ![icon] Reject Change on the Reviewing toolbar.
- Right-click a change and select Accept Change or Reject Change.
- Press Ctrl+A and click ![icon] Accept Change or ![icon] Reject Change.

Insert Comments

1. Click near or select the text or item on which you want to comment.
2. Click ![icon] Insert Comment on the Reviewing toolbar; click Insert, Comment; or press Ctrl+Alt+M.
3. Type a comment and click Close.

Create a Master Document

1. Open a document and click ![icon] Outline View or click View, Outline.
2. Enter an outline to serve as the master document's hierarchy.

3. Select a heading and click 📄 Create Subdocument.
4. Continue to mark subdocuments
5. Click 💾 Save

Add an Existing Document to a Master Document

1. Open the master document.
2. Click 📄 Master Document View on the Outlining toolbar.
3. Click a blank line where you want to add a subdocument
4. Click 📄 Insert Subdocument on the Outlining toolbar.
5. Double-click the filename you want to insert.

Apply Document Protection

1. Click File, Save As.
2. Click Tools, General Options.
3. Type a password in the Password to open text box.
4. Type a password in the Password to modify text box.
5. Click Read-only recommended.
6. Click OK, and complete Confirm Password dialog boxes, if necessary.
7. Click Save.

Create Multiple Versions of a Document

1. Click File, Versions, Save now; click 📄 Save Version on the Reviewing toolbar; or click File, Save As, Tools, Save Version.
2. Enter comments and click OK.

273

Continued

Set the Default Location for Workgroup Templates

1. Click Tools, Options, File Locations tab.
2. Select Workgroup templates, and click Modify.
3. Navigate to the location in which the templates are stored, and click OK.

Use Round Trip Documents

1. Click File, Save As.
2. In the Save as type drop-down list box, select Web Page, and click Save.
3. To reopen the Web page in Word, click ![icon] Open and double-click the file name. To save the Web page as a Word document, open the Save As dialog box, and click Word Document in the Save as type drop-down list box.

274

CHAPTER 15

Adding Spreadsheet Capabilities to Tables

Word enables you to perform calculations and include Excel spreadsheets (also called *worksheets*) within your Word documents. In some instances, spreadsheet data is stored and updated directly within the Word document; in other instances, data storage and updates occur in another document and a copy of the data displays in the Word document. To help you master Word's spreadsheet capabilities, this chapter starts with a review of performing simple table calculations and moves on to the slightly more complex tasks of embedding and linking Excel worksheets. Specifically, this chapter addresses how to:

- Perform Calculations
- Embed Worksheets
- Link Excel Data
- Modify Worksheets

OBJECTIVE 80

Perform Calculations

You can perform table calculations within a standard Word table by entering formulas in selected cells. Word assists you in creating formulas by providing the Formula dialog box, as shown in the following figure.

The Formula dialog box enables you to insert calculation fields within table cells, as illustrated in the next figure. In the figure, Column A shows the field's calculation result, and Column B shows the field's code.

You can manipulate and toggle calculation fields in the same manner that you work with other fields. For instance, you can

276

update all the calculation fields in a table by selecting the table, right clicking, and then selecting Update Field. (For more information on fields, see Chapter 11, Objective 58.)

To insert calculation formulas into a table, follow these steps:

1. Click the cell in which you want the formula result to display.

2. Open the Table menu, and click Formula. The Formula dialog box opens. By default, Word suggests a formula in the Formula text box.

3. If you do not want to use the suggested formula, delete the formula in the Formula text box, and select a formula in the Paste function list box or type a formula directly into the Formula text box.

   To reference particular cells within your formula, reference the table cells in the formula's parentheses. For example, =SUM(a2,b3) adds the number in the cell at the intersection of Column A, Row 2 to the number in the cell at the intersection of Column B, Row 3.

4. To specify a number format, select a format on the Number format drop-down list or type a format in the Number format text box.

5. Click OK.

In addition to providing the Formula dialog box calculation options, Word also includes [Σ] AutoSum on the Tables and Borders toolbar. [Σ] AutoSum enables you to quickly perform the most-frequently-used spreadsheet calculation process—adding columns or rows of data.

To find the sum of the contents of a table's column or row, your best bet is to use the Tables and Borders toolbar, like this:

- Click in the table cell at the end of the row or column for which you want to find a sum, and click [Σ] AutoSum on the Tables and Borders toolbar.

277

OBJECTIVE 81

Embed Worksheets

To expand your table-calculation prowess, you can *embed* Excel Worksheet data in your Word document or table. When you embed Excel worksheet data, you can insert a copy of pre-existing worksheet data or you can create a new blank worksheet within your document.

After a worksheet is embedded in a Word document, the Word document owns the data. The data in the embedded worksheet becomes part of the Word document. All the changes you make to an embedded worksheet in a Word document only affect the Word document—the original Excel workbook from which you copied the worksheet does not change.

If you want to synchronize an Excel worksheet's data with data displayed in a Word document, you need to link the Excel worksheet and Word document, as described in Objective 82.

Now, although the embedded-worksheet-data explanation might seem wordy, the actual process of embedding Excel worksheets and worksheet data into Word documents is straightforward. When embedding Excel information, you can choose to embed a new blank worksheet, an existing worksheet, or selected data from an existing worksheet.

Embed a New Blank Worksheet

If you embed an Excel worksheet in a Word document, you insert an Excel table directly into your document, as shown in the following figure.

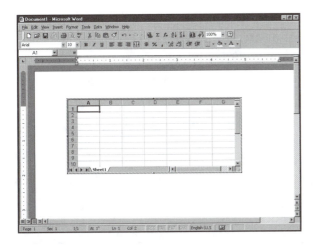

To embed a new blank worksheet, click where you want to insert a blank Excel worksheet, and then follow these steps:

1. Open the Insert menu and click Object. The Insert Object dialog box opens, as shown in the following figure. As you can see, the Create New tab is displayed by default.

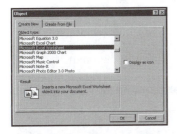

2. In the Object type list, select Microsoft Excel Worksheet, and click OK. A blank Excel worksheet displays in the Word document.

To remove an embedded worksheet, select the worksheet and press Delete.

You can copy information from an existing Excel table (including text, numbers, formulas, and formatting) into your Word document.

Embed Existing Worksheets

Part 2 • Expert Level

To embed an existing worksheet in a Word document, click where you want to insert the existing Excel worksheet information, and then follow these steps:

1. Open the Insert menu, click Object, and click the Create from File tab.

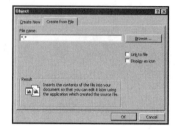

2. Click in the File name text box, and type the name of the file containing the Excel worksheet. If you don't know the name of the file, click the Browse button. The Browse window opens. Navigate to the Excel file you want to insert into your Word document and double-click the file's icon. The file name is entered on the Create from File tab in the Insert Object dialog box.

3. Click OK. The worksheet data is inserted into the Word document. The following figure shows how an Excel table looks when it is embedded in a Word document.

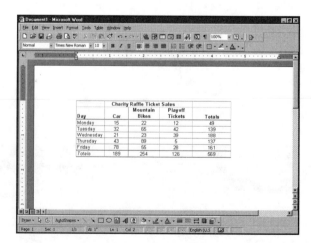

Objective 81 • Embed Worksheets

Finally, you can choose to embed selected data from an Excel worksheet. For example, you can choose to show only a few columns of an Excel table, as shown in the next figure. Notice that the Mountain Bikes, Playoff Tickets, and Totals columns do not display in the worksheet shown in the following figure.

Embed Selected Worksheet Data

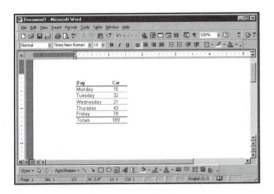

You can resize an embedded Excel worksheet's window and hide columns to show only selected data.

Embedding selected worksheet data requires you to open both the Excel file and the Word file. After both files are open, follow these steps:

1. In the Excel worksheet, select the data range you want to embed in the Word document, and click 📋 Copy on the Standard toolbar, or press Ctrl+C.

2. In the Word document, click where you want to embed the copied text, open the <u>E</u>dit menu, and click Paste <u>S</u>pecial. The Paste Special dialog box opens, as shown in the following figure.

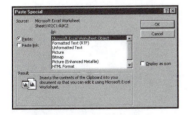

3. In the <u>A</u>s list box, click Microsoft Excel Worksheet Object, and click OK.

281

Part 2 • Expert Level

==Regardless of whether you use the Edit, Paste Special procedure or the Insert, Object method, Word inserts the entire workbook into your document whenever you embed a worksheet.== As you will see in Objective 83, you can access any portion of an embedded workbook while working in Word.

82 OBJECTIVE

Link Excel Data

Instead of embedding Excel data into a Word document, you can link an Excel worksheet to your Word document. The result appears to be the same, but the underlying data manipulation settings are distinctly different.

When you link an Excel worksheet, a connection is formed between the Excel and Word files. ==If you make changes to the Excel table, the changes appear in both the Excel worksheet and the Word document.== Fundamentally, the Word document simply borrows the Excel data whenever the Word document is opened—the Excel information is stored in the original Excel workbook.

==The process of linking Excel worksheets is similar to the process of embedding Excel worksheets in Word.== You can link entire worksheets or selected data.

To link an existing worksheet to your Word document, click in the Word document where you want the linked Excel worksheet to display, and then follow these steps:

Link Excel Worksheets

1. Open the Insert menu, click Object, and click the Create from File tab.

2. Click in the File name text box and enter the name of the Excel file you want to link to, or click the Browse button to locate the file you want to link to and double-click the file name.

3. Select the Link to file check box.

Part 2 • Expert Level

4. Click OK. The worksheet data is inserted into the Word document in much the same way an Excel table is embedded into a Word document. When data changes in the Excel worksheet, the Word document will automatically change as well.

To break the connection of a linked object, open the Edit menu, and click Links. The Links dialog box opens. In the Links dialog box, click the item you want to unlink, then click Break Link.

Link Selected Worksheet Data

Linking selected worksheet data is similar to embedding selected worksheet data. To link selected data, open both the Excel worksheet and the Word document, and follow these steps:

1. In the Excel worksheet, select the data range you want to link to the Word document, and click 📋 Copy on the Standard toolbar or press Ctrl+C.

2. In the Word document, click where you want the linked data to display, open the Edit menu, and click Paste Special.

3. In the As list box, click Microsoft Excel Worksheet Object.

4. In the Paste Special dialog box, select the Paste link radio button, and click OK.

83 OBJECTIVE

Modify Worksheets

Regardless of whether you've linked or embedded an Excel worksheet in your Word document, you can modify the worksheet. The key to modifying Excel worksheets in Word is to open the worksheet. After the worksheet is open, you can modify the worksheet using Excel commands, just as if you are working within Excel.

To open a linked or embedded Excel worksheet:

- In Word, double-click the worksheet to start Excel.

When you double-click a linked Excel worksheet, the worksheet opens in Excel. When you double-click an embedded worksheet, the workbook opens in a window, as shown in the following figure.

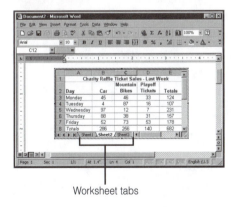

Worksheet tabs

To display Excel data as a table without formulas, copy and paste the Excel data into a Word document.

285

Notice in the figure that the workbook contains multiple worksheets. You can change which worksheet displays in a Word document by double-clicking the Excel worksheet, clicking a worksheet tab and then clicking anywhere outside of the active window to close the workbook window.

TAKE THE TEST

Task 1

Objectives covered: 80, Perform Calculations; 81, Embed Worksheets; and 83, Modify Worksheets. Open the file named Tickets_1, which is stored in the Practice folder on the enclosed CD-ROM.

1. In Table 1, calculate and insert the totals for the Car, Mountain Bikes, and Playoff Tickets columns.

2. Below the *Raffle Workbook* heading, embed the Raffle1.xls Excel workbook.

3. Modify the embedded workbook to display Sheet 2 instead of Sheet 1.

Check your work against solution file 1147XH.

Task 2

Objectives covered: 81, Embed Worksheets; 82, Link Excel Data; and 83, Modify Worksheets. Open the file named Tickets_2, which is stored in the Practice folder on the enclosed CD-ROM.

1. Embed a blank worksheet under the Table 1 heading.

2. Resize the blank worksheet so that only four columns display.

3. Below the blank worksheet, create a linked worksheet that contains the first two columns of the table on Sheet 1 of the Raffles2.xls Excel document.

Check your work against solution file 1147XI.

Cheat Sheet

Perform Calculations

- Click in the table cell, and [Σ] AutoSum.

Or

1. Click the cell that will contain the formula results.
2. Click T<u>a</u>ble, F<u>o</u>rmula.
3. Insert a formula in the <u>F</u>ormula text box.
4. Specify a number format in the <u>N</u>umber format text box, and click OK.

Embed a New Blank Worksheet

1. Click <u>I</u>nsert, <u>O</u>bject.
2. In the <u>O</u>bject type list, select Microsoft Excel Worksheet, and click OK.

Embed Existing Worksheets

1. Click <u>I</u>nsert, <u>O</u>bject, and click the Create from <u>F</u>ile tab.
2. Type a filename, or use the <u>B</u>rowse button.
3. Click OK.

Embed Selected Worksheet Data

1. In the Excel worksheet, select a data range, and click [📋] Copy or press Ctrl+C.
2. Click in the Word document, and click <u>E</u>dit, Paste <u>S</u>pecial.
3. Click Microsoft Excel Worksheet Object, and click OK.

Continued

Link Excel Worksheets

1. Click Insert, Object, and click the Create from File tab.
2. Type a file name or use the Browse button.
3. Select the Link to file checkbox.
4. Click OK.

Link Selected Worksheet Data

1. In the Excel worksheet, select a data range, and click 📋 or press Ctrl+C.
2. Click in the Word document, and click Edit, Paste Special.
3. Click Microsoft Excel Worksheet Object.
4. Select Paste link, and click OK.

Modify Worksheets

- Double-click an embedded or linked Excel worksheet, and make changes to the worksheet using Excel commands.

CHAPTER

16

Working with Advanced Graphics and Charts Features

To pass the core-level exam, you need to know how to insert clip art, pictures, and objects—you can read about those basics in Chapter 9, Objective 51. For the expert-level exam, you need to go one step further and manage the graphics and objects that you've inserted into a document. Specifically, you need to know how to:

- Add Bitmapped Graphics
- Delete Graphics
- Reposition Graphics
- Align Text with Graphics
- Create a Chart
- Modify a Chart
- Import Data into Charts

OBJECTIVE 84

Add Bitmapped Graphics

Adding bitmapped graphics to your document is fundamentally the same as adding clip art and pictures to a document. In fact, many clip art graphics and pictures are also bitmapped graphics. You can recognize bitmapped graphics because they are saved with the BMP extension. To insert a bitmapped graphic file into your document, follow the standard steps for inserting a picture from a file, which are briefly reviewed here:

1. Click where you want to insert a graphic.

2. Open the Insert menu, click Picture, and click From File; or click 🖼 Insert Picture on the Picture toolbar. The Insert Picture dialog box opens, as shown in the following figure. To open the preview window (also shown in the figure), click the 🖼 Views drop-down arrow in the Insert Picture dialog box and select Preview.

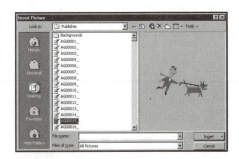

3. In the Insert Picture dialog box, navigate to the bitmapped file that you want to insert and double-click the file name's icon, or select the file and click Insert.

You can also draw a bitmapped graphic in your document. To insert a graphic box and draw your own, follow these steps:

1. Open the Insert menu and click Object. The Object dialog box opens.

2. On the Create New tab, click Bitmap Image in the Object type list box, and click OK. A graphic box opens in your document and the Word interface displays graphic editing tools, as shown in the following figure.

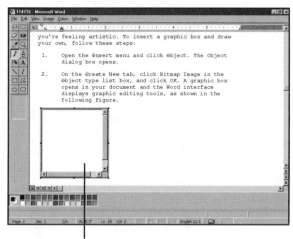

Bitmap graphic box

3. Create a bitmap graphic just as would you create a graphic in a drawing program.

OBJECTIVE 85

Delete Graphics

After you insert or create a graphic, you might find that you really don't want to include the graphic after all, or you might simply want to redesign it. Whatever the reason, you can delete graphics from your document. To delete a graphic, click the object you want to delete and then perform any of the following actions:

You can cut and paste graphics in the same manner as you cut and paste other elements.

- Click ✂ Cut on the Standard toolbar.
- Press Delete.
- Press BackSpace.
- Right-click the selected object and click Cut.

86 OBJECTIVE

Reposition Graphics

After you insert a graphic into your document, you can reposition it. To move a graphic, simply click in the middle of the graphic and drag the graphic to a new position. If you want to place a graphic more precisely, you can use the Format Picture dialog box, as described in the following steps:

1. Click the picture you want to move.

2. Open the Format Picture dialog box using any of the following methods:

   - Double-click the picture.

   - Select the picture and click [icon] Format Picture on the Picture toolbar.

   - Right-click the picture and select Format Picture.

   - Select the picture, open the Format Menu, and click Picture.

3. Click the Layout tab, click a layout option other than Inline with text, click Advanced, and click the Picture Position tab, as shown in the following figure.

4. Configure the layout settings on the Picture Position tab and then close the open dialog boxes.

295

OBJECTIVE 87

Align Text with Graphics

You can specify how text aligns with a graphic. To configure this setting, you can select a picture, open the Picture Format dialog box, and click the Layout tab, which is shown in the following figure.

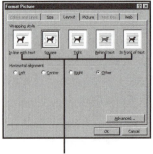

Wrapping style icons

You can drag the Text Wrapping menu to display it as the Text Wrapping toolbar while you work.

To align text relative to the selected graphic, click the Wrapping style icons on the Layout tab that references the desired text alignment style.

You can also specify text alignment relative to graphics by selecting the graphic and clicking Text Wrapping on the Picture toolbar. The Text Wrapping button displays a drop-down list, as shown in the following figure.

296

You can click any of the Text Wrapping menu items to apply the text-wrapping format. The text wrapping options include the following:

- ▣ **S̲quare**—Wraps text around all sides of the object's square bounding box.

- ▣ **T̲ight**—Wraps text around the perimeter of the selected object. You can change an object's perimeter using ▣ Edit Wrap Points.

- ▣ **Behin̲d Text**—Places the selected object behind the document text.

- ▣ **I̲n Front of Text**—Places the selected object on top of the document text.

- ▣ **To̲p and Bottom**—Wraps text above and below the selected object but not on the sides.

- ▣ **Th̲rough**—Wraps text around the perimeter and inside any open portions of the selected object.

- ▣ **E̲dit Wrap Points**—Shows the vertexes around the selected object so you can change the text-wrapping perimeter. To reshape the perimeter, drag the vertexes. Text wraps to the perimeter if you select ▣ Tight or ▣ Through.

297

OBJECTIVE 88

Create a Chart

Charts, such as pie charts and bar graphs, enable you to graphically illustrate data. From Word's perspective, a chart is simply another type of object you can add to a document. If you choose to insert a chart, Word opens a program called Microsoft Graph 2000, and you use this program to create your chart. Working with Microsoft Graph 2000 charts is similar to working with Excel charts.

Charts consist of two main components: graph and datasheet. The datasheet contains the data mapped in the graph. By default, Microsoft Graph 2000 opens a sample chart and datasheet each time you create a chart in Word.

The quickest way to understand a feature is to use it. Therefore, to review how to create a chart, follow these steps:

1. Click where you want to insert a chart, open the Insert menu, click Object, and click the Create New tab.

2. In the Object type list box, click Microsoft Graph 2000 Chart and click OK. A chart and data sheet displays in your document, as shown in the following figure. Notice that the application window displays custom tools that you can use to work with the chart and datasheet components.

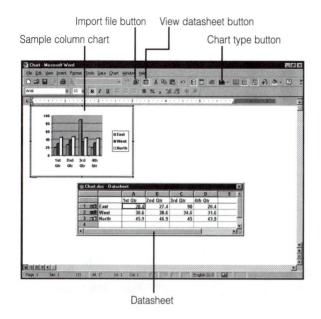

3. Click a cell on the datasheet and type your own data. Continue to replace the sample data with your own data on the datasheet.

4. Click ![icon] Chart Type drop-down arrow and select a chart style.

5. After you enter your data, click anywhere on the Word document to close the datasheet.

To hide the datasheet without closing chart view, click the View Datasheet button on the Chart view's toolbar.

OBJECTIVE 89

Modify a Chart

As in Excel, your charts aren't set in stone after you create them. You can modify charts in a variety of ways, including changing datasheet information and chart type settings.

The key to modifying a chart is reopening the Chart in Microsoft Graph 2000 chart view. To do this, double-click an existing chart. When you are in Microsoft Graph 2000 Chart view, you can use a number of procedures to modify the chart, including the following:

- **Modify a Datasheet**—Click ![icon] View Datasheet on the Chart view's Standard toolbar to open the datasheet. You can replace existing data with new data.

- **Change a Chart Type**—Click ![icon] Chart Type or open the Chart menu and click Chart Type to open the Chart Type dialog box, as shown in the following figure.

- **Format a Chart Area**—Double-click a blank area on the chart; right-click the chart and select Format Chart Area; select the chart, open the Format menu, and click Selected Chart Area; or select the chart and press Ctrl+1.

The Format Chart Area dialog box opens, as shown in the following figure.

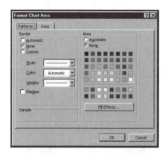

- Furthermore, to toggle the display of axis gridlines, click Category Axis Gridlines and Value Axis Gridlines on the Chart view's Standard toolbar.

- **Add Titles**—Open the Format menu, click Chart Options, and click the Titles tab. You can add a title to the chart, as well as to each axis, as shown in the following figure.

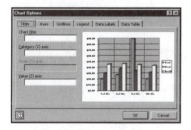

- **Format Data Elements**—Double-click a data element, such as a bar or pie area, to open the Format Data Series dialog box, as shown in the following figure.

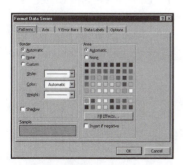

Part 2 • Expert Level

You can also open the Format Data Series dialog box by right-clicking a data element and selecting Format Data Series; clicking a data element, opening the Format menu, and clicking Selected Data Series; or clicking a data element and pressing Ctrl+1.

- **Change Axis Numbers**—Double-click the numbers on the Y-axis; right-click the numbers on the Y-axis and click Format Axis; select the numbers on the Y-axis, open the Format menu, and click Selected Axis; or select the numbers on the Y-Axis and press Ctrl+1. The Format Axis dialog box opens. Select the Number tab, as shown in the following figure, to configure the number settings.

To change the interval between axis numbers, click the Scale tab in the Format Axis dialog box.

You can also format axis numbers by clicking the Y-axis, and clicking 💲 Currency Style, ％ Percent Style, 🔢 Comma Style, 📈 Increase Decimal, 📉 Decrease Decimal, 🔽 Angle Text Downward, and 🔼 Angle Text Upward on Chart view's Formatting toolbar bar.

- **Format a Legend**—Double-click the legend; right-click the legend and click Format Legend; click the legend and press Ctrl+1; or select the legend, open the Format menu, and click Selected Legend. The Format Legend dialog box opens. You can format the patterns, fonts, or legend placement using the Format Legend dialog box. To toggle the display of the legend, click 📋 Legend in the chart view's Standard toolbar.

Objective 89 • Modify a Chart

- **Move a Chart**—Click and drag the chart to a new location on the page.

- **Resize a Chart**—Select the chart and drag a resizing handle (a small square appearing along the edge of the selected chart).

To quickly open the formatting box for any chart element, click an element (the element name displays in the Chart Objects drop-down list on the chart view's formatting toolbar) and click Format next to the drop-down list. The associated formatting dialog box opens.

OBJECTIVE 90

Import Data into Charts

Although you can create charts by entering data into the sample datasheet in Microsoft Graph 2000, you can also import existing data. You can import data from a table in Word or data stored in another program, such as Excel or Lotus. For the exam, you don't need to know the ins and outs of what particular types of data Microsoft Graph 2000 can handle and what format the data needs to be stored in. Instead, you only need to have the process of importing data mastered. The next two sections step through the procedures you'll need to take to import data into a Microsoft Graph 2000 chart.

Create a Chart from a Word Table

You can easily format table data stored in a Word document into a chart. To do so, follow these steps:

1. Create a table in Word with labels along the top and left columns.

2. Select the table (press Alt+double-click). One word of caution: If your table includes a row or column containing totals, select the entire table except for the totals row or column.

3. Open the Insert menu, click Object, and click the Create New tab.

4. In the Object type list box, select Microsoft Graph 2000 Chart and click OK.

5. Click ▲ Chart Type drop-down arrow and select a chart type.

6. Click outside the graph or datasheet to return to the Word document.

Import Data from Other Programs

As mentioned, you can also create charts from data stored in other applications. To import table data, follow these steps:

1. Create a new chart and keep the chart and datasheet open.

2. Select the cell in the datasheet where you want the upper-left corner of the data to display.

3. Open the Edit menu and click Import File or click 🔘 Import File on Chart view's Standard toolbar. The Import File dialog box opens.

4. Navigate to the location of the file and double-click the file name's icon, or select the file and click Open. The Import Data Options dialog box opens, as shown in the following figure.

5. Click OK. The data displays in the datasheet and the chart changes to reflect the imported data.

You can use standard copy and paste procedures to copy data from an application into a Microsoft Graph 2000 datasheet.

TAKE THE TEST

Task 1

Objectives covered: 84, Add Bitmapped Graphics; 85, Delete Graphics; 86, Reposition Graphics; and 87, Align Text with Graphics. Open the file named walking, which is stored in the Practice folder on the enclosed CD-ROM.

1. Delete the frog picture that displays at the top of the document.

2. In place of the frog picture, insert the picture named dog, which is stored in the Practice folder on the enclosed CD-ROM.

3. Format the dog picture so that text wraps square around the picture, and move the picture to display in the upper-left corner of the paragraph.

Check your work against solution file 1147XJ.

Task 2

Objectives covered: 88, Create a Chart; 89, Modify a Chart; and 90, Import Data into Charts. Open a blank Word document.

1. Insert a Microsoft Graph 2000 Chart into the blank document.

2. Import data into the Chart from the file named Competition.xls, which is stored in the Practice folder on the enclosed CD-ROM.

3. Set the minimum value on the Y-axis to 20, change the data bars to match the team names, and then return to Word's document view.

Check your work against solution file 1147XK.

Cheat Sheet

Add Bitmapped Graphics

- Click Insert, Picture, From File; or click ▦ Insert Picture on the Picture toolbar. Then, double-click the file name's icon, or select the file and click Insert.

- Click Insert, Object, Create New tab, click Bitmap Image in the Object type list box, click OK, and draw the graphic.

Delete Graphics

- Select the graphic and click ✂ Cut on the Standard toolbar.
- Select the graphic and press Delete.
- Select the graphic and press Backspace.
- Right-click the graphic and click Cut.

Reposition Graphics

- Click and drag the graphic to a new position.
- Select the graphic, open the Picture Format dialog box, click the Layout tab, and click Advanced.

Align Text with Graphics

- Click Text Wrapping icons on the Layout tab in the Picture Format dialog box.
- Click ▦ Text Wrapping on the Picture toolbar.

Create a Chart

1. Click Insert, Object, and Create New tab.
2. In the Object type list box, click Microsoft Graph 2000 Chart and click OK.
3. Replace the sample data on the datasheet.
4. Click anywhere on the Word document to close the datasheet.

Continued

Modify a Chart

- Click 📊 View Datasheet on the Chart view's Standard toolbar to open the datasheet.
- Click 📊 Chart Type or open the Chart menu and click Chart Type to open the Chart Type dialog box.
- Open the Format menu, click Chart Options, and click the Titles tab.
- Double-click a chart element, and then modify the settings of the resulting dialog box.
- Click 📊 Legend in the chart view's Standard toolbar.
- Click and drag the chart to a new location.
- Select the chart and drag a resizing handle.

Create a Chart from a Word Table

1. Select a table (not including rows or columns computing totals).
2. Click Insert, Object, and Create New tab.
3. Select Microsoft Graph 2000 Chart and click OK.
4. Click 📊 Chart Type drop-down arrow and select a chart style.
5. Click outside the graph or datasheet.

Import Data from Other Programs

1. Create a new chart.
2. Select the cell in the datasheet where you want the upper-left corner of the data to display.
3. Click Edit, Import File or click 📊 Import File.
4. Open the desired file.
5. Click OK.

CHAPTER 17

Designing Forms

Did you file your taxes last year? If so, you're all too familiar with completing forms! In this chapter, it's time to turn the tables a little—instead of filling in forms, you'll be creating them. Of course, this review doesn't mean you'll be sending your forms to the IRS, but you will be able to show Microsoft what you can do on the exam. In this chapter, you'll review how to:

- Create and Modify Forms
- Work with Form Controls

OBJECTIVE 91

Create and Modify Form

The purpose of this section is to debunk the notion that creating forms is complex. That's not a tall order, because most standard forms are simply tables. Therefore, if you know how to create tables (as described in Chapter 8, "Adding Columns, Tables, and Objects," Object 46 "Create a Table"), you can easily expand your repertoire of Word skills to include the art of form creation.

For the exam, you'll be required to know how to work with standard printable forms and online forms. There's one caveat: Although most forms are created using tables, you can also create forms that aren't based on tables (for example, you can insert form fields within text). On the exam, however, you will work with forms based on tables, and so that's the approach taken here. Besides, if you know how to add form elements to tables, you can easily use your skills to insert form elements into other document layouts.

When you create a form based on a table, the table cells contain labels and form elements, including check boxes, text fields, and drop-down lists. To help you create form elements, Word supplies the Forms toolbar, as shown in the following figure.

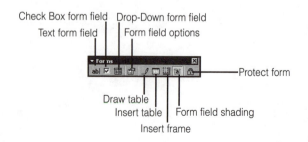

310

You can use the Forms toolbar buttons to perform the following actions:

- **Text Form Field**—Inserts a field in which users can enter text.
- **Check Box Form Field**—Inserts a check box that users can mark to specify a selection.
- **Drop-Down Form Field**—Inserts a drop-down list of items for users to choose from.
- **Form Field Options**—Displays a form field's option settings.
- **Draw Table**—Enables you to draw table boundaries and column, row, and cell divisions.
- **Insert Table**—Assists you in creating a table.
- **Insert Frame**—Creates a box, or frame, in the document.
- **Form Field Shading**—Toggles to display or hide the gray shading on form fields.
- **Protect Form**—Enables you to protect the current form's layout from changes, and it activates the online form features.

The three form field options—Text Form Field, Check Box Form Field, and Drop-Down Form Field—are discussed in more detail later in this chapter, in Objective 92.

With that brief introduction, you now know the basic supplies you can use to create a form—a table and the Forms toolbar. With these tools in hand, you're ready to create printed and online forms.

Create Printed Forms

Printed forms are just that—forms that you create and print out for people to complete either by handwriting or typing information into the form's fields. To create a printed form, follow these steps:

311

Part 2 • Expert Level

Whenever you design a form, you should always start by sketching your form's layout.

1. Click in a document where you want to insert the form.

2. Click 🧮 Insert Table on the Standard toolbar, and select the number of cells you want to create. Or, to convert existing text into a table text, select the text, open the Table menu, click Convert, select Text to Table, specify table settings in the Convert Text to Table dialog box, and click OK.

   To customize the table, click 📋 Tables and Borders in the Standard toolbar and modify cells. (You can also modify cells while you create a form or after you've inserted the form elements.)

3. If necessary, type text and labels into the appropriate table cells.

4. Open the View menu, click Toolbars, and click Forms, or right-click a toolbar and click Forms. The Forms toolbar opens.

5. Use the Forms toolbar to insert form fields. For example, to add check boxes, click in the cell where you want to insert a check box, and click ☑ Check Box Form Field on the Forms toolbar.

6. Save and print the form.

Create Online Forms

You can create an online form that people can open and complete in Word. Online forms are often used to help expedite office paperwork. For example, employees can easily use online forms to submit vacation requests, time cards, and expense reports.

To create an online form, you must create the form's layout, protect the form, and save it as a template, as described in the following steps:

1. Open the File menu and click New. The New dialog box opens.

2. On the General tab, select Blank Document, click the Template option, and click OK.

Objective 91 • Create and Modify Form

3. Create a table and insert the form's labels and form fields. (The next objective provides more information about form fields.)

4. After the form layout is complete, click 🔒 Protect Form on the Forms toolbar or open the Tools menu, click Protect Document, select Forms, and click OK.

5. Save the template. To print a complete form's data, click Tools, Options, Print tab, and select the Print data only for forms check box.

You must protect an online form before users can use the text boxes, check boxes and drop-down lists.

You can easily modify existing forms. If a form is a printable form, you can modify it as follows:

1. Open the form document.
2. Make the desired changes.
3. Save the document.
4. Print the form.

To modify an online form, you must open the form's template file to make the changes. To open a template, follow these steps:

1. Open the File menu and click Open, click 📂 Open on the Standard toolbar, or press Ctrl+O. The Open dialog box displays.

2. In the Files of type list box, select Document Templates, and display the form document in the file window.

3. Double-click the form's template icon. The template opens.

4. Open the Tools menu and click Unprotect document, or click 🔒 Protect Form on the Forms toolbar.

5. Make the desired changes to the form's layout.

6. Click 🔒 Protect on the Forms toolbar or open the Tools menu, click Protect Document, select Forms, and click OK.

7. Save and close the template.

Modify Forms

Part 2 • Expert Level

After you create a template, users can open the online form document based on the template. To use an online form, follow these steps:

1. Open the File menu and click New. The New dialog box opens.

2. Click the form template on the General tab in the New dialog box.

3. Select Document in the Create New section, and click OK.

4. After a form is opened, users can enter information into the form fields. Users can type information directly into text fields, and they can mark check boxes by pressing X. To select items on the drop-down lists, users can click the down arrow next to the field or click the field to view a pop-up menu. Furthermore, users can press F1 to view Help messages and press Tab and Shift+Tab to navigate from one field to the next.

5. Save the form.

92 OBJECTIVE

Work with Form Controls

After you create a form, you can work with the form's fields, or *form controls*, to customize your form's settings. As mentioned earlier, you can use the Forms toolbar to insert the three types of form fields. To reiterate, the three form field types and their field codes are:

- **Text Form Field**—*{ FORMCHECKBOX }*
- **Check Box Form Field**—*{ FORMDROPDOWN }*
- **Drop-Down Form Field**—*{ FORMTEXT }*

To insert a form field, click where you want to place the form field, and then click the form field button on the Forms toolbar.

After you insert a form field in a form, you need to define the field's options. Word provides form field options dialog boxes to assist in setting form field settings. You can open a form field's dialog box by performing any of the following actions:

- Double-click a form field.
- Click a form field, and click ![icon] Form Field Options on the Forms toolbar.
- Select a form field, right-click, and click Prope**r**ties.

Each field's options dialog box displays settings particular to the selected field.

When you open a Text Form field, the Text Form Field Options dialog box opens, as shown in the following figure.

To create Web forms, access the form controls on the Control Toolbox and Web Tools toolbars.

315

Part 2 • Expert Level

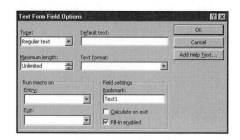

You can use the Text Form Field Options dialog box to specify the following settings:

- **Type**—Specifies the type of text that can be entered into the field, including regular text, numbers, date, current date, current time, and calculation.

- **Default text**—Indicates the text that should appear in the field (if any). Default text can include text, numbers, symbols, and spaces.

- **Maximum length**—Sets the maximum number of characters that the field can contain. By default, Unlimited is selected; 255 is the maximum number of characters that can be typed in a text form field.

- **Text format**—Specifies whether the default text will appear uppercase, lowercase, first capital, or title case.

The next form field on the agenda is the check box form field. When you open the Check Box Form Field Options dialog box, you are presented with check-box specific options, as you can see in the following figure.

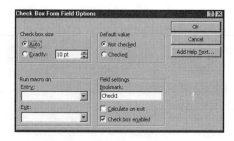

Objective 92 • Work with Form Controls

The Check Box Form Field Options dialog box enables you to set the following options:

- **Check Box Size**—Enables you to specify the size of the check box. You can choose whether to have Word automatically size the check box, or you can specify the size of the check box in points.

- **Default Value**—Indicates whether the check box will initially display selected or cleared.

The third form field options dialog box you need to review is the Drop-Down List Form Field Options dialog box. When you open the Drop-Down List Form Field Options dialog box, you are presented with drop-down list specific options, as you can see in the following figure.

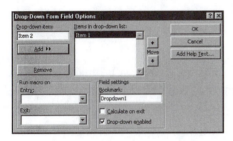

In the Drop-Down Form Field Options dialog box, you can add and remove drop-down list items by following these steps:

1. Click in the Drop-down item checkbox, type a list item name, and press Enter or click Add.

2. Continue to add entries to the drop-down list. To remove items from the list, select the item in the Items in drop-down list box and click Remove.

3. To organize list items, click an item, and click the move up and down arrows to position the item. The form's drop-down list displays the items in the order in which they appear in the Items in drop-down list box.

4. Click OK.

The first item in the Items in drop-down list box displays as the default option on the form.

317

Part 2 • Expert Level

Finally, in all three field options dialog boxes, you can use the following tools to further customize the fields:

- **Add Help Text**—Enables you to add help text relative to the selected field. When you click the Add Help Text button, the Help dialog box opens, as shown in the following figure. You can specify help text that displays in the status bar and help text that displays when a user presses F1.

Help message windows can contain up to 255 characters, and the status bar can contain up to 138 characters.

- **Run macro on**—Enables you to associate a macro with the text field. You can specify whether the macro runs when a user first clicks the field or when the user's cursor leaves the field.

- **Field settings**—Provides three field settings. You can use the Field settings options to name the text field so you can reference it when you create macros, specify whether to recalculate all the form fields after the insertion point leaves the selected field, and enable or disable the selected field.

After you set form field options, protect the form if it's an online form and save the document or template.

TAKE THE TEST

PRACTICE

Objectives covered: 91, Create and Modify Forms; and 92, Work with Form Controls. Open the file named Form1, which is stored in the Practice folder on the enclosed CD-ROM.

Task 1

1. Convert the text to a two-column table.

2. Use the existing text as form field labels, and use the Draw Table tool to create columns.

3. Insert text fields to the right of the First Name, Last Name, Date, and Time text labels.

4. Format the Date field to insert the current date, and format the Time text field to display the current time.

5. Insert check boxes to the right of the Yes and No labels.

6. Modify the check box after the word Yes so that it displays as selected.

Check your work against solution file 1147XL.

Objectives covered: 91, Create and Modify Forms; and 92, Work with Form Controls. Open the file named Form2, which is stored in the Practice folder on the enclosed CD-ROM.

Task 2

1. Open the Form2 template so that you can edit the template's settings.

2. Format the First Name text field to display the text *first name* in all uppercase letters.

3. To the right of the Birth Month label, insert a drop-down list box that contains the months of the year.

4. In the Favorite Color drop-down list, remove the *greenbacks* item, and change the Favorite Color list box to display the word *Blue* by default.

5. Turn off the field shading option.

6. Add a Help message box to the Favorite Color drop-down list that states: *Click your favorite color.*

Check your work against solution file 1147XM.

Cheat Sheet

Create Printed Forms

1. Click in a document.
2. Create a table.
3. Create labels in the table cells.
4. Click View, Toolbars, and click Forms, or right-click a toolbar and click Forms.
5. Insert form fields.
6. Save and print the form.

Create Online Forms

1. Click File, New.
2. Select Blank Document, click Template, and click OK.
3. Create a table and insert the form's labels and form fields.
4. Click 🔒 Protect Form on the Forms toolbar or click Tools, Protect Document, Forms, and click OK.
5. Save the template.

Modify Forms

1. Click File, Open; click 📂 Open; or press Ctrl+O.
2. In the Files of type list box, select Document Templates, and display the form document in the file window.
3. Double-click the form's template icon.
4. If necessary, click Tools, Unprotect document, or click 🔒 Protect Form.
5. Make the desired changes to the form's layout.
6. Click 🔒 Protect on the Forms toolbar or click Tools, Protect Document, Forms, and click OK.
7. Save and close the template.

Continued

Work with Form Controls

- Double-click a form field.
- Click a form field and click ▣ Form Field Options.
- Select a form field, right-click, and click Properties.

CHAPTER 18

Using Mail Merge

Mail merge is one of those features people tend to learn only when they really need to. If you've been fortunate enough to use Word's mail merge feature, you probably only need to brush up on the basics. If you haven't performed a mail merge in Word, you'll want to study this topic a little more closely. The expert exam takes Word's mail merge feature seriously, so, between easier tasks (like sorting lists and inserting comments), expect to see mail merge tasks. To help you prepare for mail merge questions, this chapter covers how to:

- Merge a Main Document with a Data Source
- Create a Data Source
- Create a Main Document
- Sort Merge Records
- Generate Labels
- Merge a Document Using Alternate Data Sources

OBJECTIVE 93

Merge a Main Document with a Data Source

When you perform a mail merge, you insert information, such as name and address data, into documents automatically. For example, you might want to merge a collection of addresses into a form letter. A mail merge operation involves three documents: the main document, the data source, and the merged document.

- **Data Source**—The collection of information that is inserted into a main document, such as a series of names and addresses.

- **Main Document**—The framework document that holds the text and graphics that remain the same in each merged document, along with merge field placeholders. For example, the body of a form letter can be a main document.

- **Merged Document**—The final product of a merge operation, such as a document containing a series of completed form letters or labels.

Word assists you in the complex task of conducting mail merges by providing the Mail Merge Helper, as shown in the following figure.

Because the Mail Merge Helper is integral to mail merge operations in Word, this chapter reviews this tool first. Furthermore, the Mail Merge Helper assists you in creating main documents and source data. To open and run the Mail Merge Helper, follow these steps:

1. Open the Tools menu and click Mail Merge. The Mail Merge Helper opens.

2. In the Main document section, click Create. The Create drop-down list displays and enables you to select whether you want to create form letters, labels, envelopes, or catalogs.

3. On the Create drop-down list, select the type of main document you want to create. A dialog box opens, asking you to specify whether you want to create the main document in the current document or a new document.

4. Click Active Window or New Main Document. Notice the Edit button becomes available to the right of the Create button.

5. In the Data source section, click Get Data. The Get Data drop-down list displays. The Get Data drop-down list enables you to create or open a data source.

6. Specify whether to open or create a data source.

7. Enter data into a data source (as described later in this chapter in Objective 94) or locate and click an existing data source.

To reopen the Mail Merge Helper, click Tools, Mail Merge.

325

Part 2 • Expert Level

8. If necessary, click 🔲 Mail Merge Helper in the main document's Mail Merge toolbar or click Tools, Mail Merge to redisplay the Mail Merge Helper dialog box.

9. In the Main document section, click Edit and select the document you want to edit.

10. Insert the merge fields, text, and graphics into the main document (as described in Objective 95).

11. Save the file and click 🔲 Mail Merge Helper to redisplay the Mail Merge Helper.

12. Click Merge. The Merge dialog box opens, as shown in the following figure.

13. Specify merge options, such as where to merge the information (new document, printer, email, or fax), which records to merge (all or a specified range), and whether to print blank lines if no information appears in a field.

14. Click Merge. The mail merge operation takes place.

94 OBJECTIVE

Create a Data Source

Now that you've reviewed the big picture, the next few sections break down the process into more detail. In this section, you'll review how to create a data source.

The Mail Merge Helper assists you in creating data sources. In particular, the Mail Merge Helper opens a Data Form dialog box when you are ready to create and modify data source information, as shown in the following figure.

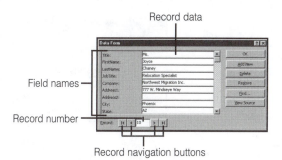

After you create a data source, you can open the data source file just as you open any other Word file. When you open a data source file, you'll see a table in which each column represents a data source field.

Part 2 • Expert Level

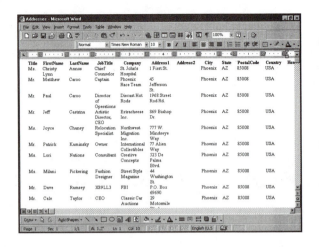

To create a data source, follow these steps:

1. In the Mail Merge Helper, click Get Data, and select Create Data Source. The Create Data Source dialog box opens.

The Create Data Source dialog box enables you to add and remove available fields from your data source document. By default, Word automatically includes common data source fields. For the exam, you won't need to add additional fields or delete any default data fields.

2. Click OK. The Save As dialog box opens.

3. Name and save the data source document. A dialog box appears stating that you have not added any records to the data source file. That's the next step.

4. Click Edit Data Source. The Data Form dialog box opens. You can open the Data Form dialog box for any data source by clicking Edit (next to Get Data) on the Mail Merge Helper and select a data source.

5. Enter information into the field name text boxes for the first record. You might have to scroll to see all the fields.

6. Press Enter or click Add New.

   To delete a record, display the record and click Delete. To undo changes to the displayed record, click Restore.

7. Continue to add records. After all the records have been added, click OK.

To edit data source information, you can reopen the Data Form dialog box at anytime from within the Mail Merge Helper or you can click ▣ Edit Data Source on the Mail Merge toolbar. Furthermore, you can open the data source document directly and make changes using standard Word editing procedures.

OBJECTIVE 95

Create a Main Document

After you create a data source, you are ready to create a main document. When you close the Data Form dialog box, Word automatically returns you to the main document. If you've closed the main document, you can reopen it just as you open any other Word document.

Basically, creating a main document consists of adding the document's standard text and graphics (if any) and inserting merge field placeholders, as shown in the following figure.

When you specify that a document is a main document, Word displays the Mail Merge toolbar, as shown in the following figure. You use the Mail Merge toolbar's buttons to insert merge fields into your main document.

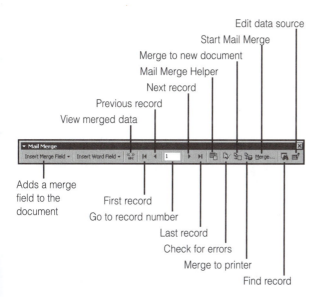

In this section, you'll review how to create a basic form letter. Later in the chapter, you'll review how to create labels. To create a form letter, follow these steps:

1. In the main document, enter any text and graphics that you want to display in every form letter.

2. When you want to enter variable information from the data source, click Insert Merge Field button on the Mail Merge toolbar, and select the merge field name you want to place in the document. A merge field placeholder displays in the document.

3. To preview your form letter, click [icon] View Merged Data to see the information from the first record displayed in the main document.

4. Save the document and click Merge on the Mail Merge toolbar. The Merge dialog box opens as shown earlier in this chapter.

5. Specify the merge settings and click Merge. The form letters are created in a single Word document, and each letter is offset by a section break.

Add spaces and commas around merge field placeholders as you would add spaces and commas around inserted text.

331

OBJECTIVE 96

Sort Merge Records

Often, you can save quite a bit of time by sorting source data before you print. For example, if you're using the merge feature to create letters and labels, you probably won't want to spend a few extra hours matching up the labels with the letters. Therefore, Word enables you to sort data source information. To do so, follow these steps:

1. Open the main document and display the Mail Merge Helper (click Tools, Mail Merge or click ![] Mail Merge Helper on the Mail Merge toolbar).

2. In the Merge the data with the document section, click Query Options. The Query Options dialog box opens.

3. Click the Sort Records tab. The Sort Records tab displays as shown in the following figure.

4. In the Sort by drop-down list, click a data field to sort by and mark whether you want to sort in Ascending or Descending order. If desired, select data fields in the subsequent Then by text boxes.

5. Click OK.

97 OBJECTIVE

Generate Labels

Merging mailing labels is a combination of conducting a mail merge and printing a label. (Printing labels is covered in Chapter 10, Objective 56.) In this section, you'll review how to create labels by merging a data source with a main document. This section assumes you've already created a data source. (On the exam, you won't be required to create a complete data source—you'll simply need to modify and work with an existing data source.)

To generate mailing labels, follow these steps:

1. Open the Mail Merge Helper and select Mailing Labels on the Create drop-down list

2. Open a data source, and click Set Up Main Document. The Label Options dialog box opens.

3. On the Label Options dialog box, specify the printer settings, a label product number, and a label product number.

4. Click OK. The Create Labels dialog box opens.

333

Part 2 • Expert Level

5. Click the Insert Merge Field button and select merge field names on the drop-down list. Selecting merge field enters merge field placeholders into the Create Labels dialog box, as shown in the following figure.

6. Click OK.

7. Click Merge in the Mail Merge Helper, and then click Merge in the Merge dialog box.

Your mailing labels main document should appear similar to the following figure.

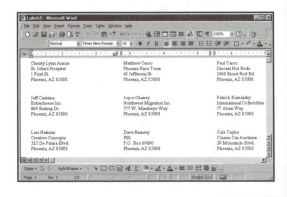

334

98 OBJECTIVE

Merge a Document Using Alternate Data Sources

You can use just about any type of data source to conduct a mail merge operation, including Word tables, Outlook contact lists, Excel worksheets, Access databases, and text files.

The one caveat is that alternate data sources must have a header section. This means that the very top row of the data source must contain the field names you will use for the mail merge. Consequently, the corresponding data must be listed properly under each header/field name label.

For the exam, you will not need to create an alternate data source. Instead, you will need to merge data from an alternate data source to conduct a mail merge. Using data from an alternate data source means that when you select a data source on the Mail Merge Helper, you will have to specify the file type in the Open Data Source dialog box. To do so, follow these steps:

1. In the Mail Merge Helper, click Get Data, and click Open Data Source. The Open Data Source dialog box displays.

2. In the Files of type drop-down list box, select the file type of the alternate data source, such as MS Excel Worksheets.

3. Navigate to the location of the alternate data source file,

select the file, and click <u>O</u>pen. ==An application-specific dialog box might appear.== For example, if you are opening an Excel worksheet, you can choose to open the entire workbook or a specified range. Click the appropriate options in the application-specific dialog box.

4. Insert the merge fields, text, and graphics into the main document.

5. Save the file and click 🗐 Mail Merge Helper to redisplay the Mail Merge Helper.

6. Click <u>M</u>erge, specify merge options, and click <u>M</u>erge.

Objectives covered: 93, Merge a Main Document with a Data

TAKE THE TEST

Task 1 — source; 94, Create a Data Source; 95, Create a Main Document; and 96, Sort Merge Records. Open the file named Letter, which is stored in the Practice folder on the enclosed CD-ROM.

1. After the word *Dear*, insert fields for title, first name, and last name.

2. Add a data source record to the Address data source consisting of the following information: Mr. Matthew Roberts, Entomologist, Bughouse Research, 65 Cicada Circle, Phoenix, AZ 85008.

3. Sort the Address data source records by last name and then first name in ascending order.

4. Merge the Address data source with the main document named letter.

Check your work against solution file 1147XN.

Objectives covered: 93, Merge a Main Document with a Data Source; 97, Generate Labels; and 98, Merge a Document Using Alternate Data Sources. Open a new blank document.

Task 2

1. Create Avery Standard labels (product number 5160) that contain first and last names on the first line, job titles on the second line, and company names on the third line. Use the data source named Excel_Addresses, which is an Excel document stored in the Practice folder on the enclosed CD-ROM.

Check your work against solution file 1147XO.

Cheat Sheet

Merge a Main Document with a Data Source

1. Click Tools, Mail Merge.
2. Click Create, and select a main document type.
3. Click Active Window or New Main Document.
4. Click Get Data, and specify whether to open or create a data source.
5. Enter data into a data source or open an existing data source.
6. In the Main document section, click Edit and select the document you want to edit.
7. Insert the merge fields, text, and graphics into the main document and save the file.
8. Click 🗐 Mail Merge Helper.
9. Click Merge, specify merge options, and click Merge.

Create a Data Source

1. In the Mail Merge Helper, click Get Data, select Create Data Source, and click OK.
2. Name and save the data source document, and click Edit Data Source.
3. Enter information into the Data Form.
4. Press Enter or click Add New.
5. Continue to add records.
6. Click OK.

Create a Main Document

1. Enter any text and graphics that you want to display in the main document.
2. Click Insert Merge Field on the Mail Merge toolbar, to enter merge field placeholders in the document.

3. Click ![icon] View Merged Data to preview the document.

   4. Save the document and click <u>M</u>erge on the Mail Merge toolbar.

   5. Specify the merge settings and click M<u>e</u>rge.

Sort Merge Records

   1. Open the main document and display the Mail Merge Helper.

   2. Click <u>Q</u>uery Options.

   3. Click the S<u>o</u>rt Records tab.

   4. In the S<u>o</u>rt by drop-down list, click a data field to sort by and mark whether you want to sort in <u>A</u>scending or <u>D</u>escending order. Select data fields in the subsequent Then <u>b</u>y text boxes.

   5. Click OK.

Generate Labels

   1. Open the Mail Merge Helper and select <u>M</u>ailing Labels on the <u>C</u>reate drop-down list. *choose Active Window or New main Document*

   2. Open a data source, and click <u>S</u>et Up Main Document. *click Get Data*

   3. On the Label Options dialog box, specify the printer settings, a label product name, and a label product number.

   4. Click OK.

   5. Use the Insert Merge Field button to enter merge field placeholders into the Create Labels dialog box, and click OK.

   6. Click <u>M</u>erge in the Mail Merge Helper, and then click <u>M</u>erge in the Merge dialog box.

Merge a Document Using Alternate Data Sources

   1. In the Mail Merge Helper, click <u>G</u>et Data, and click <u>O</u>pen Data Source.

   2. In the Files of <u>t</u>ype drop-down list box, select the file type of the alternate data source, such as MS Excel Worksheets.

Continued

3. Navigate to the location of the alternate data source file, select the file, and click <u>O</u>pen.
4. Complete application-specific dialog boxes if necessary.
5. Insert the merge fields, text, and graphics into the main document, and save the file.
6. Click Mail Merge Helper.
7. Click <u>M</u>erge, specify merge options, and click <u>M</u>erge.

CHAPTER

19

Activating Macros and Customizing Toolbars

Working with macros is the topic of discussion in this book's concluding chapter. But don't let the topic's position within the text lull you into complacency. In Microsoft's eyes, knowing all about macros is an integral skill for expert-level Word users. As you will see, the exam thoroughly covers macros—from running and modifying existing macros to copying macros from one document to another. Therefore, before you take the exam, ensure that you know how to:

- Create, Apply, and Edit Macros
- Copy, Rename, and Delete Macros
- Customize Toolbars

OBJECTIVE 99

Create, Apply, and Edit Macros

A macro consists of a series of Word commands and instructions combined into a single command that you assign to a toolbar, menu, or keyboard combination. The tasks that you perform repeatedly are perfect candidates for becoming macros. Instead of continually opening a dialog box or repeatedly performing multiple steps to format an element, you can create and run a single macro.

Record a Macro

The act of creating a macro is referred to as *recording* a macro. This is because Word provides a tool that acts similar to a tape recorder, as shown in the following figure.

Stop button — Pause button

Looking at the big-picture, the process of recording a macro is straightforward—you open the recorder, perform the actions you want to automate, stop the recorder, and save your changes. Word saves your actions as Visual Basic code. You'll need to know at least a little about Visual Basic to pass the Word expert exam, and so you should review some Visual Basic code and become familiar with its appearance and organization.

One important point to remember when you're recording macros pertains to mouse movements. You can record click commands and options, but the macro recorder doesn't record mouse movements within a document window. Therefore, to work around this, you need to select text before opening the macro recorder or use the keyboard equivalents for selecting text, if necessary.

Now that you've reviewed the basics, you're ready to walk through the following steps, which describe how to record a macro:

1. ==Determine the exact actions you want to record before you create a macro.== Figure out the most direct route to the end result. The more actions you record in a macro the longer it takes for the macro to run.

2. Open the <u>T</u>ools menu, click <u>M</u>acro, and click <u>M</u>acros or press Alt+F8. The Macros window opens, as shown in the following figure.

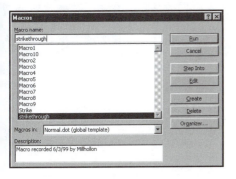

3. In the Macros window, click <u>R</u>ecord New Macro. The Record Macro dialog box appears.

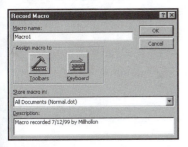

343

Part 2 • Expert Level

Macro names must begin with a letter and can contain up to 80 letters and numbers; spaces and symbols are not allowed.

4. Type a name in the Macro name text box.
5. In the Store macro in list box, select the template or document in which you want to store the new macro. By default, All Documents (Normal.dot) is selected.
6. Type a description of the macro in the Description box.
7. Select an icon to assign the macro to a toolbar button or a keyboard command, or you can choose to have it assigned to neither:

   - **If you select Toolbars**—The Commands tab in the Customize dialog box displays, as shown in the following figure.

   In the Commands list box, click the icon next to the macro name, and drag the icon to a toolbar or menu. Then, click the Modify Selection button in the Customize dialog box to configure the settings for the button. After you've added the toolbar button or menu item, click Close to begin recording the macro.

   - **If you select Keyboard**—The Customize Keyboard dialog box appears, as shown in the following figure.

Objective 99 • Create, Apply, and Edit Macros

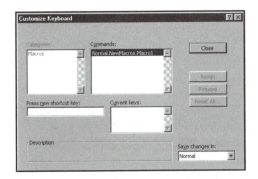

Select the macro name in the Commands list box, and press the keyboard shortcut you want to assign to the macro. The keyboard combination displays in the Press new shortcut key text box. The text below the text box indicates whether the keyboard shortcut is currently unassigned or if it is assigned to another task. After you've added the keyboard command, click Close to begin recording the macro.

- **If you opt to select neither Toolbars nor Keyboard**—Click OK in the Record Macro dialog box to begin recording the macro.

8. Perform the steps necessary to create the macro. When you're recording a macro, the recorder displays on your screen and a small cassette tape graphic accompanies your mouse pointer.

9. When you've finished recording the macro, click ▪ Stop Recording on the recorder.

Run a Macro

As described in the previous section, when you record a macro, you can assign the macro to a toolbar, menu, or a keyboard command. Therefore, to run a macro, do any of the following:

- Click the macro's toolbar button.
- Choose the macro's menu command.
- Press the macro's keyboard combination.

345

Part 2 • Expert Level

- Press Alt+F8 to open the Macros dialog box, select a macro, and click <u>R</u>un.

- Open the <u>T</u>ools menu, click <u>M</u>acro, click <u>M</u>acros, select a macro, and click <u>R</u>un.

Edit a Macro

You can edit macros in two ways—you can rerecord the macro or you can alter the Visual Basic text. ==On the exam, you'll be required to alter Visual Basic text at the most rudimentary level.== The key is to demonstrate that you know how to access a macro's Visual Basic code, and after you've accessed it, to show that you can make enough sense out of the code to understand what's going on.

One of the easiest ways to practice editing a macro is to delete unnecessary code. Not only does this help you become familiar with Visual Basic code, but it also helps to speed up your macros. Whenever a macro recording is created by selecting an option in a dialog box, the recorder tracks all the settings. The macro does not need to know which settings are inactive to perform correctly. Therefore, you can remove the unnecessary properties by deleting the extra code lines. To illustrate, the following figure shows the Visual Basic code for a macro design to draw a strikethrough mark through a letter whenever the Alt+Z keyboard combination is pressed.

Visual Basic code window

Because the macro doesn't involve formatting settings, such as Bold, Italic, Doublestrike, Outline, and so forth, those code lines can be deleted. On the exam, you will be told which code lines you need to modify or delete. Therefore, read the instructions carefully to ensure that you modify the macro properly.

To edit a macro (without rerecording it), follow these steps:

1. Press Alt+F8 or open the <u>T</u>ools menu, click <u>M</u>acro, and click <u>M</u>acros. The Macros dialog box appears.
2. In the <u>M</u>acro name list box, select the macro you want to edit.
3. Click <u>E</u>dit. The Microsoft Visual Basic window opens.
4. Edit the Visual Basic code by replacing, deleting, or adding text.
5. Click 💾 Save
6. Open the <u>F</u>ile menu, click <u>C</u>lose and Return to Microsoft Word or press Alt+Q.

To open the Visual Basic window directly, click Tools, Macro, Visual Basic Editor or press Alt+F11.

347

OBJECTIVE 100

Copy, Rename, and Delete Macros

You can manage macros in much the same way you manage styles. You can copy, rename, and delete macros in an Organizer window, as shown in the following figure.

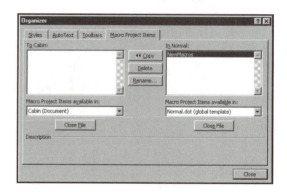

In the next few sections, you'll review how to copy, rename, and delete macros. After that, you'll know enough about macros to become a certified expert-level Word specialist.

Copy a Macro

To copy a macro from one document to another, you must first open the Organizer dialog box. In the Organizer dialog box, you select and copy macro names from one document and copy them to another. The specific steps required to copy macros are as follows:

1. Press Alt+F8 or open the Tools menu, click Macro, and click Macros. The Macros dialog box appears.

2. Click Organizer. The Organizer dialog box appears. By default, the right box displays the current document's macros and the left box displays the `Normal.dot` template's macros. ==You can change which document's macros display in either box by clicking the Close File button.== When you close a file, the button changes to Open File. Click the Open File button, and open the desired document.

3. Select the macro you want to copy, and click <u>C</u>opy. The copied macro displays in both boxes.

4. Click Close.

Practice using the Organizer—you need to copy macros from one specified document to another on the exam.

Rename a Macro

The Organizer dialog box comes into play when you rename macros. The process of renaming a macro is similar to copying a macro. To rename a macro, follow these steps:

1. Press Alt+F8 or open the <u>T</u>ools menu, click <u>M</u>acro, and click <u>M</u>acros. The Macros dialog box appears.

2. Click Organizer. The Organizer dialog box appears.

3. Select the macro you want to rename, click <u>R</u>ename, enter the macro's new name, and click OK.

4. Click Close, and click Yes.

Delete a Macro

Of the three tasks—copying, renaming, and deleting—deleting entails the fewest steps. To delete a macro, you don't have to open the Organizer window (although you can, if you prefer). Instead, ==you can delete a macro within the Macros dialog box,== as described here:

1. Press Alt+F8 or open the <u>T</u>ools menu, click <u>M</u>acro, and click <u>M</u>acros. The Macros dialog box appears.

2. Select the macro you want to delete, and click <u>D</u>elete. Click Yes to delete the macro.

3. Click Close.

You can delete macros in the Macros dialog box or in the Organizer dialog box.

OBJECTIVE 101

Customize Toolbars

Frequently, you'll find that Microsoft offers a toolbar button that you can use in place of creating a macro. Fortunately, you can easily customize existing toolbars as well as create custom toolbars to make accessing often-used buttons a snap (or, more accurately, a click). In the next few sections, you'll review how to add and remove toolbar buttons, as well as reset Word's default settings to predefined toolbars. Finally, you'll review how to create a custom toolbar.

Add and Remove Toolbar Buttons

Word 2000 makes adding and removing toolbar buttons to existing toolbars extremely easy. You might have noticed that most docked toolbars have a drop-down list button along the far-right edge and floating toolbars have a drop-down arrow to the left of the toolbar name. If you click the drop-down arrow, you'll see an option to add or remove buttons, as shown in the figure.

To add and remove toolbar buttons, follow these steps:

1. Show the toolbar you want to change.

2. Click the <u>A</u>dd or Remove Buttons drop-down arrow, and point to <u>A</u>dd or Remove Buttons on the shortcut menu. A second shortcut menu that shows the buttons available for the current toolbar opens, as shown in the following figure.

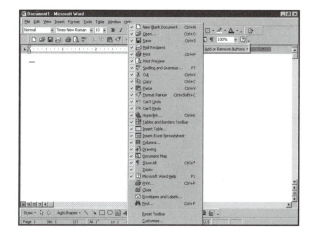

To remove a toolbar bar button quickly, press Alt and drag the button off the toolbar.

3. On the button menu, click toolbar icons to select or clear the check boxes. Items displaying a check box are included on the toolbar.

You can also modify existing toolbars by opening the Customize dialog box and dragging icons, as described later in this chapter in the "Create Custom Toolbars" section.

Reset Toolbars

You can reset a built-in toolbar that has been changed. When you reset a toolbar, the toolbar's display reverts to Word's default settings. The method used to reset a toolbar is similar to adding and removing buttons. To reset a toolbar, follow these steps:

1. Show the toolbar you want to reset.

2. Click the Add or Remove Buttons drop-down arrow, and point to Add or Remove Buttons on the pop-up menu.

3. On the button pop-up menu, click Reset toolbar. The toolbar reverts to Word's default settings.

You can also reset a toolbar using the Tools menu. To do so, open the Tools menu, click Customize, and display the Toolbars tab. Then, select the toolbar name, and click Reset.

351

Part 2 • Expert Level

Create Custom Toolbars

You can create custom toolbars that contain only the buttons you need. You can add existing Word buttons to a custom toolbar, or you can add macro toolbar buttons to a custom toolbar. You can manipulate and manage custom toolbars in the same way you work with other toolbars in Word.

To create a custom toolbar, you must first open the Toolbar tab in the Customize dialog box, as shown in the following figure.

While the Customize dialog box is open, you can click and drag icons on open toolbars to reposition/remove them.

Notice that checkmarks display next to currently open toolbars. The Customize dialog box is helpful for displaying, creating, renaming, deleting, and resetting toolbars. To create a custom toolbar, follow these steps:

1. Open the Tools menu, and click Customize; open the View menu, click Toolbars, and click Customize; or open the Add or Remove Buttons menu from any toolbar and click Customize. The Customize dialog box appears.

2. Click the Toolbars tab, if necessary.

3. Click New. The New Toolbar dialog box appears, as shown in the figure.

Objective 101 • Customize Toolbars

4. In the Toolbar name text box, type a toolbar name.

5. Click the Make toolbar available to drop-down arrow and select the template or document in which you want to save the toolbar. By default, custom toolbars are saved in the Normal template.

6. Click OK. A small empty toolbar displays on screen.

7. In the Customize dialog box, click the Commands tab, select a category in the Categories list, and drag buttons from the Commands list onto the newly created toolbar. To remove buttons, drag them off the toolbar while the Customize dialog box is still open.

8. After you've added all the necessary buttons to the toolbar, click Close.

To delete a toolbar, select the toolbar name in the Toolbars tab on the Customize dialog box and click Delete.

353

PRACTICE

TAKE THE TEST

Task 1

Objectives covered: 99, Create, Apply and Edit Macros; and 100, Copy, rename, and delete macros. Open a new document.

1. In a new document, enter text, and create a macro named Strikethrough that creates strikethrough text when you press Alt+1.

2. Edit the Strikethrough macro Visual Basic code to remove extra formatting (false) settings.

3. Copy the macro named Mountains from the Vacation.doc file to the Cabin.doc file.

4. Delete the Rustic macro in the Cabin.doc file.

Check your work in Steps 1 and 2 against the Visual Basic code found in solution file 1147XP.

Task 2

Objectives covered: 101, Customize Toolbars. Open a blank document.

1. Modify the Standard toolbar to include the Find button.

2. Create a custom toolbar named Break Time that includes the Page Break and Time buttons from the Insert category.

Check your work against the figure shown in solution file 1147XQ.

Cheat Sheet

Record a Macro

1. Click Tools, Macro, Macros or press Alt+F8.
2. Click Record New Macro.
3. Type a name in the Macro name text box.
4. In the Store macro in drop-down list box, select a template or document.
5. Type a description in the Description box.
6. Select icons to assign the macro to a toolbar, a keyboard command, or neither.
7. Perform the steps necessary to create the macro.
8. Click ■ Stop Recording on the recorder.

Run a Macro

- Click the macro's toolbar button.
- Choose the macro's menu command.
- Press the macro's keyboard combination.
- Press Alt+F8 to open the Macros dialog box, select a macro, and click Run.
- Open the Tools menu, click Macro, click Macros, select a macro, and click Run.

Edit a Macro

1. Press Alt+F8 or open the Tools menu, click Macro, and click Macros.
2. In the Macro name list box, select a macro.
3. Click Edit.
4. Edit the Visual Basic code by replacing, deleting, or adding text.

Continued

5. Click 🖫 Save.
6. Open the <u>F</u>ile menu, click <u>C</u>lose and Return to Microsoft Word or press Alt+Q.

Copy a Macro

1. Press Alt+F8 or open the <u>T</u>ools menu, click <u>M</u>acro, and click <u>M</u>acros.
2. Click Organizer.
3. Select a macro, and click <u>C</u>opy.
4. Click Close.

Rename a Macro

1. Press Alt+F8 or open the <u>T</u>ools menu, click <u>M</u>acro, and click <u>M</u>acros.
2. Click Organizer.
3. Select the macro you want to rename, click <u>R</u>ename, enter the macro's new name, and click OK.
4. Click Close, and click Yes.

Delete a Macro

1. Press Alt+F8 or open the <u>T</u>ools menu, click <u>M</u>acro, and click <u>M</u>acros.
2. Select the macro you want to delete, and click <u>D</u>elete.
3. Click Close.

Add and Remove Toolbar Buttons

1. Show the toolbar you want to change.
2. Click the toolbar's <u>A</u>dd or Remove Buttons drop-down arrow, and point to <u>A</u>dd or Remove Buttons on the shortcut menu.

3. Click toolbar icons to select or clear the check boxes.

Reset Toolbars

1. Show the toolbar you want to reset.
2. Click the Add or Remove Buttons drop-down arrow, and point to Add or Remove Buttons on the pop-up menu.
3. On the button pop-up menu, click Reset toolbar.

Create Custom Toolbars

1. Open the Tools menu, and click Customize; open the View menu, click Toolbars, and click Customize; or open the Add or Remove Buttons menu from any toolbar and click Customize.
2. Click the Toolbars tab, if necessary.
3. Click New.
4. Type a toolbar name.
5. Select the template or document that you want to save the toolbar in.
6. Click OK.
7. Click the Commands tab, select a category, and drag buttons onto the newly created toolbar. To remove buttons, drag them off the toolbar.
8. Click Close.

PART III

Appendices

- Student Preparation Guide
- Objectives Index

APPENDIX A

Student Preparation Guide

Microsoft's certified professional program has certainly been a plus in my line of work. Not only has my career flourished, but I've also become much more adept in streamlining my work tasks in Office products. Most relative to this book, I've passed both the MOUS Word core-level and expert-level exams.

From my personal test-taking experience, discussions with other test-takers, communication with computer-industry professionals, and my experience in writing, developing, and editing computer-training books, I've gleaned some practical test-taking knowledge. For your convenience, this section presents some hints and directions that you might find valuable when preparing for the MOUS Word exams.

Test Specs

The exams are hands on. In other words, there are no multiple choice, Yes/No, or fill-in-the blank questions. You will be asked to follow directions and use the MS Word application to complete tasks. After completing each task, you click the Next button to move to the next task. You cannot return to preceding tasks after you've clicked the Next button. Therefore, try your best to complete each task, but, if completing a particular a task seems to be taking too much time (2-3 minutes), you should move on.

Passing is 75 to 80% correct. You will be given about one hour to complete the test. A small amount of leeway is given to read the questions, about 20 minutes. This means that you are given 60 minutes for actual working time and 80 minutes total time to complete the exam. As soon as you start to work on a task, the one-hour clock starts. The number of questions varies with each Word exam, but you should expect from 40 to 50 questions.

During the Test

The most important piece of advice concerning the Word MOUS tests is to read each question carefully and don't do any more or less than the question asks. Try to imagine that someone has asked you to perform a task and that he or she will now look at your terminal screen to see the results.

One test-taker asked why they had failed the exam. They had been working with Word for years, and the questions were not that hard to answer. The reason turned out to be that they had done what the instructions asked and then they saved and closed the document. Unless specifically asked to do so, leave the answer exposed on the screen when you move to the next question.

Don't change the view unless asked to do so. The view of the answer should not be obscured by leaving dialog boxes or toolbars floating over the screen.

Follow the instructions given to you at the test site. If you have any problems with your machine at the testing center, immediately bring it to the administrator's attention. For example, during the exam, your screen should always show the menu bar, Standard toolbar, and Formatting toolbar. If basic window elements are missing or the system freezes, notify the test administrator as soon as possible.

Be Prepared

You will have a limited amount of time to complete the test. Do not count on being able to use the Help file to find information, although ScreenTips display. Try to learn more than one way to complete a job. There is usually a keyboard equivalent for items on the menu bar. You will be scored on your results. In the past, some options have been grayed out, forcing users to find alternate means.

The *Word 2000 Cheat Sheet* book is designed to help you learn alternative methods of accomplishing tasks. After each Practice element, the book includes a Cheat Sheet short list, which details, in abbreviated form, any steps or terms used in the chapter.

The tear card inside the front cover of this book also includes tables that outline the various methods for issuing a command: keyboard shortcuts, toolbar buttons, and Menu command strings. Tear out the card and use it to review the shortcuts in the last few minutes before stepping into the exam room.

You will not be allowed to bring any books or papers into the testing area. So, use the Tear Card and Cheat Sheets for review, but do not become dependent on them.

Appendix A • Student Preparation Guide

For More Information

The main web site for information about the exams is `http://www.mous.net`. This site will also give you directions to an Authorized Testing Center (ATC). Call 1-800-933-4493 if you need more details.

The program is international. If you live in Japan, Brazil, or Latin America, there is information concerning test sites and local variations.

Several newsgroups have formed to discuss the tests. Try `msnews.microsoft.com`, `microsoft.public.cert.exam.mous`, or `microsoft.public.certification.office`.

Also, there is an online e-zine `http://OfficeCert.com`. OfficeCert.com has a discussion forum and articles relating to the examinations, applications, and job-hunting techniques.

Take a Break

The standard advice you receive for every potentially stressful testing situation applies to the MOUS exams as well.

Review the information before going to sleep and then get a good night's rest before the test. The Tear Card and Cheat Sheets will give you an opportunity to review the skills to be used on the day of the test, but they are not a substitute for some good practice sessions.

After you get into the testing room, relax. Sit comfortably (don't cross your legs!), and accept that you'll do your best. Think of the entire experience as a fun adventure, and enjoy the challenge.

When the test is over, you'll see your score on the computer screen, and the administrator will give you a printout of your certificate if you pass. (The official certificate arrives by snail mail within a few weeks.) The printed certificate also points out areas of weakness if you missed particular topics or took an extended amount of time to complete a task. If you don't meet the exam's breakpoint, you receive a printout that suggests areas of study.

After the test, you can review your score and weak areas. The *Word 2000 Cheat Sheet* book is developed using the Objectives and Activities that make up the examination. Appendix B includes the core-level and expert-level objective lists and the location in the book for a discussion of each task.

When you see that you have passed, pat yourself on the back and treat yourself to some small pleasure. (The testing center I regularly attend is right next door to a Borders bookstore and coffee shop!). Keep your printout and wait for about four to six weeks for your certificate.

Good luck to you. You can do it.

APPENDIX B

Nivo #	Objective	Page #
W2000.1	**WORKING WITH TEXT**	
W2000.1.1	Use the Undo, Redo, and Repeat command	40
W2000.1.2	Apply font formats (Bold, Italic, and Underline)	52
W2000.1.3	Use the Spelling feature	110
W2000.1.4	Use the Thesaurus feature	113
W2000.1.5	Use the Grammar feature	115
W2000.1.6	Insert page breaks	135
W2000.1.7	Highlight Text in document	64
W2000.1.8	Insert and move text	28, 31
W2000.1.9	Cut, copy, Paste, and Paste Special using the Office Clipboard	37
W2000.1.10	Copy formats using the Format Painter	65
W2000.1.11	Select and change font and font size	59
W2000.1.12	Find and replace text	37
W2000.1.13	Apply character effects (superscript, subscript, strikethrough, small caps, and outline)	56
W2000.1.14	Insert date and time	42
W2000.1.15	Insert symbols	43
W2000.1.16	Create and apply frequently used text with AutoCorrect	44
W2000.2	**WORKING WITH PARAGRAPHS**	
W2000.2.1	Align text in paragraphs (Center, Left, Right, and justified)	80
W2000.2.2	Add bullets and numbering	72, 75
W2000.2.3	Set character, line, and paragraph spacing options	83
W2000.2.4	Apply borders and shading to paragraphs	86
W2000.2.5	Use indentation options (Left, Right, First Line, and Hanging Indent)	91
W2000.2.6	Use Tabs command (Center, Decimal, Left, and Right)	94
W2000.2.7	Create an outline style numbered list	77
W2000.2.8	Set tabs with leaders	97

Appendix B

Nivo #	Objective	Page #
W2000.3	**WORKING WITH DOCUMENTS**	
W2000.3.1	Print a document	184
W2000.3.2	Use print preview	180
W2000.3.3	Use Web Page Preview	183
W2000.3.4	Navigate through a document	106
W2000.3.5	Insert page numbers	120
W2000.3.6	Set page orientation	130
W2000.3.7	Set margins	131
W2000.3.8	Use GoTo to locate specific elements in a document	119
W2000.3.9	Create and modify page numbers	120
W2000.3.10	Create and modify headers and footers	122
W2000.3.11	Align text vertically	133
W2000.3.12	Create and use newspaper columns	144
W2000.3.13	Revise column structure	144
W2000.3.14	Prepare and print envelopes and labels	185, 189
W2000.3.15	Apply styles	138
W2000.3.16	Create sections with formatting that differs from other sections	136
W2000.3.17	Use click and type	28
W2000.4	**MANAGING FILES**	
W2000.4.1	Use Save	16
W2000.4.2	Locate and open an existing document	4
W2000.4.3	Use Save As (different name, location, or format)	17
W2000.4.4	Create a folder	22
W2000.4.5	Create a new document using a Wizard	7
W2000.4.6	Save as a Web Page	17
W2000.4.7	Use templates to create a new document	7
W2000.4.8	Create Hyperlinks	61
W2000.4.9	Use the Office Assistant	117
W2000.4.10	Send Word documents via e-mail	10
W2000.5	**USING TABLES**	
W2000.5.1	Create and format tables	147
W2000.5.2	Add borders and shading to tables	147
W2000.5.3	Revise tables (insert & delete rows and columns, change cell formats)	154
W2000.5.4	Modify table structure (merge cells, change height and width)	157
W2000.5.5	Rotate text in a table	159

Appendix B

Nivo #	Objective	Page #
W2000.6	**WORKING WITH PICTURES AND CHARTS**	
W2000.6.1	Use the drawing toolbar	166
W2000.6.2	Insert graphics into a document (WordArt, ClipArt, Images)	171
W2000.1	**WORKING WITH PARAGRAPHS**	
W2000.1.1	Apply paragraph and section shading	89
W2000.1.2	Use text flow options (Widows/Orphans options and keeping lines together)	198
W2000.1.3	Sort lists, paragraphs, tables	205
W2000.2	**WORKING WITH DOCUMENTS**	
W2000.2.1	Create and modify page borders	219
W2000.2.2	Format first page differently than subsequent pages	216
W2000.2.3	Use bookmarks	236
W2000.2.4	Create and edit styles	225
W2000.2.5	Create watermarks	217
W2000.2.6	Elements	209
W2000.2.7	Balance column lengths (using column breaks appropriately)	229
W2000.2.8	Create or revise footnotes and endnotes	221, 224
W2000.2.9	Work with master documents and subdocuments	257
W2000.2.10	Create and modify a table of contents	240
W2000.2.11	Create cross-references	238
W2000.2.12	Create and modify an index	243
W2000.3	**USING TABLES**	
W2000.3.1	Embed worksheets in a table	278
W2000.3.2	Perform calculations in a table	276
W2000.3.3	Link Excel data as a table	283
W2000.3.4	Modify worksheets in a table	285
W2000.4	**WORKING WITH PICTURES AND CHARTS**	
W2000.4.1	Add bitmapped graphics	292
W2000.4.2	Delete and position graphics	294, 295
W2000.4.3	Create and modify charts	298, 300
W2000.4.4	Import data into charts	304
W2000.5	**USING MAIL MERGE**	
W2000.5.1	Create a main document	330
W2000.5.2	Create a data source	327
W2000.5.3	Sort records to be merged	332
W2000.5.4	Merge main document and data source	324
W2000.5.5	Generate labels	333
W2000.5.6	Merge a document using alternate data sources	335

Appendix B

Nivo #	Objective	Page #
W2000.6	**USING ADVANCED FEATURES**	
W2000.6.1	Insert a field	202
W2000.6.2	Create, apply, and edit macros	342
W2000.6.3	Copy, rename, and delete macros	348
W2000.6.4	Create and modify form	310
W2000.6.5	Create and modify a form control (e.g., add an item to a drop-down list)	315
W2000.6.6	Use advanced text alignment features with graphics	296
W2000.6.7	Customize toolbars	350
W2000.7	**COLLABORATING WITH WORK GROUPS**	
W2000.7.1	Insert comments	255
W2000.7.2	Protect documents	261
W2000.7.3	Create multiple versions of a document	263
W2000.7.4	Track changes to a document	250
W2000.7.5	Set default file location for workgroup templates	265
W2000.7.6	Round Trip documents from HTML	267

Index

Symbols

_ (underscore), 237
2 pages per sheet option, 132

A

Accept or Reject Changes dialog box, 253
accepting revisions, 253-254
accessing Go To feature, 119
actions
  redoing, 40
  repeating, 41
  undoing, 40
Add button, 111
Add Help Text button, 318
Add or Remove Buttons menu commands (Customize), 352
adding
  borders
    pages, 219-220
    paragraphs, 86-88
    tables, 152-153
  documents to master documents, 259-260
  entries to drop-down lists, 317
  hyperlinks, 61
  page numbers, 120-121

POSTNET bar codes to envelopes, 186
shading
  paragraphs, 89-90
  tables, 153
text, 28-30
titles to charts, 301
toolbar buttons, 350-351
WordArt, 172
adjusting spacing
  lines, 84
  characters, 83-84
  paragraphs, 83
After text box, 85
Align Left button, 82
Align Right button, 82
aligning text
  (with) graphics, 296-297
  justifying, 81
  left, 81
  paragraphs, 80-82
  right, 81
  vertically, 133-134
Alignment list box, 81
All button, 79
Apply to drop-down list, 132
Apply to text box, 88
applying
  character effects, 52, 56-57
  styles, 138-139
Ascending radio button, 207

assigning
  custom template styles, 241
  TOC (table of contents) fields, 240
associating macros with text fields, 318
attached envelopes, 187
  modifying, 187-188
  printing, 188
attaching envelopes to documents, 187
audio files, inserting, 172
AutoCorrect, 44
  customizing, 45
  deleting entries, 45
AutoCorrect button, 111
AutoCorrect command (Tools menu), 45
AutoCorrect dialog box, 44
AutoCorrect list, 45
AutoFit (column widths), 148
AutoFit to window (column widths), 149
AutoFormat button, 149
Automatically save a version on close check box, 264
AutoNumber command (Footnote menu), 222
AutoShape, 169-170
AutoShapes command (Picture menu), 218

Word 2000 Cheat Sheet

AutoShapes menu, 170
axis numbers (charts), 302

B

balancing column
 breaks, 229-230
Based on drop-down
 list, 226
Before list box, 85
Behind Text command
 (Text Wrapping
 menu), 297
bitmapped graphics,
 inserting, 292-293
Blank Document icon, 7
blocks of text, selecting, 33
BMP extension, 292
Boder button, 86
bold text, formatting, 53
Bookmark command
 (Insert menu), 237
Bookmark dialog box, 237
bookmarked text,
 deleting, 237
Bookmark name
 text box, 237
bookmarks, 236
 creating, 236
 deleting, 237
Bookmarks check box, 236
Border and Shading
 Options dialog box, 220
Border button, 152
borders, adding
 page, 219-220
 paragraphs, 86-88
 tables, 152-153
Borders and Shading
 command (Format
 menu), 86, 152, 219

Borders and Shading
 dialog box, 86,
 152-153, 219
Break command (Insert
 menu), 135-137, 229
Break dialog box, 137
Break menu commands
 Column break, 229
 Continuous, 230
Browse button, 280
bulleted lists
 creating, 72-74
 customizing, 73
Bullets and Numbering
 command (Format
 menu), 73
Bullets and Numbering
 dialog box, 73
Bullets button, 73
buttons
 Add, 111
 Add Help Text, 318
 Align Left, 82
 Align Right, 82
 All, 79
 AutoCorrect, 111
 AutoFormat, 149
 Border, 86, 152
 Browse, 280
 Bullets, 73
 Center, 82
 Change
  Grammar checker, 116
  spell checker, 111
 Change All, 111
 Change Text
  Direction, 159
 Change Title, 20
 Check Box Form
  Field, 311
 Clear Formatting, 211
 Collapse, 79
 Columns, 145

Customize, 73
Cut, 156
Decrease Indent, 91
Demote, 79, 258
Distribute Columns
 Evenly, 150
Distribute Rows
 Evenly, 150
Document Map, 109
Draw Table, 311, 150
Drop-Down Form
 Field, 311
Edit, 325
Eraser, 150, 157
Expand, 79
Find Next, 38
Font, 186
Font Color, 58
Form Field Options, 311
Form Field Shading, 311
Format, 121, 210, 227
Full Screen View, 182
Go To, 119
Hide/Show, 94
Highlight, 64
Horizontal Line, 88
Ignore
 Grammar checker, 116
 spell checker, 111
Ignore All, 111
Ignore Rule, 116
Increase Indent, 91
Insert, 43
Insert Frame, 311
Insert Merge Field, 331
Insert Table, 311
 Standard toolbar,
  147-148
 Tables and Borders
  toolbar, 154
Justify, 82
Less, 209
Magnifier, 181

Index

Merge Cells, 157
Microsoft Word
  Help, 117
Modify Selection, 344
More, 37, 209
Move Down, 79
Move Up, 79
Multiple Pages, 181
Next, 119
Numbering, 75
One Page, 181
Options, 111, 186,
  222, 241
OVR, 29
Previous, 119
Print, 181
Promote, 79, 258
Protect Form, 311
Redo, 41
Save, 16
ScreenTip, 62
Shading, 153
Show Heading, 79
Show Next, 124
Show Previous, 124
Show Toolbar, 86
Shrink to Fit, 182
Special, 210
Spelling and Grammar,
  110, 115
Split Cells, 158
Tab style, 95
Table AutoFormat, 149
Tables and Borders, 150
Tabs, 94
Text Form Field, 311
Text Wrapping, 296
toolbar, adding/
  removing, 350-351
Tools, 261
Undo, 40
Up One Level, 5
View Datasheet, 299
View Ruler, 181

C

calculation fields,
  updating, 277
calculations (tables),
  performing, 276-277
Categories list, 203
cells (tables)
  height/width, 157
  merging, 157
  selecting, 151
  splitting, 158
Center button, 82
centering text, 81
Change All button (spell
  checker), 111
Change button
  Grammar checker, 116
  spell checker, 111
Change Text Direction
  button (Tables and
  Borders toolbar), 159
Change Title button, 20
changing
  axis numbers (charts),
    302
  chart types, 300
  font families, 59
  fonts, 59
  size (fonts), 59-60
  text color, 58
  WordArt, 172
character effects,
  applying, 52, 56-57
Character Spacing tab, 83
character styles, 225
characters
  spacing, adjusting, 83-84
  selecting, 32
chart areas,
  formatting, 301
Chart menu commands
  (Chart Type), 300

Chart Options command
  (Format menu), 301
Chart Type command
  (Chart menu), 300
Chart Type dialog
  box, 300
chart types, changing, 300
charts
  adding titles, 301
  axis numbers,
    changing, 302
  creating, 298-299
  data, formatting, 301
  datasheets, 298
  formatting, 303
  graphs, 298
  importing data, 304-305
  legends, formatting, 302
  modifying, 300
  moving, 303
  resizing, 303
check box form field, 316
Check Box Form Field
  button, 311
Check Box Form Field
  Options dialog
  box, 316-317
check boxes
  Automatically save a
    version on close, 264
  Bookmarks, 236
  Check grammar, 115
  Check grammar as you
    type, 115
  Check spelling as you
    type, 112
  Continue previous
    list, 76
  default value, setting, 317
  Different first page, 216
  Drop-down item, 317
  Highlight changes on
    screen, 252

371

Word 2000 Cheat Sheet

Insert as hyperlink, 239
Keep lines together, 199
Keep with next, 200
Line between, 146
Outline, 57
Page break before, 135
Print data only for
 forms, 313
Read-only, 262
Right-align page
 numbers, 241
Show number on first
 page, 216
Show page numbers, 241
size, setting, 317
Small caps, 57
Subscript, 57
Superscript, 57
Tab characters, 94
Update automatically, 42
Use return address, 189
Widow/Orphan, 198
Check grammar as you
 type check box, 115
Check grammar check
 box, 115
Check spelling as you type
 check box, 112
checking
 grammar, 115-116
 spelling, 110-112
Clear Formatting
 button, 211
Click and Type, 30
clip art, 172
 formatting, 173
 inserting, 172-173
 resizing, 174
Clip Art command
 (Picture menu), 172, 218
Clipboard, 31, 34
Clipboard command
 (Toolbars menu), 31, 35

closing Document
 Map, 109
code (underlying),
 viewing, 203
Collapse button, 79
color (text), changing, 58,
 153
Column break command
 (Break menu), 229
column breaks, 229-230
columns
 creating, 145-146
 customizing, 146
 deleting, 155-156
 format, deleting, 146
 inserting, 154-155
 rule lines, inserting
  between, 146
 selecting, 151
 sizing, 157
 widths, 148
Columns button (Standard
 toolbar), 145
Columns command
 (Format menu), 146
Columns dialog
 box, 145-146
commands
 Add or Remove Buttons
  menu (Customize), 352
 Break menu
  Column break, 229
  Continuous, 230
 Chart menu (Chart
  Type), 300
 Convert menu (Text to
  Table), 312
 Custom mark menu
  (Symbol), 222
 Draw menu (Rotate or
  Flip), 170
 Edit menu
  Copy, 35
  Cut, 34

Find, 37
Go To, 119
Import File, 305
Links, 284
Paste, 35
Paste Special, 36
Repeat Typing, 40, 155
Replace, 38
Select All, 33
Undo Typing, 40
File menu
 New, 7-8, 312
 Open, 4
 Page Setup, 130, 216
 Print, 184
 Print Preview, 181
 Save, 16
 Save As, 17-18, 261
 Versions, 264
 Web Page Preview, 183
Footnote menu
 AutoNumber, 222
 Custom mark, 222
Format menu
 Borders and Shading,
  86, 152, 219
 Bullets and Numbering,
  73
 Chart Options, 301
 Columns, 146
 Font, 52, 83
 Paragraph, 78, 80,
  135, 199
 Picture, 173, 295
 Selecte Chart Area, 301
 Selected Data
  Series, 302
 Selected Legend, 302
 Style, 139, 226
 Tabs, 94
Get Data menu
 Create Data
  Source, 328
 Open Data Source, 335

Index

Help menu
  Hide the Office
    Assistant, 118
  Microsoft Word
    Help, 117
  What's This?, 83
Insert menu
  Bookmark, 237
  Break, 135-137, 229
  Comment, 256
  Cross-reference, 238
  Date and Time, 42
  Fields, 202
  Footnote, 221
  Index and Tables, 240
  Object, 293
  Page Numbers, 216
  Page Numbers command, 120
  Picture, 170, 218, 292
  Symbol, 43, 201
  Text Box, 218
Picture menu
  AutoShapes, 218
  Clip Art, 127, 218
  From File, 174,
    218, 292
  WordArt, 171
Protect Document menu
  (Forms), 313
Rotate or Flip menu
  Flip Horizontally, 170
  Flip Vertically, 170
Save As menu
  (Tools), 264
Table menu
  Convert, 312
  Convert, Text to
    Table, 148
  Delete, Cells, Delete
    entire column, 156
  Delete, Cells, Delete
    entire row, 156

  Draw Table, 150
  Formula, 277
  Insert, 154
  Insert, Columns to the
    Left, 154
  Insert, Columns to the
    Right, 154
  Insert, Rows above, 155
  Insert, Rows Below, 155
  Insert, Table, 148
  Select Row, 151
  Sort, 207
  Table AutoFormat, 149
  Table Properties, 152
  Text Wrapping menu
    Behind Text, 297
    Edit Wrap Points, 297
    In Front of Text, 297
    Square, 297
    Through, 297
    Tight, 297
    Top and Bottom, 297
Toolbars menu
  Clipboard, 31, 35
  Customize, 352
  Drawing, 166
  Forms, 312
  Reviewing, 251
  Tables and Borders, 86
Tools menu
  AutoCorrect, 45
  Customize, 351-352
  Envelopes and
    Labels, 189
  Language, Thesaurus,
    113
  Macro, 343
  Mail Merge, 325
  Options, 94, 112, 115,
    236, 252
  Protect Document, 313
  Save Version, 264

  Spelling and Grammar,
    111, 115
  Track Changes, 252
  Unprotect document,
    313
View menu
  Document Map, 109
  Header and Footer,
    122, 218
  Outline, 79, 258
  Ruler, 95, 132
  Toolbars, 31, 35, 86,
    166, 251, 312, 352
  Toolbars, Tables and
    Borders, 150
Commands list box, 344
Commands tab, 344, 353
Comment command
  (Insert menu), 256
comments
  deleting, 256
  editing, 256
  inserting, 255-256
  viewing, 256
comments feature, 255
Comments pane, 255
Confirm Password dialog
  box, 262
Continue previous list
  check box, 76
Continuous command
  (Break menu), 230
Continuous section
  breaks, 136
controlling text flow, 198
Convert command (Table
  menu), 312
Convert menu commands
  (Text to Table), 148, 312
Convert Text to Table
  dialog box, 312
Copy command (Edit
  menu), 35

373

Word 2000 Cheat Sheet

copying
  macros, 348-349
  text, 35
Create Data Source
  command (Get Data
  menu), 328
Create Data Source dialog
  box, 328
Create drop-down
  list, 325, 333
Create from File tab, 280
Create Labels dialog
  box, 333
Create New tab, 293, 298
creating
  AutoShapes, 170
  bookmarks, 236
  charts, 298-299
  column breaks, 229
  data sources, 327-329
  documents, 7, 12
    master, 258-259
    templates, 7-9
    wizards, 9
  folders, 22
  form letters, 331
  forms, 310-311
    online, 312
    printed, 311-312
  hanging indents, 93
  hyperlinks, 61-63
  index entries, 243-245
  indexes, 243
  labels, 333-334
  lists
    bulleted, 72-74
    numbered, 75-76
  macros, 342-345
  main documents,
    330-331
  section breaks, 137
  shapes, 168-169
  small caps, 57

styles, 226-227
toolbars, 352-353
watermarks, 217-218
Cross-reference command
  (Insert menu), 238
Cross-Reference dialog
  box, 238
cross-references
  deleting, 239
  inserting, 238-239
  updating, 239
cross-references
  hyperlinks, 238
Custom mark command
  (Footnote menu), 222
Custom mark menu
  commands
  (Symbol), 222
custom template styles,
  assigning, 241
Customize Bulleted List
  dialog box, 73
Customize button, 73
Customize command
  Add or Remove Buttons
    menu, 352
  Toolbars menu, 352
  Tools menu, 351-352
Customize dialog
  box, 344, 351
Customize Keyboard
  dialog box, 344
customizing
  AutoCorrect, 45
  bulleted lists, 73
  cells, 157
  columns, 146
  fields, 318
  headers and footers, 124
  page numbers, 121
  toolbars, 350
Cut button (Standard
  toolbar), 156

Cut command (Edit
  menu), 34
cutting
  graphics, 294
  text, 34

data
  charts
    formatting, 301
    importing, 304-305
    embedding, 281-282
    linking, 283-284
Data Form dialog box, 327
data source files,
  opening, 327
data sources, 324
  alternate (mail
    merge), 335-336
  creating, 327-329
  editing, 329
datasheets, 298
  hiding, 299
  modifying, 300
dates, inserting, 42
Date and Time command
  (Insert menu), 42
Date and Time dialog
  box, 42
Decrease Indent
  button, 91
decreasing paragraph
  indents, 91-92
default text (fields),
  setting, 316
default value (check
  boxes), setting, 317
Delete, Cells, Delete entire
  column command (Table
  menu), 156

Index

Delete, Cells, Delete entire row command (Table menu), 156
deleting
  AutoCorrect entries, 45
  bookmarked text, 237
  bookmarks, 237
  column formatting, 146
  comments, 256
  cross-references, 239
  graphics, 294
  indexes, 245
  lines (tables), 150
  macros, 349
  page breaks, 135
  rows/columns (tables), 155-156
  section breaks, 137
  tables of contents, 242
  text, 33
Demote button, 79, 258
Descending radio button, 207
dialog boxes
  Accept or Reject Change, 253
  AutoCorrect, 44
  Bookmark, 237
  Border and Shading Options, 220
  Borders and Shading, 86, 152-153, 219
  Break, 137
  Bullets and Numbering, 73
  Chart Type, 300
  Check Box Form Field, 316-317
  Columns, 145-146
  Confirm Password, 262
  Convert Text to Table, 312
  Create Data Source, 328
  Create Labels, 333

Cross-Reference, 238
Customize, 344, 351
Customize Bulleted List, 73
Customize Keyboard, 344
Data Form, 327
Date and Time, 42
Drop-Down List Form Field Options, 317
Edit WordArt Text, 171
Envelope Options, 186
Explorer-type, 5
Field, 202
Field Options, 203
Find, 5
Find and Replace, 37, 209
Go To tab, 119
opening, 37
Font, 52, 83, 186
Footnote and Endnote, 221
form field, opening, 315
Format Axis, 302
Format Chart Area, 301
Format Data Series, 301
Format Legend, 302
Format Picture, 173, 295
Formula, 276
Help, 117-118, 318
Highlight Changes, 251
Horizontal Line, 88
Hyperlink, 62
Import Data Options, 305
Import File, 305
Index and Tables, 240
Insert ClipArt, 172
Insert Hyperlink, 61
Insert Picture, 174, 292
Insert Subdocument, 260
Insert Table, 148-149
Label Options, 190, 333

Labels, 189
Links, 284
Mail Merge Helper, 326
Mark Index Entry, 243
Merge, 326
Microsoft Word Help, 118
Modify Location, 266
Modify Style, 227
New, 7-8, 312
New Style, 226-227
New Toolbar, 352
Notes Options, 222
Object, 293
Open, 4
Open Data Source, 335
Options, 252, 265
Organizer, 348
Page Number Format, 121
Page Numbers, 120, 216
Page Setup, 124, 130, 184
Paragraph, 78-80, 198
Paste Special, 36, 281
Print, 184
Query Options, 332
Record Macro, 343
Save, 261
Save As, 17-18, 261
Save Version, 264
Set Hyperlink ScreenTip, 62
Set Page Title, 21
Sort, 207
Sort Table, 207
Sort Text, 208
Spelling & Grammar options, 111
Spelling and Grammar, 110-111, 115-116
Style, 226-227
Symbol, 43, 222

375

Word 2000 Cheat Sheet

Table AutoFormat, 149
Table Properties, 158
Tabs, 94
Text Form Field
 Options, 315-316
Thesaurus, 113-114
Versions, 263-264
Different first page check
 box, 216
displaying
 AutoShapes menu as
  toolbar, 170
 Borders and Shading
  dialog box, 152
 Document Map
  sections, 109
 documents, 4, 11, 78-79
 headers and footers, 122
 Help dialog box, 117
 index markers, 244
 Replace tab, 38
 ruler, 95
 tab marks, 94
 Tables and Borders
  toolbar, 149
 Window/Orphan
  Control, 199
Distribute Columns
 Evenly button (Tables
 and Borders
 toolbar), 150
Distribute Rows Evenly
 button (Tables and
 Borders toolbar), 150
.DOC file extension, 7
Document Map
 closing, 109
 document navigation,
  108-109
 opening, 109
Document Map button
 (Standard toolbar), 109

Document Map command
 (View menu), 109
document sections
 (Document Map),
 displaying, 109
documents
 creating, 7, 12
 templates, 7-9
 wizards, 9
 displaying, 4, 11, 78-79
 envelopes, attaching, 187
 first page
  formatting, 216
  hiding page
   numbers, 216
 locating, 5
 main, 324
  creating, 330-331
  inserting merge
   fields, 330
 managing, 257-258
 master, 257-258
  adding documents
   to, 259-260
  creating, 258-259
  saving, 259
 merged, 324
 navigating, 106
  Document Map,
   108-109
  Go To feature, 119
  keyboard commands,
   106-107
  scroll bar, 107-108
 opening, 6
 password protecting,
  261-262
 previewing, 180-182
 printing, 184
 round trip, 267-269
 saving, 15-18
  different format, 19
  different location,
   18-19

 different name, 18
 Web page, 19-21
 selecting all text, 33
 sending as email
  messages, 10-11
 sharing, 267-269
 tracking changes,
  250-251
 versions, saving, 263-264
.DOT file extension, 7
dragging and dropping
 text, 34
Draw menu commands
 (Rotate or Flip), 170
Draw Table button, 150,
 311
Draw Table command
 (Table menu), 150
drawing
 lines, 167
 tables, 149-151
Drawing command
 (Toolbars menu), 166
Drawing toolbar, 58,
 166-167
Drop-Down Form Field
 button, 311
Drop-down item
 check box, 317
drop-down list boxes
 Items in, 317
 Look in, 5
 Tab leader, 241
 Zoom, 181
Drop-Down List Form
 Field Options dialog
 box, 317
drop-down lists
 adding/removing
  entries, 317
 Apply to, 132
 Based on, 226
 Create, 325, 333
 Envelope size, 186

376

Index

Files of type, 335
Formats, 241
Line Spacing, 84
List, 227
Reference type, 239
Save as type, 268
Style, 138

E

Edit button, 325
Edit menu commands
  Copy, 35
  Cut, 34
  Find, 37
  Go To, 119
  Import File, 305
  Links, 284
  Paste, 35
  Paste Special, 36, 281
  Repeat Typing, 40, 155
  Replace, 38
  Select All, 33
  Undo Typing, 40
Edit WordArt Text dialog box, 171
Edit Wrap Points command (Text Wrapping menu), 297
editing
  comments, 256
  data sources, 329
  footnotes, 223
  macros, 346-347
  styles, 227-228
email messages, sending documents as, 10-11
embedded worksheets, 278
  opening, 285
  removing, 279
embedding
  data, 281-282
  worksheets

existing, 279-280
new, 278-279
endnotes, inserting, 224
Envelope Options dialog box, 186
envelope size, selecting, 186
Envelope size drop-down list, 186
Envelope tab, 185
envelopes
  attached, 187
  modifying, 187-188
  printing, 188
  attaching to documents, 187
  fonts, setting, 186
  POSTNET bar codes, adding, 186
  printing, 185-187
Envelopes and Labels command (Tools menu), 185, 189
Eraser button, 150, 157
Even section breaks, 137
Expand button, 79
Explorer-type dialog box, 5
extensions (BMP), 292

F

Feed icon, 187
feed methods, 187
Field codes text box, 203
Field dialog box, 202
Field names list, 203
Field Options dialog box, 203
fields, 202
  calculation, updating, 277
  customizing, 318
  default text, setting, 316

form
  inserting, 315
  setting options, 315
  inserting, 202-204
  maximum characters, setting, 316
  merge, inserting in main documents, 330
  setting, 318
  Text Form, 315
  text format, setting, 316
  TOC (table of contents), assigning, 240
  type of text, setting, 316
  underlying code, viewing, 203
Fields command (Insert menu), 202
file extensions
  .DOC, 7
  .DOT, 7
  .WIZ, 9
File List pane, 5
File Locations tab, 265
File menu commands
  New, 7-8, 312
  Open, 4
  Page Setup, 130, 216
  Print, 184
  Print Preview, 181
  Save, 16
  Save As, 17-18, 261
  Versions, 264
  Web Page Preview, 183
File name text box, 20
File types list, 266
files (data source), opening, 327
Files of type drop-down list, 335
Files of type list box, 313
Find and Replace dialog box, 37, 119, 209

377

Word 2000 Cheat Sheet

Find command (Edit menu), 37
Find dialog box, 5
Find Next button, 38
Find tab, 37
Find tool, 37
Find what text box, 38
finding
  specific elements, 119, 236
  text, 37-38
finding and replacing, 209
  formats, 209-211
  special characters, 210-211
First Line indent marker, 92
first lines (paragraphs), indenting, 92
first pages (documents)
  formatting, 216
  hiding page numbers, 216
fixed column widths, 148
Flip Horizontally command (Rotate or Flip menu), 170
Flip Vertically command (Rotate or Flip menu), 170
flipping AutoShapes, 170
folders
  creating, 22
  managing, 22
  renaming, 22-23
Font button, 186
Font Color button, 58
Font command (Format menu), 52, 83
Font dialog box, 52, 83, 186
font families, changing, 59
Font list, 43

fonts
  changing, 59
  envelopes, setting, 186
  size, changing, 59-60
footers
  creating, 122-124
  customizing, 124
  displaying, 122
Footnote and Endnote dialog box, 221
Footnote command (Insert menu), 221
Footnote menu commands
  AutoNumber, 222
  Custom mark, 222
footnotes, 221
  editing, 223
  inserting, 221-223
  modifying, 223
  moving, 223
  renumbering, 223
For which text box, 239
form controls, 315-318
form field dialog boxes, opening, 315
Form Field Options button, 311
Form Field Shading button, 311
form fields
  check box, 316
  inserting, 315
  setting options, 315
form letters
  creating, 331
  previewing, 331
Format Axis dialog box, 302
Format button, 121, 210, 227
Format Chart Area dialog box, 301
Format Data Series dialog box, 301

Format Legend dialog box, 302
Format menu commands
  Borders and Shading, 86, 152, 219
  Bullets and Numbering, 73
  Chart Options, 301
  Columns, 146
  Font, 52, 83
  Paragraph, 78, 80, 135, 199
  Picture, 173, 295
  Selected Axis, 302
  Selected Chart Area, 301
  Selected Data Series, 302
  Selected Legend, 302
  Style, 139, 226
  Tabs, 94
Format Painter icon, 65
Format Painter tool, 65
Format Picture dialog box, 173, 295
formats
  finding and replacing, 209-211
  saving documents, 19
Formats drop-down list, 241
formatting
  chart areas, 301
  charts, 303
  clip art, 173
  documents, 216
  legends (charts), 302
  paragraphs, 71
  sections, 137
  tables of contents, 241
  text
    bold, 53
    character effects, applying, 52, 56-57
    italics, 54

378

Index

outlined, 57
underlining, 54-55
formatting settings
  (paragraphs), viewing, 83
Formatting toolbar, 52, 226
forms
  creating, 310-311
  data, printing, 313
  modifying, 313
  online, 312-314
  printed, 311-312
  protecting, 313
Forms command
  Protect Document menu, 313
  Toolbars menu, 312
Forms toolbar, 310-312
Formula command (Table menu), 277
Formula dialog box, 276
Formula text box, 277
From File command
  (Picture menu), 174, 218, 292
Full Screen View button, 182

G

generating
  indexes, 245
  tables of contents, 240-241
Get Data menu commands
  Create Data Source, 328
  Open Data Source, 335
Go To button, 119
Go To command (Edit menu), 119
Go To feature, 119, 236
Go To tab, 119

Go to what list, 236
grammar
  checking, 115-116
  spell checking, 110-112
  Thesaurus, 113-114
Grammar checker, 115-116
graphics
  aligning text with, 296-297
  cutting and pasting, 294
  deleting, 294
  moving, 295
graphs, 298
Gutter position option, 132
gutter space, 131

H

hanging indents, creating, 93
hard page breaks, 135
Header and Footer command (View menu), 122, 218
Header and Footer option, 132
Header and Footer toolbar, 123, 218
Header and Footer view, 122-124
headers
  creating, 122-124
  customizing, 124
  displaying, 122
height (cells), 157
help, 117-118
Help dialog box, 117-118, 318
Help icon, 203

Help menu commands
  Hide the Office Assistant, 118
  Microsoft Word Help, 117
  What's This?, 83
Hide the Office Assitant command (Help menu), 118
Hide/Show button, 94
hiding
  datasheets, 299
  Help dialog box, 117
  Office Assistant, 118
  outline information, 79
  page numbers, 216
  paragraph marks, 73
Highlight button, 64
Highlight Changes dialog box, 251
Highlight changes on screen check box, 252
highlighting text, 64
horizontal and vertical rulers, 132
Horizontal Line button, 88
Horizontal Line dialog box, 88
HTML (Hypertext Markup Language) source ccode, 19-21
Hyperlink dialog box, 62
hyperlinks, 61
  adding, 61
  creating, 61-63
  cross-reference, 238
Hypertext Markup Language (HTML) source code, 19-21

379

Word 2000 Cheat Sheet

I

icons
  Blank Document, 7
  Feed, 187
  Format Painter, 65
  Help, 203
  Insert Clip, 173
  Normal View, 269
  Office Assistant, 116
  Print Layout View, 269
  Select Objects, 168
  Shortcut bar, 5
  subdocument, 260
  Template, 8
  Text Wrapping, 174
  Wizard, 9
Ignore All button, 111
Ignore button, 111, 116
Ignore Rule button, 116
images, inserting, 173-174
Import Data Options
  dialog box, 305
Import File command
  (Edit menu), 305
Import File dialog
  box, 305
importing data (charts),
  304-305
In Front of Text command
  (Text Wrapping
  menu), 297
Increase Indent button, 91
increasing paragraph
  indents, 91-92
indenting
  first line (paragraphs), 92
  paragraphs, 91
indents
  hanging, 93
  paragraph, 91-92
Indents and Spacing
  tab, 81

Index and Tables
  command (Insert
  menu), 240
Index and Tables dialog
  box, 240
index entries,
  creating, 243-245
index markers,
  displaying, 244
indexes
  creating, 243
  deleting, 245
  generating, 245
  updating, 245
Insert as hyperlink check
  box, 239
Insert button, 43
Insert Clip icon, 173
Insert ClipArt dialog
  box, 172
Insert command (Table
  menu), 154
Insert Frame Field
  button, 311
Insert Hyperlink dialog
  box, 61
Insert menu commands
  Bookmark, 237
  Break, 135-137, 229
  Comment, 256
  Cross-reference, 238
  Date and Time, 42
  Fields, 202
  Footnote, 221
  Index and Tables, 240
  Object, 293
  Page Numbers, 120, 216
  Picture, 170, 218, 292
  Symbol, 43, 201
  Text Box, 218
Insert Merge Field
  button, 331
Insert mode, 28

Insert Picture dialog
  box, 174, 292
Insert reference to
  list box, 239
Insert Subdocument
  dialog box, 260
Insert Table button, 311
  Standard toolbar,
  147-148
  Tables and Borders
  toolbar, 154
Insert Table dialog
  box, 148-149
Insert, Columns to the
  Left command (Table
  menu), 154
Insert, Columns to the
  Right command (Table
  menu), 154
Insert, Rows Above
  command (Table
  menu), 155
Insert, Rows Below
  command (Table
  menu), 155
Insert, Table command
  (Table menu), 148
inserting
  audio files, 172
  bitmapped graphics,
  292-293
  clip art, 172-173
  comments, 255-256
  cross-references, 238-239
  date/time, 42
  endnotes, 224
  fields, 202-204
  footnotes, 221-223
  form fields, 315
  images, 173-174
  lines, 166
  merge fields, 330
  multiple rows/
  columns, 155

380

Index

nonbreaking spaces, 201
page breaks, 135
rows/columns, 154-155
rule lines between
   columns, 146
shapes, 166
symbols, 43
tables, 147-149
text, 28-29
video files, 172
WordArt, 171-172
italics (text),
   formatting, 54
Items in drop-down
   list box, 317

J-L

Justify button, 82
justifying text, 81

Keep lines together check
   box, 199
Keep with next check
   box, 200
keyboard commands
   document navigation,
      106-107
   finding and replacing
      formats, 210
   special characters, 210
   inserting fields, 204

Label Options dialog
   box, 190, 333
labels
   creating, 333-334
   printing, 189-190
Labels dialog box, 189
Labels tab, 189
Landscape orientation, 130
Landscape radio
   button, 130

Language, Thesaurus
   command (Tools
   menu), 113
Layout tab, 134, 216, 295
Layout view (Click and
   Type), 30
leading tabs, 97
left aligning text, 81
legends (charts),
   formatting, 302
Less button, 209
Line and Page Breaks
   tab, 81, 199
Line between check
   box, 146
line of text, selecting, 32
line spacing, adjusting, 84
Line Spacing drop-down
   list, 84
lines
   drawing, 167
   inserting, 166
   moving, 168
   reformatting, 168
   resizing, 168
   selecting, 168-169
   tables, deleting, 150
linked worksheets,
   opening, 285
linking
   data, 283-284
   worksheets, 283
Links command (Edit
   menu), 284
Links dialog box, 284
list boxes
   Alignment, 81
   Before, 85
   Commands, 344
   Files of type, 313
   Insert reference to, 239
   Object type, 293
   Size, 60
   Store macro in, 344

Style, 139
Tab stop position, 97
List drop-down list, 227
lists
   AutoCorrect, 45
   bulleted
      creating, 72-74
      customizing, 73
   Categories, 203
   Field names, 203
   File types, 266
   Font, 43
   Go to what, 236
   numbered, 75-76
   Style, 88, 227
locating documents, 5
Look in drop-down
   list box, 5

M

Macro command (Tools
   menu), 343
Macro name text box, 344
macros, 342
   associating with text
      fields, 318
   copying, 348-349
   deleting, 349
   editing, 346-347
   managing, 348
   recording, 342-345
   renaming, 349
   running, 345-346
Macros window, 343
Magnifier button, 181
mail merge, 323-326
   alternate data
      source, 335-336
   data source, 324
   main documents, 324
   merged documents, 324

381

Word 2000 Cheat Sheet

Mail Merge command
    (Tools menu), 325
Mail Merge Helper,
    324-327
Mail Merge Helper dialog
    box, 326
Mail Merge toolbar, 326
main document, 324
    creating, 330-331
    inserting merge
        fields, 330
Main entry text box, 244
managing
    documents, 257-258
    folder, 22
    macros, 348
Margins tab, 131-132
Mark Index Entry dialog
    box, 243
markers (First Line
    indent), 92
marking subdocuments,
    259
Master Document
    view, 260
master documents,
    257-258
    adding documents
        to, 259-260
    creating, 258-259
    saving, 259
maximum characters
    (fields), setting, 316
Merge Cells button, 157
Merge dialog box, 326
merge fields, inserting, 330
merge records, sorting, 332
merged document, 324
merging cells, 157
Microsoft Graph 2000,
    298
Microsoft Word Help
    button, 117

Microsoft Word Help
    command (Help
    menu), 117
Microsoft Word Help
    dialog box, 118
Mirror margins
    option, 132
modes
    Insert, 28
    Overtype, 28
Modify Location dialog
    box, 266
Modify Selection
    button, 344
Modify Style dialog
    box, 227
modifying
    attached envelopes,
        187-188
    charts, 300
    datasheets, 300
    footnotes, 223
    forms, 313
    subdocuments, 260
    worksheets, 285-286
More button, 37, 209
Motion Clips tab, 172
Move Down button, 79
Move Up button, 79
moving
    charts, 303
    footnotes, 223
    graphics, 295
    lines, 168
    objects, 168
    sections, 79
    tables of contents, 242
    text, 34
    watermark objects, 218
multiple
    lines, selecting, 169
    objects, selecting, 169
Multiple Pages button, 181

N

Name text box, 226
navigating documents, 106
    Document Map,
        108-109
    Go To feature, 119
    keyboard commands,
        106-107
    scroll bar, 107-108
nested tables, 149
New command (File
    menu), 7-8, 312
New dialog box, 7-8, 312
New Style dialog
    box, 226-227
New Toolbar dialog
    box, 352
newsgroups, Word MOUS
    exams, 363
Next button, 119
Next Page section
    breaks, 136
nonbreaking spaces,
    inserting, 201
Normal View icon, 269
Notes Options dialog
    box, 222
numbered lists,
    creating, 75-76
Numbered tab, 76
Numbering button, 75

O

Object command (Insert
    menu), 293
Object dialog box, 293
Object type list box, 293
objects
    moving, 168
    reformatting, 168

Index

resizing, 168
selecting, 168-169
Odd section breaks, 137
Office Assistant, 117-118
Office Assistant icon, 116
Office Clipboard, 31, 34
One Page button, 181
online forms, 312-314
Open command (File menu), 4
Open Data Source command (Get Data menu), 335
Open Data Source dialog box, 335
Open dialog box, 4
opening
  dialog boxes
    Find and Replace, 37
    form field, 315
    Format Picture, 173
    Hyperlink, 62
    Page Numbers, 120
    Paragraph, 80
    Print, 184
    Thesaurus, 113
  Document Map, 109
  documents, 6
  Drawing toolbar, 166
  files (data source), 327
  Grammar checker, 115
  spell checker, 111
  subdocuments, 260
  worksheets, 285
Options button, 111, 186, 222, 241
Options command (Tools menu), 94, 112, 115, 236, 252
Options dialog box, 252, 265
Organizer dialog box, 348
Organizer window, 349

orphans, 198
Outline check box, 57
Outline command (View menu), 79, 258
Outline feature, 77
outline information, hiding/showing, 79
Outline toolbar, 79
Outline view, 78
  displaying documents in, 78-79
  moving sections, 79
outlined text, formatting, 57
Outlining toolbar, 258
Overtype mode, 28
overtyping text, 28-30
OVR button, 29

P

Page Border tab, 219
page borders, adding, 219-220
Page break before check box, 135
Page break radio button, 135
page breaks
  deleting, 135
  hard, 135
  inserting, 135
  preventing, 199-200
Page Breaks tab, 135
page margins, setting, 131-132
Page Number Format dialog box, 121
page numbers
  adding, 120-121
  customizing, 121
  hiding, 216

Page Numbers command (Insert menu), 120, 216
Page Numbers dialog box, 120, 216
page orientation, setting, 130
Page range bookmark radio button, 244
Page Setup command (File menu), 130, 216
Page Setup dialog box, 124, 130, 184
Page Size tab, 130
panes
  Comments, 255
  File List, 5
Paper Size tab, 130
Paragraph command (Format menu), 78-80, 135, 199
Paragraph dialog box, 78-80, 198
paragraph indents, 91-92
paragraph marks, 71-73
paragraph styles, 225-227
paragraphs
  borders, 86-88
  first line, indenting, 92
  formatting, 71
  formatting settings, viewing, 83
  indenting, 91
  selecting, 33
  shading, adding, 89-90
  sorting, 205-207
  spacing
    above, 85
    adjusting, 83
    below, 85
  text, aligning, 80-82
password protecting documents, 261-262

383

Word 2000 Cheat Sheet

Password to modify
 text box, 262
Password to open
 text box, 262
Paste command (Edit
 menu), 35
Paste Special, 36
Paste Special command
 (Edit menu), 36, 281
Paste Special dialog
 box, 36, 281
pasting
 graphics, 294
 text, 35-36
performing calculations
 (tables), 276-277
Picture command
 Format menu, 173, 295
 Insert menu, 170,
  218, 292
Picture menu commands
 AutoShapes, 218
 Clip Art, 172, 218
 From File, 174, 218, 292
 WordArt, 171
Picture Position tab, 295
Picture toolbar, 174
placeholder text, 8
placing tabs, 94-96
Portrait orientation, 130
Portrait radio button, 130
positioning table text, 159
POSTNET (POSTal
 Numeric Encoding
 Technique) bar code, 186
pre-formatted shapes, 169
preparing for Word
 MOUS exams, 361
preventing page
 breaks, 199-200
previewing
 documents, 180-182
 form letters, 331
 Web pages, 183

Previous button, 119
Print button, 181
Print command (File
 menu), 184
Print data only for forms
 check box, 313
Print dialog box, 184
Print Layout view, 132,
 122, 218
Print Layout View
 icon, 269
Print Preview, 180-182
Print Preview command
 (File menu), 181
Print Preview toolbar, 181,
 184
Print tab, 313
printed forms,
 creating, 311-312
printing
 attached envelopes, 188
 data (forms), 313
 documents, 184
 envelopes, 185-187
 labels, 189-190
Printing Options tab, 187
Promote button, 79, 258
Protect Document
 command (Tools
 menu), 313
Protect Document menu
 commands (Forms), 313
Protect Form button, 311
protecting forms, 313

Q-R

Query Options dialog
 box, 332
radio buttons
 Ascending, 207
 Descending, 207

Landscape, 130
Page break, 135
Page range
 bookmark, 244
Portrait, 130
Update the style to reflect
 recent changes?, 227
Read-only recommended
 check box, 262
Record Macro dialog
 box, 343
recording macros, 342-345
Redo button, 41
redoing actions, 40
Reference type drop-down
 list, 239
reformatting
 lines, 168
 objects, 168
rejecting revisions,
 253-254
removing
 embedded worksheets,
  279
 entries from drop-down
  lists, 317
 toolbar buttons, 350-351
renaming
 folders, 22-23
 macros, 349
renumbering
 footnotes, 223
Repeat Typing command
 (Edit menu), 40, 155
repeating actions, 41
Replace command (Edit
 menu), 38
Replace tab, 38
Replace text box, 45
Replace tool, 38-39
Replace with text box, 38
replacing text, 38-39
resetting toolbars, 351

384

Index

resizing
  charts, 303
  clip art, 174
  columns/rows, 157
  lines, 168
  objects, 168
  watermark objects, 218
  windows (worksheets), 281
Reviewing command (Toolbars menu), 251
Reviewing toolbar, 251
revisions
  accepting, 253-254
  rejecting, 253-254
  viewing, 252
revisions feature, 250-251
right aligning text, 81
Right-align page numbers check box, 241
Rotate or Flip command (Draw menu), 170
Rotate or Flip menu commands
  Flip Horizontally, 170
  Flip Vertically, 170
rotating table text, 159
round trip documents, 267-269
rows (tables)
  deleting, 155-156
  inserting, 154-155
  inserting multiple, 155
  selecting, 151
  sizing, 157
rule lines, inserting between columns, 146
ruler, displaying, 95
Ruler command (View menu), 95, 132
running macros, 345-346

S

Save As command (File menu), 17-18, 261
Save As dialog box, 17-18, 261
Save as type drop-down list, 268
Save button, 16
Save command (File menu), 16
Save dialog box, 261
Save Version command (Tools menu), 264
Save Version dialog box, 264
saving documents, 15-18
  different format, 19
  different location, 18-19
  different name, 18
  master, 259
  versions, 263-264
  Web page, 19-21
ScreenTip button, 62
scroll bars, document navigation, 107-108
section breaks, 136-137
sections
  formatting, 137
  moving, 79
Select All command (Edit menu), 33
Select Objects icon, 168
Select, Row command (Table menu), 151
Selected Axis command (Format menu), 302
Selected Chart Area command (Format menu), 301

Selected Data Series command (Format menu), 302
Selected Legend command (Format menu), 302
selecting
  envelope size, 186
  feed methods, 187
  lines, 168-169
  objects, 168-169
  paragraphs, 33
  sentences, 33
  table components, 151
  tables, 151
  text, 31-32
    blocks of, 33
    characters, 32
    documents, 33
    line of, 32
    words, 32
sending documents as email messages, 10-11
sentences, selecting, 33
Set Hyperlink ScreenTip dialog box, 62
Set Page Title dialog box, 21
setting
  default text (fields), 316
  default value (check boxes), 317
  fonts (envelopes), 186
  form fields options, 315
  maximum characters (fields), 316
  page orientation, 130
  pages margins, 131-132
  size (check boxes), 317
  tab style, 95
  text format (fields), 316
  type of text (fields), 316
settings (fields), 318

385

Word 2000 Cheat Sheet

shading, adding
  paragraphs, 89-90
  tables, 153
Shading button, 153
Shading tab, 89, 153
shapes
  creating, 168-169
  inserting, 166
  pre-formatted, 169
  stylizing, 169
sharing documents,
  267-269
Shortcut bar icons, 5
shortcut keys (styles), 139
Show Heading buttons, 79
Show levels text box, 241
Show Next button, 124
Show number of first page
  check box, 216
Show page numbers
  check box, 241
Show Previous button, 124
Show Toolbar button, 86
showing
  outline information, 79
  paragraph marks, 73
Shrink to Fit button, 182
size
  check boxes, setting, 317
  fonts, changing, 59-60
Size list box, 60
Size text box, 60
sizing columns/rows, 157
small caps, creating, 57
Small caps check box, 57
Sort command (Table
  menu), 207
Sort dialog box, 207
Sort Records tab, 332
Sort Table dialog box, 207
Sort Text dialog box, 208

sorting, 205
  merge records, 332
  paragraphs, 205, 207
  tables, 207-208
Sounds tab, 172
spacing
  characters, 83-84
  lines, 84
  paragraphs, 83-85
Special button, 210
special characters, finding
  and replacing, 210-211
Special Characters tab, 201
specifying
  location (workgroup
    templates), 265-266
  tracking color, 252
spell checking, 110-112
Spelling & Grammar
  options dialog box, 111
Spelling and Grammar
  button, 110, 115
Spelling and Grammar
  command (Tools
  menu), 111, 115
Spelling and Grammar
  dialog box, 110-111,
  115-116
Spelling and Grammar
  tab, 112, 115
Split Cells button, 158
splitting cells, 158
spreadsheets, 275
Square command (Text
  Wrapping menu), 297
Standard toolbar, 4
  buttons
    Columns, 145
    Cut, 156
    Document Map, 109
    Insert Table, 147-148

Spelling and Grammar,
  110, 115
Tables and Borders, 150
Store macro in
  list box, 344
strikethrough text, 57
Style command (Format
  menu), 139, 226
Style dialog box, 226
Style drop-down list, 138
Style list, 88
Style text box, 226-227
Style type text box, 226
styles, 225
  applying, 138-139
  character, 225
  creating, 226
  editing, 227-228
  paragraph, 225-227
  shortcut keys, 139
  tabs, setting, 95
  viewing, 138
Styles dialog box, 227
Styles list, 227
Styles list box, 139
stylizing shapes, 169
subdocument icons, 260
subdocuments, 257-258
  marking, 259
  modifying, 260
  opening, 260
Subentry text box, 244
Subscript check box, 57
subscripts, 57
Superscript check box, 57
superscripts, 57
Symbol command
  Custom mark menu, 222
  Insert menu, 43, 201
Symbol dialog box, 43,
  222

Index

symbols, inserting, 43
synonyms, 113

T

Tab characters check box, 94
Tab leader drop-down list box, 241
tab leaders, 97
tab marks, displaying, 94
Tab stop position list box, 97
Tab stop position text box, 97
tab style, setting, 95
Tab style button, 95
Table and Borders toolbar, 89
Table AutoFormat button, 149
Table AutoFormat command (Table menu), 149
Table AutoFormat dialog box, 149
Table menu commands
 Convert, 312
 Convert, Text to Table, 148
 Delete, Cells, Delete entire column, 156
 Delete, Cells, Delete entire row, 156
 Draw Table, 150
 Formula, 277
 Insert, 154
 Insert, Columns to the Left, 154
 Insert, Columns to the Right, 154
 Insert, Rows Above, 155
 Insert, Rows Below, 155
 Insert, Table, 148
 Select Row, 151
 Sort, 207
 Table AutoFormat, 149
 Table Properties, 152
Table of Contents tab, 240-241
Table Properties command (Table menu), 152
Table Properties dialog box, 158
Table tab, 148
tables, 158. *See also* columns, rows
 borders, adding, 152-153
 cells
  height/width, 157
  merging, 157
  splitting, 158
 components, selecting, 151
 creating, 147-151
 deleting rows/columns, 155-156
 drawing, 149-151
 importing data from, 304-305
 inserting rows/columns, 154-155
 lines, deleting, 150
 nested, 149
 performing calculations, 276-277
 selecting, 151
 shading, adding, 153
 sorting, 207-208
 text, rotating, 159
Tables and Borders button, 150
Tables and Borders command (Toolbars menu), 86
Tables and Borders toolbar, 149-150, 207, 277
tables of contents, 240
 deleting, 242
 formatting, 241
 generating, 240-241
 moving, 242
 updating, 242
tabs
 Character Spacing, 83
 Commands, 344, 353
 Create from File, 280
 Create New, 293, 298
 Envelope, 185
 File Locations, 265
 Find, 37
 Go To, 119
 Indents and Spacing, 81
 Labels, 189
 Layout, 134, 216, 295
 Line and Page Breaks, 81, 199
 Margins, 131-132
 Motion Clips, 172
 Numbered, 76
 Page Border, 219
 Page Breaks, 135
 Page Size, 130
 Picture Position, 295
 placing, 94-96
 Print, 313
 Printing Options, 187
 Replace, 38
 Shading, 89, 153
 Sort Records, 332
 Sounds, 172
 Special Characters, 201
 Spelling and Grammar, 112, 115
 Table, 148
 Table of Contents, 240-241
 Toolbars, 351

387

Track Changes, 252
User Information, 252
View, 236
Tabs button, 94
Tabs command (Format menu), 94
Tabs dialog box, 94
taking Word MOUS exams, 362-364
template icon, 8
templates
  creating documents, 7-9
  placeholder text, 8
  wizards, 9
  workgroup, specifying location, 265-266
text
  adding, 28
  aligning
    (with) graphics, 296-297
    justifying, 81
    left, 81
    right, 81
    vertically, 133-134
  bookmarked, deleting, 237
  centering, 81
  copying, 35
  cutting, 34
  deleting, 33
  dragging and dropping, 34
  fields, setting, 316
  finding, 37-38
  formatting
    applying character effects, 52, 56-57
    bold, 53
    italics, 54
    outlined, 57
    underlining, 54-55
  highlighting, 64
  inserting, 28-29
  moving, 34
  overtyping, 29-30
  paragraphs, aligning, 80-82
  pasting, 35-36
  replacing, 38-39
  selecting, 31-32
    block, 33
    characters, 32
    line of, 32
    words, 32
  selecting all in document, 33
  tables, rotating, 159
Text Box command (Insert menu), 218
text boxes
  After, 85
  Apply to, 88
  Bookmark name, 237
  Field codes, 203
  File name, 20
  Find what, 38
  For which, 239
  Formula, 277
  Macro name, 344
  Main entry, 244
  Name, 226
  Password to modify, 262
  Password to open, 262
  Replace, 45
  Replace with, 38
  Show levels, 241
  Size, 60
  Style, 226-227
  Style type, 226
  Subentry, 244
  Tab stop position, 97
  Toolbar name, 353
  With, 45
  text color, changing, 58
text fields, associating macros with, 318
text flow, controlling, 198
Text Form field, 315
Text Form Field button, 311
Text Form Field Options dialog box, 315-316
text format (fields), setting, 316
text strikethrough, 57
Text to Table command (Convert menu), 312
Text Wrapping button, 296
Text Wrapping icon, 174
Text Wrapping menu commands
  Behind Text, 297
  Edit Wrap Points, 297
  In Front of Text, 297
  Square, 297
  Through, 297
  Tight, 297
  Top and Bottom, 297
Text Wrapping toolbar, 296
Thesaurus, 113-114
Thesaurus dialog box, 113-114
Through command (Text Wrapping menu), 297
Tight command (Text Wrapping menu), 297
time, inserting, 42
titles (charts), adding, 301
TOC (table of contents) fields, assigning, 240
Toolbar name text box, 353
toolbars
  buttons, adding/ removing, 350-351
  creating, 352-353

Index

customizing, 350
Drawing, 58, 166-167
Formatting, 52, 226
Forms, 310-312
Header and Footer, 123, 218
Mail Merge, 326
Outline, 79
Outlining, 258
Picture, 174
Print Preview, 181, 184
resetting, 351
Revieiwng, 251
Standard, 4
Tables and Borders, 89, 149-150, 207, 277
Text Wrapping, 296
WordArt, 172
Toolbars command (View menu), 31, 35, 86, 150, 166, 251, 312, 352
Toolbars menu commands
Clipboard, 31, 35
Customize, 352
Drawing, 166
Forms, 312
Reviewing, 251
Tables and Borders, 86, 150
Toolbars tab, 351
tools
Find, 37
Format Painter, 65
Replace, 38-39
Tools button, 261
Tools commands (Save As menu), 264
Tools menu commands
AutoCorrect, 45
Customize, 351-352
Envelopes and Labels, 185, 189

Language, Thesaurus, 113
Macro, 343
Mail Merge, 325
Options, 94, 112, 115, 236, 252
Protect Document, 313
Save Version, 264
Spelling and Grammar, 111, 115
Track Changes, 252
Unprotect document, 313
Top and Bottom command (Text Wrapping menu), 297
Top, Bottom, Left, Right, and Gutter option, 131
Track Changes command (Tools menu), 252
Track Changes tab, 252
tracking changes in documents, 250-251
tracking color, specifying, 252
turning on/off revisions feature, 251
Window/Orphan Control, 199
typefaces, 59

U

underlining text, 54-55
underlying code (fields), viewing, 203
underscore (_), 237
Undo button, 40
Undo Typing command (Edit menu), 40
undoing actions, 40
unlinking worksheets, 284

Unprotect document command (Tools menu), 313
Up One Level button, 5
Update automatically check box, 42
Update the style to reflect recent changes? radio button, 227
updating
calculation fields, 277
cross-references, 239
indexes, 245
tables of contents, 242
URLs, 63
Use return address check box, 189
User Information tab, 252

V

versions (documents), saving, 263-264
Versions command (File menu), 264
Versions dialog box, 263-264
vertically aligning text, 133-134
video files, inserting, 172
View Datasheet button, 299
View menu commands
Document Map, 109
Header and Footer, 122, 218
Outline, 79, 258
Ruler, 95, 132
Toolbars, 31, 35, 86, 166, 251, 312, 352
Toolbars, Tables and Borders, 150
Web Layout, 183

389

Word 2000 Cheat Sheet

View Ruler button, 181
View tab, 236
viewing
  Clipboard, 31
  comments, 256
  formatting settings
    (paragraphs), 83
  HTML source code
    (Web pages), 20-21
  revisions, 252
  styles, 138
  underlying code
    (fields), 203
views
  Header and Footer, 122, 124
  Layout (Click and Type), 30
  Master Document, 260
  Outline, 78
    displaying documents in, 78-79
    moving sections, 79
  Print Layout, 122, 132, 218
  Web Layout, 183

W-Z

watermark objects, 218
watermarks, 217-218
Web addresses, 63
Web Layout command
  (View menu), 183
Web Layout view, 183
Web Page Preview, 183
Web Page Preview
  command (File
  menu), 183

Web pages
  HTML source code,
    viewing, 20-21
  previewing, 183
  saving documents
    as, 19-21
Web sites (Word MOUS
  exams), 363
What's This? command
  (Help menu), 83
Widow/Orphan
  Control, 199
Widow/Orphan Control
  check box, 198
widows, 198
width
  cells, 157
  columns, 148
windows
  Macros, 343
  Organizer, 349
  worksheets, resizing, 281
Windows Explorer,
  opening documents, 6
With text box, 45
.WIZ file extension, 9
Wizard icon, 9
wizards
  creating documents, 9
  templates, 9
Word MOUS exams
  description, 361
  newsgroups, 363
  preparing for, 361
  taking, 362-364
  Web site, 363
WordArt, 171-172
WordArt command
  (Picture menu), 171
WordArt Gallery, 171

WordArt toolbar, 172
words, selecting, 32
workgroup templates
  (location), specifying,
  265-266
worksheets
  embedded, 278-279, 285
  embedding, 278-280
  linked, opening, 285
  linking, 283
  modifying, 285-286
  unlinking, 284
  windows, resizing, 281
worksheets, 275

Zoom drop-down
  list box, 181

Read This Before Opening the Software

By opening this package, you are agreeing to be bound by the following agreement:

You may not copy or redistribute the entire CD-ROM as a whole. The installer and code from the author(s) is copyrighted by the publisher and the author.

This software is sold as-is, without warranty of any kind, either expressed or implied, including but not limited to the implied warranties of merchantability and fitness for a particular purpose. Neither the publisher nor its dealers or distributors assumes any liability for any alleged or actual damages arising from the use of this program. (Some states do not allow for the exclusion of implied warranties, so the exclusion may not apply to you.)

This CD-ROM uses long and mixed-case filenames requiring the use of a protected-mode CD-ROM driver.

CD-ROM Installation

If Windows 95 is installed on your computer and you have the AutoPlay feature enabled, the START.EXE program starts automatically whenever you insert the disc into your CD-ROM drive.

Windows 95 Installation Instructions

1. Insert the CD-ROM disc into your CD-ROM drive.
2. From the Windows 95 desktop, double-click on the My Computer icon.
3. Double-click on the icon representing your CD-ROM drive.
4. Double-click on the icon titled START.EXE to run the CD-ROM interface.

Windows NT Installation Instructions

1. Insert the CD-ROM disc into your CD-ROM drive.
2. From File Manager or Program Manager, choose Run from the File menu.
3. Type <drive>\START.EXE and press Enter, where <drive> corresponds to the drive letter of your CD-ROM. For example, if your CD-ROM is drive D:, type D:\START.EXE and press Enter. This will run the CD-ROM interface.